The publisher and the University of California Press
Foundation gratefully acknowledge the generous support
of the Philip E. Lilienthal Imprint in Asian Studies, established
by a major gift from Sally Lilienthal.

Collaborative Settler Colonialism

Collaborative Settler Colonialism

Japanese Migration to Brazil in the Age of Empires

Sidney Xu Lu

UNIVERSITY OF CALIFORNIA PRESS

University of California Press
Oakland, California

Suggested citation: Xu Lu, S. *Collaborative Settler Colonialism: Japanese Migration to Brazil in the Age of Empires.* Oakland: University of California Press, 2025. DOI: https://doi.org/10.1525/luminos.221

This title is freely available in an open access edition made possible by generous contributions from the Fondren Library at Rice University.

A portion of chapter 1 was published in Sidney Xu Lu, "A Great Convergence: The American Frontier and the Origins of Japanese Migration to Brazil," *Journal of Global History*, 17, no. 1, (2021), 109–127, and is reproduced by permission of Cambridge University Press.

Library of Congress Cataloging-in-Publication Data

Names: Lu, Sidney Xu, 1981– author.
Title: Collaborative settler colonialism : Japanese migration to Brazil in the age of empires / Sidney Xu Lu.
Description: Oakland, California : University of California Press, [2025] | Includes bibliographical references and index.
Identifiers: LCCN 2024026610 (print) | LCCN 2024026611 (ebook) | ISBN 9780520404328 (cloth) | ISBN 9780520404335 (ebook)
Subjects: LCSH: Settler colonialism—Brazil—History—20th century. | Foreign workers, Japanese—Brazil—History—20th century.
Classification: LCC JV231 .L78 2025 (print) | LCC JV231 (ebook) | DDC 331.6/25608100904—dc23/eng/20241114

LC record available at https://lccn.loc.gov/2024026610
LC ebook record available at https://lccn.loc.gov/2024026611

33 32 31 30 29 28 27 26 25 24
10 9 8 7 6 5 4 3 2 1

CONTENTS

ILLUSTRATIONS

FIGURES

MAPS

TABLES

ACKNOWLEDGMENTS

Writing is a lonely journey, yet I am blessed with the company of colleagues, friends, and family who support me with love and kindness. At Rice University, I express my gratitude to my chair, Lisa Balabanlilar, for her enthusiasm for this project. Sonia Ryang and Sayuri Shimizu read the manuscript and provided inspiring feedback. A book workshop funded by Rice's Humanities Research Center was pivotal in developing the manuscript, and I am grateful to all participants and supporters of this event. The writing retreat for associate professors at Rice in 2023 gave me the opportunity to revisit the project's focus, and for that, I thank the retreat organizers, Tracy Volz and Jennifer Wilson, for imparting their wisdom. My research assistant, Hoang Nguyen, has been instrumental in refining the manuscript. I am grateful to Anne Chao for her encouragement and to Anna Shparberg for her support at Fondren Library.

I extend my thanks to my colleagues and friends at Michigan State University (MSU), whose support was crucial to the initial development of this book. Peter Beattie warmly accepted me as a colleague and enriched our many lunches and conversations with his extensive knowledge of and fervor for modern Brazil. Edward Murphy graciously permitted me to audit his remarkable course on Latin America and the world. David Wheat shared his perspectives on settler colonialism, prompting me to consider Latin America from a wider viewpoint. Tom Summerhill's insights into settler colonialism in U.S. history have been invaluable. I am appreciative of Charles Keith, Ronan Steinburg, Paula and Michael Koppisch, Pero Dagbovie, Emine Evered, Liam Brockey, LaShawn Harris, Sean Foner, Nwando Achebe, Jamie Monson, Naoko Wake, Andrea Louie, Anna Pegler-Gordon, Xian Wu, Yulian Wu, Emily Tabuteau, Tze-lan Sang, Mindy Smith, Ethan Segal, Siddharth Chandra, Michael Stamm, and Walter Hawthorne for their friendship

xi

and encouragement. This research was supported by grants from the Diversity Research Network, the Asian Studies Center, and the Center for Latin American and Caribbean Studies. I am eternally grateful to Mary Jo Zeter, Spanish and Portuguese studies librarian at the MSU Library, for her unwavering support. Her timely procurement of a series of scarce resources on Japanese immigrants from São Paulo was indispensable for this project.

Further, I thank Louise Young, Jordan Sand, and Martin Dusinberre for reading an early version of the manuscript and offering their valuable comments. The insights and encouragement of Victor Seow, Jeffrey Lesser, Tian Huang, Toyomi Asano, Jun'ichi Isomae, Pedro Iacobelli, Takashi Fujitani, Seth Jacobowitz, Shellen Wu, Sophie Esch, Alida Metcalf, Ran Zwigenberg, Nick Kapur, John Kanbayashi, and many other friends and colleagues are greatly appreciated. Research and completion of this book would have been unthinkable without the generous and professional support of librarians and archivists across the globe. I am grateful to Tanaka Naoki at the Japanese Striving Society, Kaoru Ueda at the Hoover Institution, Tokiko Bazzell at the University of Hawai'i, Daniel McKee at Cornell University, and the staff members at the Museo de la Inmigración Japonesa en Brasil in São Paulo, the Japanese Overseas Migration Museum in Yokohama, the Japanese National Diet Library, and the Diplomatic Archives of the Ministry of Foreign Affairs of Japan in Tokyo. I am indebted to Eiichiro Azuma, Frederick Dickinson, Ayako Kano, Siyen Fei, and other mentors and peers at the University of Pennsylvania for their continuous inspiration long after my graduation. The Fondren Library's OA Book Subvention Fund at Rice University made it possible for this book to be published as open access. I am immensely thankful for the professional and invaluable guidance from my editor, Enrique Ochoa-Kaup, at the University of California Press.

I wrote a significant portion of this book during the pandemic years. My heartfelt thanks go to my dear wife, Eileen, whose love, encouragement, and sacrifices made my daily writing and reflection possible throughout the lockdown. Parenting our daughter Noëlla at home for a year due to school closures and witnessing her daily growth has been immensely fulfilling as a father. The birth of Natalie amid the lockdown brought incredible joy and hope to us in a time of uncertainty. It is to them that I dedicate this book.

Parts of Chapters 1 and 4 have been previously published in different formats as "A Great Convergence: The American Frontier and the Origins of Japanese Migration to Brazil," *Journal of Global History* 17, no. 1 (2022); and "Toward a Prototype of the Total Empire: Japanese Migration to Brazil and Japanese Colonial Expansion in Asia, 1921–1934," in *The Japanese Empire and Latin America*, edited by Pedro Iacobelli and Sidney Xu Lu (Honolulu: University of Hawai'i Press, 2023). They are reprinted with permission.

NOTE ON NAMES, TERMS, AND TRANSLATIONS

Except for names of scholars and historical figures who have written and published their works in English, Japanese, Korean, and Chinese names in this book are in the original order, with family names first. The romanization of Japanese names and terms follows the revised Hepburn system. Exceptions are place-names and terms in standard English usage, such as Tokyo, Kobe, Hokkaido, Sapporo, and Osaka. Chinese names and terms follow the Pinyin system. All translations in the book, unless otherwise noted, are the author's.

Introduction

In 1893, Chicago hosted the World's Columbian Exposition to commemorate the 400th anniversary of Columbus's arrival in the Americas. It was here, at an American Historical Association meeting, that Frederick Jackson Turner introduced his seminal frontier thesis in an essay titled "The Significance of the Frontier in American History."[1] Turner's thesis heralded the end of American westward expansion and underscored the frontier's pivotal role in shaping U.S. culture and societal norms.[2] Concurrently, in San Francisco, Japanese Consul Chinda Sutemi was visited by a member of the Brazilian delegation to the same event in Chicago. This Brazilian envoy was investigating the condition of Chinese neighborhoods on the Pacific Coast. Given the First Republic's renewed invitation to immigrants from Qing China and Meiji Japan, he met with Chinda to discuss the prospects of Japanese immigration to Brazil.[3] This encounter marked the first dialogue on the topic of immigration between Japanese and Brazilian officials. This set in motion Japanese migration to Brazil in the twentieth century, turning Brazil into the home of the largest Japanese-descent population outside of Japan, the number of which now has surpassed two million.[4]

The co-occurrence of the closure of the frontier in the American West and the start of Japanese emigration to Brazil was by no means a coincidence. The great success of U.S. settler colonialism in the nineteenth century, which simultaneously involved the influx of European immigrants and massive emigration from the east side of the Mississippi to the American West, was studied by aspiring empire builders in other parts of the world. Among them were leaders of both Meiji Japan and independent Brazil. What the Japanese and Brazilian expansionists saw in the American westward expansion were two distinct but indelibly entwined modes of settler colonialism—one driven by emigration and the other by immigration.

Elites in Meiji Japan chose to embrace the former because they were convinced that emigration would be a central means of colonial expansion through which the Japanese, people of a superior race just like the Anglo-Saxons, would claim their rightful share of power, wealth, and land in the world as a modern empire. Educated Brazilians, on the other hand, believed that an influx of superior races through immigration was crucial not only to improve Brazil's racial composition but also to claim and utilize the vast land in the country's interior in the mode of the American westward expansion.[5]

Unsurprisingly, imperial visionaries of Japan and Brazil also saw the World's Columbian Exposition in the United States, which celebrated both modes of Anglo-American settler colonialism, as a perfect opportunity to present their own colonial accomplishments.[6] In a booklet that advertised Japan's exhibition in Chicago, the prominent Japanese scholar and politician Nitobe Inazō praised Meiji Japan's recent colonization of Hokkaido as a *mission civilisatrice*. Though the land of Hokkaido was endowed with "magnificent natural resources," he claimed, it was wasted in the hands of "a barbarian folk known as Ainu" and "untouched" until the Meiji government brought civilization to this frontier.[7] The Brazilian exhibition, on the other hand, demonstrated the new republic's technological development and contrasted it with exotic dances performed by "live Indians" from its interior.[8]

Through the lens of Japanese migration to Brazil, this book uses the concept "collaborative settler colonialism" to capture the complex connections between migration and settler colonialism in the modern world.[9] One may rightly argue that *all* forms of settler colonialism are collaborative, especially when considering the partnership between the colonial state and non-state actors such as farmers, merchants, intellectuals, and religious groups that participate in Indigenous dispossession in one way or another. However, by "collaborative," this book refers to three levels of collaboration exemplified by the history of Japanese migration to Brazil in which migration and settler colonialism became intertwined.

At the first level, Japanese immigration to and community building in Brazil revealed the often-unintentional collaboration between the two settler colonial regimes in Japan and Brazil. Both strove to turn migrants into vanguards of colonial expansion and saw migration itself as a means of improving the racial stock. At the second level, Japanese immigrants served as collaborators of the Brazilian state in the latter's efforts to colonize Indigenous land. Existing literature has well documented the indisputable fact that Japanese immigrants were victims of Brazil's ethnic nationalism.[10] At the same time, however, Japanese immigrant laborers and farmers were also contributors to and beneficiaries of state-led Indigenous dispossession in Brazil. At the third level is the partnership between Japanese immigrants and Japanese colonialism, which I examine by placing the origin, development, and transformation of the Japanese community in Brazil in the context of the fate of Japan's colonial empire in Asia. I explain how Japanese colonial expansion had continuously influenced the identity-making process of the Japanese community in Brazil. Japanese Brazilians, in turn, participated in Japan's project of empire making in Asia. Through analyses at these three levels, this book aims to provide new insights into our existing understanding of the Japanese empire, the history of immigration in Brazil and Latin America, and settler colonialism in the modern world.

COLLABORATION OF SETTLER COLONIAL REGIMES: MIGRATION STATES AND IDEOLOGIES OF RACE

On the first level, the concept of collaboration captures the fact that Japanese migration and community making in Brazil were a product of interactions between Japanese and Brazilian settler colonialism. While both were deeply inspired by the U.S. westward expansion, Japan and Brazil exemplified two different modes of settler colonialism. These were the emigration-driven expansion and the immigration-driven expansion, which became closely entwined in Brazil during the nineteenth and twentieth centuries. This was a period that saw waves of European and Asian immigration into Brazil, on the one hand, and the escalating appropriation of Indigenous land, on the other. Japanese migration and the subsequent process of community formation in Brazil were part of this historical convergence, when emigration-driven Japanese settler colonialism mingled with immigration-driven settler colonialism in Brazil.

By "collaboration," I do not refer exclusively to the diplomatic cooperation between the Japanese and Brazilian governments, though negotiations between Tokyo and Rio de Janeiro constituted an important part of the story. Instead, I also refer to the convergence and interactions between the Japanese empire and Brazil in their respective processes of settler colonial expansion. Usually without explicit intention, these two processes developed in tandem. At the heart of this collaboration were the interactions of two "migration states" and two shifting ideologies of race.

Here "migration state" means a government that has devoted itself to the promotion and management of migration through diplomacy, laws, social policies, and financial aid.[11] The critical roles played by a modern government in facilitating and controlling migration at both the sending and receiving ends have been extensively discussed.[12] The concept of migration state in this book, though, refers specifically to the role of the state not only in facilitating migration but also in turning migration into an essential act of settler colonialism. This research joins scholarship in recent decades that has begun examining the cooperation and comparability of modern empires. A number of scholars have analyzed how empires learned from one another in terms of policies, strategies, and ideologies to consolidate their colonial rule.[13] However, these connections and collaborations among settler colonial regimes remain insufficiently examined and largely West-centered.[14]

Through the concept "migration state," this book aims to contribute to the existing scholarship by exploring the intersections between Japan and Brazil, two non-Western regimes of settler colonialism.

The decades between the late nineteenth and early twentieth centuries saw the rise of migration states in both Japan and Brazil. On the one hand, Japan's migration state played a crucial role in promoting and managing emigration that was central to the development of Japan's emigration-driven settler colonialism. On the other hand, the migration state of Brazil at both the central and local levels was pivotal for the influx of immigrants, the essential force of Brazil's immigration-driven internal settler colonialism. As the primary engines of settler colonialism in Japan and Brazil, both migration states functioned according to the modern logic of race and a racialized ideology of expansionism.

Meiji elites were quick to embrace the modern concept of race from the West and the worldview on which it was centered. An example can be found in the widely circulated book *Sekai kunizukushi*, by Fukuzawa Yukichi, one of the most prominent intellectuals of modern Japan, that was published right after the formation of the Meiji government. Based on a wide range of history and geography books imported to Japan in recent years, Fukuzawa divided different human races into four categories and ranked them according to the evolutionary narrative of human history. At the bottom were Indigenous peoples such as those in Australia and Africa. In his view, they were the most backward and inferior, as many of them still lived in a cannibalistic and lawless manner. At the other end of the spectrum were civilized people who engaged in farming, arts, and academics; they were moderate in their emotions. Examples of the latter were white Europeans and white Americans. Between these two categories were those he termed barbarian and half-civilized. The entire world, in his description, was organized according to such a racialized hierarchy of civilizations in which white Europeans and Americans were at the top and Indigenous people were at the bottom. Not only was this book a best-seller, but it was later used as a geography textbook. It became a fundamental part of the Japanese understanding of race and racial hierarchy in the world.

The Meiji categorization of race was simultaneously rigid and fluid. It was rigid in the sense that the hierarchy of civilization was strictly arranged according to color lines. As Fukuzawa famously proclaimed, Indigenous people in the Americas were red; Pacific Islanders, brown; Africans, black; Asians, yellow; and Europeans, white. Later, this classification was adopted by generations of school textbooks in modern Japan to illustrate the global hierarchy of human beings.[15]

The Meiji perception of race was fluid because it allowed for ambiguity when it came to categorizing the Japanese themselves. For Fukuzawa, the location of the Japanese in the global racial hierarchy was yet to be defined; that is, the Japanese occupied a liminal space between Asians and whites. While he was confident in Japanese racial superiority over the Chinese and Koreans, who he defined as half-civilized, he believed that the Japanese had to lift themselves up in order to

FIGURE 1. This image was featured in *Chikyū sanbutsu zasshi*, an illustrated book translated from French in 1872, which aimed to familiarize Japanese students and the general public with the world's geography and human races. This image ranked white people as the first class, yellow people as the second, and Black people as the third. Source: Horikawa Kensai, trans., *Chikyū sanbutsu zasshi* (Tokyo: Izumiya Hanbei, 1872).

join the white people's ranks.[16] Many Japanese elites of the day shared this view, and racial improvement (*jinshū kairyō*) became a central topic in public debate. For example, in 1884, Takahashi Yoshio, a student of Fukuzawa, published *Nihon jinshu kairyōron* (On Japanese Racial Improvement). Based on the logic of Social Darwinism, this book not only emphasized the absolute necessity for the Japanese to improve their racial stock but also presented a wide range of methods to achieve this goal. These included promoting physical education and body training, avoiding consanguine marriages, and engaging in racial mixing with white people, though the last idea had rarely been practiced in modern Japan.[17]

As a natural extension of his call for Japan to join Western civilization and leave Asian traditions behind, Fukuzawa saw emigration-based overseas expansion and settler colonialism as a means of racial improvement. In particular, he urged his countrymen to migrate to North America as this would allow them to join white Americans and participate in the settler colonial construction of the American West. He further envisioned Japanese migration to the United States as the first step to establish new settler nations across the globe.[18]

The Meiji leaders sought to establish Japan's racial superiority in Asia first through emigration and settler colonialism. Around the same time that Fukuzawa populated his racial categories and hierarchy, the imperial government rolled out its very first project of expansion, a state-sponsored campaign that sent declassed samurai to Hokkaido as colonial settlers. These migrants were promised free land and farming tools after completing a certain period of stay in the empire's newly acquired northern territory. The Ainu, the Indigenous people of Hokkaido, were deprived of their ancestral land. The Meiji leaders justified this policy by contrasting the supposed inferiority and backwardness of the Ainu with the racially superior Japanese settlers who were armed with scientific knowledge, the capitalist spirit, and a laudable commitment to national expansion.[19]

To be sure, racism against Indigenous people in Japan was—and remains—a complex and sophisticated issue. In addition to the ideas and acts of exclusion, it involved assimilation and integration. Inspired by the General Allotment Act of 1887 in the United States, the Imperial Diet passed the Hokkaido Former Natives Protection Act in 1899. Modeled after U.S. policies regarding Indigenous peoples, this act aimed to assimilate the Ainu people by encouraging them to engage in agriculture and learn Japanese language and culture. In effect, the government sought to transform the Ainu people into loyal and productive Japanese subjects by eradicating their language, customs, and values.[20]

Beginning in the last two decades of the nineteenth century, Tokyo began to officially allow overseas emigration; it negotiated diplomatic treaties and agreements that enabled Japanese subjects to immigrate to various destinations in Asia and the Americas. Japanese policy makers and intellectuals promoted emigration-driven expansion for a variety of reasons, including solving the nation's perceived overpopulation problem, increasing remittances, and expanding Japan's international trade networks. At the same time, the issue of race remained critical. As Japan's leaders designed emigration policies and diplomatic strategies, two of their central concerns were rejecting the notion of Japanese racial inferiority to the whites while asserting their superiority to nonwhites.[21]

On the other side of the globe, as soon as the Empire of Brazil declared its independence from Portugal, its migration state started to take shape. Without taking the existence and rights of Indigenous people into consideration, the Brazilian elites deemed this newly independent empire underpopulated and called for immigrants to work the land. In their minds, immigrants would not only help defend the empire's territory but also expand its smallholding agricultural economy.[22] Its constitution, promulgated in 1824, made the empire's commitment to immigration clear; though a Roman Catholic state, it allowed people of all religions to practice their faith in private. It also extended citizenship to all people born in Brazilian territory and to any woman who married a Brazilian citizen. Offering subsidies, Rio brought in immigrants from Europe, the Middle East, and Qing China by working with plantation owners and private immigration companies.[23] The empire's eventual transition to a republic and the abolition of slavery brought Brazil's migration state into its new phase, creating new demands for immigrants in Brazil both as plantation laborers and as land colonizers. Rio not only allowed people the freedom to practice their religions in public but also partnered with state governments, making governmental financial subsidies and land grants much more attractive than before. This ushered in the era of mass immigration that saw 2.6 million immigrants arriving in Brazil between 1890 and 1919.[24]

The concept of race was crucial to the operation of Brazil's migration state. Similar to their Japanese counterparts, the Brazilian elites saw race as both a fixed and a fluid concept. On the one hand, they embraced the idea of white supremacy and the rigid racial hierarchy it created as scientific truth. In their minds, the centuries-long practice of racial mixing among white colonists, African slaves, and Indigenous peoples had made the Brazilian race inferior to pure-blood whites. On the other hand, like their Japanese counterparts, they believed that Brazilian racial stock and the position of the Brazilians in the global racial hierarchy were changeable. Similar to the Japanese case, the supposed inferiority of Brazil's Indigenous people served as a foil to the superiority of the Brazilian race. In 1910, the Brazilian government established the Indian Protection Service (IPS) under the influence of Cândido Mariano da Silva Rondon, a Brazilian politician and military officer who accompanied Theodore Roosevelt during what became known as the Roosevelt-Rondon Scientific Expedition to the Amazon.[25] While it had the stated goal of protecting Indigenous peoples' right to land and preventing further violent conflict between them and settlers, IPS's programs in fact facilitated the central government's penetration into the hinterland. They also reduced the diverse and heterogeneous Indigenous peoples in Brazil to a generic and state-created "Indian" category. They reinforced the racial hierarchy between Brazilians and Indigenous peoples and sought to assimilate the latter into Brazilian nationhood through the mission of civilization.[26]

Between the late nineteenth century and the early twentieth century, the elites in Brazil, as well as other Latin American nations, also embraced the ideology

FIGURE 2. *Ham's Redemption* (*A Redenção de Cam*), painted by Modesto Brocos in 1895. The painting depicts three generations of a family. At the center sits the mother of mixed African and European descent with a white baby in her arms. Her husband, a white man, sits next to her. On the other side, the African grandmother raises her arms to express her gratitude for the baby's whiteness. Source: Museu Nacional de Belas Artes, Rio de Janeiro.

of racial whitening (*branqueamento*), a combination of Social Darwinism and eugenics. In their minds, the Brazilian racial stock could and should be improved by white immigrants from Europe and North America. Perhaps one of the best illustrations of this idea was the 1895 painting *Ham's Redemption* by Modesto Brocos, which won a gold medal at Brazil's National Salon of Fine Arts. It showcased the contemporary belief that generations of the same family could be gradually whitened through marriage with white Europeans. Brazil's policy makers and immigration advocates expected that immigration would "whiten" the existing Brazilian race through interracial marriage, thereby improving Brazilians' racial quality.[27]

Indeed, the start of Japanese migration to Brazil was a joint product of these two migration states and marked the convergence of Japanese and Brazilian racial ideologies. In order to pacify anti-Japanese sentiment in the United States, Tokyo voluntarily ended U.S.-bound labor migration. To the Japanese expansionists, Brazil then became an attractive alternative: the Japanese would join white Europeans as a master race and colonize the land of the racially inferior Indigenous peoples.[28] On the other hand, Brazilian leaders initially equated the Japanese with the Chinese as people of the Mongolian race and deemed them undesirable due to their racial inferiority. However, Japan's quick rise in East Asia as a modernizing and expanding empire altered the Brazilian elites' perception of the Japanese race. After Japan's stunning victories in the Sino-Japanese War and, more importantly, the Russo-Japanese War, the Brazilian elites began to see the Japanese as the white people of Asia, believing they could contribute to Brazil's ongoing process of racial whitening.[29]

Some Japanese expansionists too justified Japan's migration and settler colonialism in Brazil and other Latin American countries by the idea of racial mixing. Fukuhara Hachirō, a Japanese businessman who played a central role in starting Japanese migration to the Brazilian Amazon, claimed after an investigative trip to the Amazon that the Indigenous peoples there looked "exactly like the Japanese" and that the two peoples bore a close resemblance in manners and customs.[30] Since Indigenous Brazilians had Asiatic or Mongol origins, miscegenation between Japanese and Brazilians would only strengthen the Brazilian race.[31] Around the same time, Japanese immigrants in the Andes were exploring a possible link between themselves and the ancient Inca civilization. After witnessing the architectural artistry of the Inca ruins, the settlers thought that the Japanese were potentially the progenitors of the Inca people.[32] Aoyagi Ikutarō, who spearheaded Japanese migration to both Brazil and Peru, even described Peru-bound migration as a homecoming for the Japanese.[33]

While most of the Japanese immigrants started out as contracted plantation laborers, more than half of them had become independent farmers by the outbreak of the Pacific War in 1941. The continuation of immigration and social changes in the Japanese community in Brazil depended on the work of both migration states. Japan's central and prefectural governments played a vital role not only in mobilizing Japanese subjects for emigration and transporting them to the Brazilian shores but also in securing farmland for them in Brazil. Likewise, both Rio and state governments in Brazil were instrumental in distributing land to Japanese immigrants. The late 1920s marked a turning point in Japanese migration to and community making in Brazil. On the one hand, stimulated by the Great Kantō Earthquake and the racial exclusion of the Japanese from North America, the Japanese government undertook a series of structural changes to maximize its capacity to mobilize its subjects for Brazil-bound emigration. On the other hand, the global economic depression and the sharp drop in coffee prices on the international market substantially reduced the demand for immigrant labor in Brazil. Rio, accordingly, began to restrict immigration. This shift in policy was formally institutionalized by the constitution of 1934, which imposed a 2 percent immigration quota based on national origin. However, through diplomatic negotiation and compromise, Tokyo and Rio agreed to delay the restriction on Japanese immigration for two years. Even after the quota took effect and the number of Japanese immigrants sharply declined under the ultranationalist regime of Getúlio Vargas, the Brazilian government at the central and local levels continued to see Japanese immigrants as instrumental to Brazil's ongoing process of settler colonialism.[34]

COLLABORATORS OF SETTLER COLONIALISM: RELOCATING JAPANESE IMMIGRANTS IN BRAZIL AND LATIN AMERICA

At the second level, the concept of collaboration explains the role played by Japanese immigrants in facilitating Brazil's own settler colonial expansion. The bulk of existing scholarship on the Japanese community in Brazil has been written through the lens of ethnography and generally falls into the domain of ethnic studies in Latin America. It has documented how Japanese immigrants, through their industry and perseverance, successfully proved their worth in Brazil and turned themselves from unwelcome foreigners into what Takeyuki Gaku Tsuda calls the "positive minority."[35] To this day, this narrative continues to dominate the ways the history of Japanese immigration has been told in the realms of both academic research and public history.[36] While the approach of ethnic studies remains necessary, this book moves beyond national and disciplinary boundaries and reexamines migration and community building in the context of settler colonialism in Brazil and Latin America in a broader sense.

In 1906, two years before the *Kasato Maru* reached the Port of Santos, the state of São Paulo signed a financial agreement in the city of Taubaté with coffee producers in the state.[37] In the agreement, the state government promised to buy excess coffee; in exchange, the coffee producers had to restrict the production of low-quality beans.[38] This marked an important step in the São Paulo state government's intervention in and management of the state's coffee production and trade. The state's intervention in the coffee economy was also part of the overall expansion of state power, which spearheaded railway construction and land distribution in its hinterland. Japanese immigrants, like their counterparts from Europe, participated in this process as collaborators of the state.

By recognizing the partnership between Japanese immigrants and the Brazilian settler colonial state, the concept of collaborative settler colonialism allows us to reposition Japanese immigrants in Brazilian society by moving beyond the framework of ethnic studies. Seeing Japanese immigration and community making as part of the development of Brazilian settler colonialism by no means takes away from the fact that Japanese immigrants were targeted and victimized by racism in Brazil. It is undeniable that the Japanese community suffered from various forms of Brazilian ethnic nationalism throughout the twentieth century, from that of racial whitening to the ideology of racial democracy.[39] Racial discrimination against the Japanese undergirded the Brazilian government's legalization of the immigration quota on Japanese immigration in 1934, as well as its ban of Japanese-language schools and newspapers by the beginning of the Pacific War. These policies were also a result of what Erika Lee calls "hemispheric Orientalism," namely, the trans-American anti-Asian racism that revealed the impact of white supremacy in North America on rising ethnic nationalism in Latin America.[40]

However, starting the history of Japanese immigration to Brazil with orientalism and ending it with the celebration of their status as a "positive minority" according to the ethnic studies framework is insufficient to capture the complexity of Japanese experiences in Brazil. Viewing Japanese immigrants only as victims of Brazilian ethnic nationalism, for example, cannot explain why only two organized anti-Japanese political campaigns in Brazil at the national level existed in the first half of the twentieth century—and why only the campaign in the 1930s, amid an upheaval of the federal government itself, succeeded. Nor can the ethnic studies framework explain why the Brazilian elites who imposed a quota on Japanese immigration uniformly denied their racism against the Japanese. Instead of referring to the Japanese as racially inferior, they rationalized the quota primarily by the argument of the Japanese failure to assimilate.[41] Brazilian elites' disavowal of their racism against the Japanese as well as their rather abrupt and delayed success in legalizing the quota can only be understood by acknowledging the more consistent pattern of collaboration between Japanese immigrants and the Brazilian state. In other words, the history of Japanese migration and community building in Brazil was marked by a long-term partnership between Japanese immigrants and the Brazilian government in the latter's land colonization efforts. The two notable anti-Japanese campaigns in the 1920s and 1930s, as well as Rio's wartime policies against the Japanese community, were in fact anomalies in the long history of collaboration.

Aside from being victims of Brazil's ethnic nationalism and contributors to its economic prosperity and cultural diversity, Japanese immigrants benefited from Brazil's ongoing process of settler colonialism. Like other groups of immigrants, they acted as the Brazilian state's agents by occupying and farming appropriated Indigenous land. By the same process, over half of the Japanese population in the Brazilian countryside became landowners by the beginning of the Pacific War.

The Brazilian government's land policies were also crucial for the economic success of Japanese coffee and cotton cultivators in São Paulo and Paraná as well as jute farmers in the Amazon.

The convergence of Japanese and Brazilian settler colonialism was further revealed by the ways the Japanese settlers identified themselves. Before the end of World War II, the settler elites saw Japanese immigrants in Brazil as *shokumin*, literally, "colonists."[42] It resonated with the discourse of emigration-driven overseas expansion (*kaigai hattenron*) in the Japanese empire that equated emigration with settler colonialism and defined Japanese emigrants abroad as trailblazers of the empire's expansion.[43] On the other hand, the Brazilian elites commonly called immigrant communities *colônias*, which can be translated as "colonies."[44] The double meaning of this term, immigrants and colonists, reflected the fact that immigration and land colonization were two sides of the same coin in the history of Brazilian settler colonialism. In the 1950s, Japanese settler elites in Brazil embraced the term "Nikkei koronia" to refer to their community. This was their strategy to improve the image of the Japanese community in Brazil, which was severely damaged by the crimes and violence committed by ultranationalist settlers who refused to accept Japan's defeat in World War II. By adopting this new term, the settler elites exploited the historical convergence between Japanese and Brazilian settler colonialism by celebrating the settlers as contributing members in the national histories of both Japan and Brazil.

The experience of Japanese migration to Brazil mirrors the overall history of Japanese migration to Latin America. Admittedly, Brazil was unique not only as the sole Portuguese-speaking country on the continent but also as the home of the largest number of Japanese immigrants in Latin America. Brazil stood out as a highly attractive destination because of its vast territory, abundance of natural wealth, and prosperous, agriculture-centered economy. On the other hand, Brazil resembled other Latin American countries that were also destinations of both European and Asian immigration such as Peru, Mexico, Argentina, Bolivia, Chile, and Uruguay before World War II. Japanese migration to all of these countries started in response to anti-Japanese campaigns in North America. The vast majority of Japanese immigrants arrived in Latin America as contract laborers. In one way or another, they fell prey to ethnic nationalism in their host countries.[45]

The late nineteenth and early twentieth centuries were a critical era for Latin America in general. At a time when waves of immigrants from Europe and Asia reached their shores, the newly independent Latin American nation-states escalated their appropriation of Indigenous land.[46] Japanese immigration and community building in Latin America as a whole were a result of the convergence of these two historical processes on the continent. Immigrants from Japan and other countries served as effective agents of Latin American regimes' own settler colonialism. Recent scholarship on Japanese history and Latin American history has critically engaged the Anglo-American-centered literature of settler colonialism.[47]

However, scholars of Japanese settler colonialism and those of Latin American settler colonialism have rarely been in conversation with each other. The concept of collaborative settler colonialism, then, allows one to bring these two innovative yet separated academic endeavors into serious dialogue.

More specifically, through the experience of Japanese immigration, this book joins recent scholarship in Latin American history that has begun to revise the definitions of *settlers* and *indigenes* in the scholarship of settler colonialism in Latin America, which traditionally drew a clear line between immigrants and settlers.[48] This conceptual separation of immigrants and settlers was derived from the conventional wisdom of settler colonialism in the British and American experiences. In both North America and British Australia, for example, the formation of the colonial states took place hand in hand with the seizure of Indigenous land. The settlers were defined as those who arrived during the formative period of the colonial states, while those who arrived later were categorized as immigrants.[49] In Latin America, while the settlers' exploitation of and violence against the indigenes had taken place since the very beginning of the colonial period, the massive appropriation of Indigenous land happened long after the formation of the colonial states.[50] This was because unlike the Anglo-American colonial settlers who saw Indigenous land as their primary target from the start, colonial settlers in Latin America initially focused on exploiting Indigenous labor and wealth, only targeting land centuries later. The systematic dispossession of Indigenous land did not happen until there was an influx of European and Japanese immigrants.[51]

Thus the late nineteenth and early twentieth centuries, this study argues, were a turning point in the history of Latin America: collaborative settler colonialism emerged and developed across the continent at around this time. This process was marked by the confluence of the experience of immigration and that of settler colonialism, as foreign immigrants effectively acted as colonial settlers who deprived the Indigenous peoples of their land. This was also the period when empire builders of both East Asia and Latin America turned to U.S. settler colonialism in the American West for inspiration. Japanese and Brazilian leaders' efforts to reproduce the two modes of settler colonialism derived from American frontier expansion were shared by elites of other modernizing powers in East Asia and Latin America.[52]

During the last decades of the Qing empire, China's own expansionists shared the Meiji elites' enthusiasm for emigration. The iconic reformer Kang Youwei, for example, envisioned the establishment of a new China in Brazil through emigration as a means of survival, as the Qing empire was in danger of being partitioned by Western and Japanese powers at the end of the nineteenth century.[53] Post-independence nations in Latin America such as Argentina, Uruguay, and Chile also utilized foreign immigration as an effective means to expand the government's control over interior land and borders.[54] In 1858, the Republic of Chile introduced a law that defined lands to the south of the Biobío River and to the north of Copiapó as unowned, offering them to foreign immigrants for free.[55] Juan B. Alberdi, who drafted the Argentine constitution of 1853, forcefully called for European immigrants to populate and civilize the primitive land in Argentina, much like what they had done in the American West.[56] It was during this period that Japan's emigration-driven expansionism became deeply entwined with the immigration-driven mode of settler colonialism in Brazil. For this reason, this book uses "immigrants" and "settlers" interchangeably when referring to the Japanese community in Brazil.

In addition to redefining the concept of settlers, the study revises the term "indigenes" in the context of Latin America. Centuries-long practices of racial mixing among white settlers, African slaves, and Indigenous peoples on the continent have complicated the conventional narratives of settler colonialism in the British and American contexts, which were centered on the binary of white settlers versus Indigenous peoples. Before the colonial governments carried out systemic appropriation of Indigenous land, a large portion of land in Latin America was occupied by squatters without legal titles, who were usually independent farmers of mixed European and Indigenous ancestries. Known as *caboclos* in Brazil, these squatters obtained their own plots on the periphery of large plantations by burning down forests; there they would cultivate subsistence crops and form interdependent relationships with the plantations nearby.[57] While the practice of intermarriage may be seen as what Patrick Wolfe called racial "elimination" of the indigenes, the caboclos also carried biological features of Indigenous people and were critical for the survival of Indigenous identity and culture.[58] In addition, similar to the Indigenous people, the caboclos were victims of both state-sanctioned white supremacy ideology and land dispossession. Because of these connections and similarities, this study treats the land squatted on by the caboclos also as Indigenous land and caboclos themselves as victims of settler colonialism.

The Brazilian state dispossessed the caboclos and the Indigenous peoples of their land by means of a thorough transformation of land tenure, a process in which the European and Japanese immigrants were both catalysts and beneficiaries. During this process, governments at both the federal and state levels were able to substantially expand and consolidate their control over land in the interior. During the long colonial period and the early phase of the empire, *sesmaria*, or land granted by the crown, was the only title to land recognized by the courts.[59] Because of the very limited government control over the vast land in the country, it was common for plantation owners and individual farmers to occupy new land without legal titles. The Land Law of 1850 marked a major shift in land tenure by banning further royal land grants. Under this law, one was only allowed to obtain a legal land title through purchase.[60] Though it served as a critical step in the capitalization of land that allowed it to be traded, the law's actual impact was limited at best. While some large landholders managed to purchase legal titles for the land they occupied, most impoverished and isolated squatters did not due to poverty and illiteracy.[61] As the government remained small and incapable of exerting effective control over the bulk of land in its territory, squatting continued to be a common practice. The caboclos who lived and farmed around the borders of the legally titled land were the primary beneficiaries of squatting.

Brazil's Proclamation of the Republic in 1889 turned once nationally owned land into the property of individual states, making state governments the primary agents of land colonization. This institutional shift took place around the time the southeastern states, led by São Paulo, embraced modern capitalism. Centered on coffee cultivation and trade, this capitalist economy was marked by three interconnected aspects: transportation modernization, land exploration, and immigration. In all three aspects, state governments played a decisive and central role. First, in order to gain greater access and control over the interior land, the state governments encouraged railway construction. Second, in order to expand coffee cultivation, state governments granted interior land to land-developing companies and railway companies, tasking them with its development and redistribution. Third, in order to attract immigrants, including the Japanese, who constituted the backbone of this state-driven land colonization, state governments provided subsidies. Some immigrants started out as plantation laborers but later became farmers; others arrived as farming settlers. Most of the Japanese immigrants belonged to the former category. Either way, they served as agents to enforce state power by taking interior land from the caboclos and the Indigenous peoples.

BRAZIL AND A NEW CHRONOLOGY OF JAPANESE SETTLER COLONIALISM

In addition to explaining the role of Japanese migrants as collaborators of the state-led land colonialization process in Brazil, this book recognizes migration as a part of Japan's emigration-driven settler colonial expansion.[62] It analyzes the connections between the Japanese community in Brazil and the evolution of Japan's colonial empire and its transition to a nation-state after World War II.[63] By transcending conventional temporal and geographic boundaries, this book revises the existing understanding of the Japanese empire in a number of ways.

First, it joins a recent body of scholarship that examines the impact of white racism on Japanese colonialism.[64] More specifically, this book demonstrates how racial exclusion of Asian immigrants in the United States propelled Japanese expansion into Latin America. The closure of the frontier in the American West, observed by Turner, took place hand in hand with the closure of the American gates to Chinese immigration. The Chinese exclusion campaigns on the U.S. West Coast stimulated Meiji elites to cast their colonial gaze on Latin America. Fearing that Japanese migrants in the United States would suffer the same fate as the Chinese, Japanese diplomats in Tokyo and San Francisco turned to countries south of the U.S. border as alternative destinations for Japanese migration. It was in this context that Meiji Japan began diplomatic negotiations with several Latin American countries, such as Brazil, Peru, and Mexico, at the end of the nineteenth century. A notable product of these efforts was the short-lived "Enomoto Colony" that the former minister of foreign affairs, Enomoto Takeaki, and his followers established in southern Chiapas, Mexico, in 1897.[65]

The history of Japanese migration to Brazil is especially illustrative of this connection. While Chinese exclusion in the United States at the end of the nineteenth century brought Tokyo to the negotiation table with Rio, it was the Gentlemen's Agreement in 1907, which effectively ended Japanese labor migration to the United States, that finally jumpstarted official Japanese migration to Brazil. Less than a year after the signing of the Gentlemen's Agreement, the *Kasato Maru* reached the shores of Santos with 781 Japanese subjects on board. They became known as the first official group of Japanese immigrants in Brazil. The U.S. Immigration Act of 1924 that formally terminated Japanese immigration to the United States marked another turning point in the history of Japanese migration to Brazil. It propelled a series of changes in Japanese policies that substantially increased the government's capacity to manage Brazil-bound migration. Tokyo's political and financial supports not only led to a sharp increase in the annual number of migrants but also accelerated the Japanese community's socioeconomic transition from laborers to owner-farmers in Brazil.

Second, looking at migration to Brazil from the lens of the Japanese empire allows us to recognize the roles played by individuals associated with the migration and community formation in Brazil in Japan's own process of empire building and its transition to a nation-state. Leaders of the Japanese community in Brazil, throughout different periods, actively participated in political and intellectual debates within Japan; they connected their efforts of community building in Brazil with the agenda for Japanese expansion in Asia. First-generation elites such as Saibara Seitō, Nagata Shigeshi, and Koseki Tokuya returned to Asia in the 1930s and 1940s. They advocated for accelerated imperial expansion and sought to build Japanese settler communities in Southeast Asia in order to support Japan's war in Asia-Pacific.

On the other hand, in the years immediately following World War II, new Japanese Brazilian leaders closely associated their efforts to rebuild their community in Brazil with the reinvention of Japan's identity as a "cultured nation." These included first-generation intellectuals such as Yamamoto Kiyoshi and Suzuki Tei'ichi, as well as second-generation elites like Saitō Hiroshi. They joined both Japanese and Western scholars in the collective invention of Japan's cultural and national identity during the Cold War, which laid the intellectual foundation for the popularization of the theory of the Japanese in the 1970s. *Nihonjinron*, as it was popularly known, celebrated the unique cultural and racial character of the Japanese as the key to the nation's splendid success in economic growth and modernization.

Third, the book offers a new chronology of Japanese settler colonialism. Most existing scholarship of Japanese settler colonialism has adhered to the formal timeline of the Japanese colonial empire, which itself has been in question. Conventional wisdom defines Japan's annexation of Taiwan as the starting point of the empire and sees the empire's collapse at the end of World War II as its historical conclusion.[66] More recent scholarship has extended the timeline of the empire by dating its origin to the early Meiji era, recognizing the colonization of Hokkaido and the annexation of the Ryukyu Islands as the initial chapters of the Japanese empire.[67] Scholars have also begun to acknowledge the historical continuity before and after the collapse of the colonial empire by examining the complicated process of decolonization in East Asia.[68] Such revisions, though immensely significant, are still confined by the territory-bound narrative of the Japanese empire that is centered on the relationship between the colonies, both informal and formal, and the metropole.[69]

A focus on Japanese emigration to Brazil allows us to reevaluate the significance of Japanese expansion beyond the relationship between the imperial metropole and the colonies. By not taking the temporal and geographic boundaries of the empire for granted, this book presents a new chronology of Japanese settler colonialism. My examination of Japanese settler colonialism starts with its colonial migration to Hokkaido at the beginning of the Meiji era and concludes with the celebration of the seventieth anniversary of Japanese migration to Brazil in 1978 in São Paulo. As Patrick Wolfe so powerfully declared, settler colonialism "is a structure not an event."[70] A history of the Japanese empire through the lens of settler colonialism is, therefore, a history of the present and does not have an endpoint. Nevertheless, the event of 1978 marked the cultural separation of Japan and Japanese Brazilians, the largest Japanese population outside of the archipelago. As the last anniversary held by the Issei, this celebration also symbolized the end of the community leadership of the Issei, the first generation of settlers who carried the personal ties and collective memories of the empire. The end of Issei leadership in the Japanese community in Brazil was coupled with the demolition of Japan's emigration-centered migration state in the same decade.[71] As Japan's rapid economic growth generated a huge demand for labor, it quickly changed from a migration-sending into a migration-receiving country. While this is the concluding point of the book, as a "structure" Japanese settler colonialism does not end here. Instead, Japanese settler colonialism entered a new phase with new connections between Japan and Japanese overseas communities. It was marked by the migration of people of Japanese ancestry from Brazil and other Latin American countries to Japan as laborers, a topic beyond this book's coverage.

The history of Japanese settler colonialism in this book is divided into four periods. In the first period, the Meiji empire reproduced the mode of the U.S. westward expansion in its own colonial frontier in Hokkaido. The colonial migration of declassed samurai to Hokkaido in early Meiji laid the intellectual and material foundation for subsequent Japanese settler colonial projects in Asia and across the Pacific.[72] The decades between the 1880s and the 1900s constitute the second period. In the conventional narrative of the empire, this period is more commonly known for the empire's triumph in the Sino-Japanese War and Russo-Japanese War and for its colonization of Taiwan and Korea. However, these years were also crucial for the confluence of Japanese overseas emigration and settler colonial expansion. In particular, the 1880s marked a turning point in Japanese settler colonialism because they saw the beginning of Japan's emigration-driven expansion abroad: the Japanese government officially lifted the ban on overseas emigration, resulting in an exodus of laborers, students, travelers, and political exiles to Hawai'i and North America, on the one hand, and merchants to the Korean Peninsula, on the other. This immediate increase in the outflow of Japanese subjects and their endeavors on both sides of the Pacific also ushered in the convergence of emigration and settler colonialism.[73] In response to the Chinese Exclusion Act and the rise of anti-Japanese sentiment in the United States, Japanese expansionists, both in and outside of policy-making circles, cast their gaze to the South Seas and Latin America as alternative destinations for Japanese emigration. It was precisely in this context that Tokyo established diplomatic relationships with several Latin American countries, such as Mexico (1891), Brazil (1897), Chile (1902), and Peru (1909). Japanese emigrants also began to reach Latin American shores in the same period.[74]

The sailing of the *Kasato Maru* to Brazil marked the beginning of the third period (1908–36) of Japanese settler colonialism. Apart from the rise of farmer-centered Japanese settler colonialism in both Asia and the Americas, this period saw the expansion of state power into the field of emigration promotion and management. The Gentlemen's Agreement led to a paradigm shift in Japanese settler colonialism, from the migration of laborers to that of farmers. Japan's empire builders learned two important lessons from their setbacks in the United States. First, they concluded that farmers, not temporary laborers, were the most suited to putting down roots for the empire in foreign countries because they had an intrinsic desire to acquire land. Second, they urged Tokyo to take a bigger role in promoting, managing, and financially supporting the emigration process as well as the emigrants' community formation abroad.[75]

This paradigm shift was clearly seen in Japanese expansion in the Asia-Pacific region, especially with the formation of the semigovernmental organization Tōyō Takushoku Gaisha (Oriental Development Company, or Tōtaku) in 1908 and its subsequent migration schemes in Northeast Asia.[76] Across the Pacific, Brazil-bound emigration was similarly illustrative of this change. Not only was it conceived with the goal of establishing a Japanese farming community; the migration process was also carried out with increasing involvement by and support from the Japanese government. The formation of the Kaigai Kōgyō Kabushiki Gaisha (Overseas Development Company, or Kaikō) and the enactment of the Overseas Emigration Cooperatives Law, for example, were two important government measures directly aimed at promoting and managing Brazil-bound migration.

TABLE 1 Annual number of Japanese emigrants to Brazil, 1929–1938

	1929	1930	1931	1932	1933	1934	1935	1936	1937	1938
Number of emigrants	15,597	13,741	5,565	15,092	23,299	22,960	5,745	5,357	4,675	2,563

SOURCE: Gaimushō Ryōji Ijūbu, *Waga kokumin no kaigai hatten: ijū hyakunen no ayumi, shiryōhen* (Tokyo: Gaimushō Ryōji Ijūbu, 1971), 140.

A closer look at Japanese expansion and community building in Brazil in the 1920s and 1930s also challenges the conventional view that the Manchurian Incident in 1931 and subsequent formation of Manchukuo was a turning point in the history of Japanese expansion. The formation of Manchukuo had little effect on the existing pattern of Japanese settler colonialism. Several attempts by the Kwangtung Army to relocate Japanese subjects to Manchuria in the first half of the 1930s proved unsuccessful.[77] In the meantime, as table 1 illustrates, the volume of Japanese emigration to Brazil continued to grow after the Manchurian Incident and reached its zenith in the following years. The watershed moment came only in 1935, when the volume of Brazil-bound Japanese emigration declined sharply due to an immigration quota imposed by the Brazilian government a year before. In 1936, Tokyo launched a state-led mass migration program to Manchuria, marking a true geographic shift in Japanese settler colonialism.

In addition, the focus on Brazil in the 1930s offers us a better understanding of the economic vibrancy of Japan's wartime empire. The decline in Japanese emigration took place hand in hand with Japanese economic expansion into Brazil. After the delegation from Japan's Chamber of Commerce and Industry visited Brazil in 1935, Japanese importation of raw cotton from Brazil skyrocketed. This crop, largely cultivated by Japanese settlers in São Paulo, allowed many Japanese immigrant farmers to finally become independent landowners in rural São Paulo. After India restricted raw cotton exportation to Japan, Brazilian cotton became essential for the empire's textile industry.[78] In fact, increased trade between Japan and Brazil was critical to sustaining Japan's manufacturing industries during the second half of the 1930s, a period when Japan urgently needed alternative sources of raw materials as well as markets in the face of mounting trade embargos imposed by the United States and the Commonwealth nations.[79]

The fourth and final period of discussion in this book (1936–78) is from the beginning of Japan's total war in Asia to the celebration of the seventieth anniversary of Japanese immigration in São Paulo in 1978. The experience of the Japanese community in Brazil during World War II and its aftermath offers a unique prism through which to analyze Japanese settler colonialism during the empire's transition to a nation-state. The bitter split among the Japanese settlers in São Paulo did not stop at the end of the war; in fact, the rift only deepened in the following decade. On the other hand, the repatriation of Japanese colonial settlers in Asia proceeded concurrently with the resumption of Japanese migration to Brazil and other Latin American countries; the migration state's apparatuses established during the time of the empire were revived for this purpose.[80] This series of events jointly challenge the usefulness of the year 1945 as a dividing line of history. Examining the largely neglected role of the Japanese Brazilian community in Japan's national reinvention during the Cold War also offers a new endpoint of Japan's empire-to-nation transition itself. This process concluded with Japan's consolidation of its position as the second-largest economy in the world and its cultural separation from the Japanese overseas communities. This separation occurred together with the termination of the Japanese government–sponsored programs of overseas emigration.

CHAPTER OUTLINE

This book, organized chronologically, contains eight chapters that are divided into four parts, and each part examines one of the four periods in the history of Japan's collaborative settler colonialism. Part 1, comprising the first two chapters, examines the origins and the initial period of Japanese collaborative settler colonialism in Brazil. Chapter 1 illustrates the surprising parallels between the two countries' historical trajectories in the nineteenth century in terms of empire building. It explains how both Meiji leaders and Rio de Janeiro's political elites, inspired by ongoing U.S. westward expansion, associated the notion of migration with that of colonial expansion. At the turn of the twentieth century, the convergence of Japan and Brazil in their processes of migration-driven expansion brought the two countries together to negotiate the start of Japanese migration to Brazil. Chapter 2 explains how the sailing of the *Kasato Maru*, the ship that brought the first official group of Japanese immigrants to Brazil, was a joint product of several historical processes happening concurrently across the Pacific Ocean: the Japanese expansionists' push for overseas emigration, the rise of anti-Japanese sentiment in the United States, and the rapid expansion of Brazil's coffee economy all served as indispensable factors at the start of the migration.

Part 2, comprising chapters 3 and 4, analyzes the emergence and growth of Japanese settler villages in southeastern Brazil in relation to Japanese colonialism in Asia during the critical period of the 1910s and 1920s. Chapter 3 details the origin, development, and expansion of Japanese farming villages in southeastern Brazil through the end of World War I. I explain this process by placing it in three distinct but interconnected contexts: Brazil's railway construction and new policies of land distribution in the state of São Paulo, the development of Japanese colonialism in the Korean Peninsula and the South Seas, and the emergence of a new world order following World War I. Chapter 4 examines how the historical rise of Kobe as a military and commercial port of the empire developed concurrently with the growth of Brazil-bound emigration. A series of structural changes within the Japanese government maximized its capacity to promote and manage the emigration. These changes not only led to a golden decade of Japanese migration to Brazil from the 1920s to the early 1930s but also established the institutional foundation for the Japanese government's relocation of its subjects to Asia during the late 1930s and the 1940s.

Part 3, comprising chapters 5 and 6, examines the minds and lives of Japanese Brazilian leaders and illustrates how they associated their ideas and activities in South America with contemporaneous Japanese colonial expansion in Asia from the 1930s to the end of World War II. Chapter 5 analyzes the process by which Japanese Brazilian opinion leaders created and cultivated a settler colonial identity among ordinary Japanese farmers in São Paulo. They did so through newspapers, school textbooks, and public events in the Japanese community with support from Tokyo. Individual settlers, men and women, first generation and second, rural and urban, began to connect with one another through a new imagined collective identity. Chapter 6 examines and compares the regimes of ethnic nationalism in Japan and Brazil in the decade right before World War II and explains how they worked together in unexpected ways to plunge the Japanese settler community into an identity crisis. It analyzes the different choices and actions of Japanese Brazilian elites, some of whom called for returning to Japan and joining the empire's expansion while others advocated for staying and pledging their allegiance to the flag of Estado Novo. The chapter concludes with an analysis of the impact this split had on the course of the Japanese empire in Asia and the Japanese community in Brazil.

Part 4 consists of the last two chapters. It sheds light on the continuity of Japan's collaborative settler colonialism before and after World War II. Chapter 7 delves into the details of the often-overlooked but critical history of Japanese migration and investment in the Brazilian Amazon and emphasizes both the transnational and transwar nature of Japanese collaborative settler colonialism in the rainforest. It not only illustrates its connections with Japanese colonial expansion in the Asia-Pacific region but also puts Japanese presence in the Amazon in the context of Brazil's own settler colonialism and U.S. expansion in the same region. The Brazilian Amazon was also the restarting point of Japanese migration after World War II because of the continuity in the ideology and practice of settler colonialism in both Japan and Brazil. Chapter 8 explains the close relationship between the cultural reinvention and socioeconomic transformation of the Japanese community in Brazil and Japan's reemergence onto the world stage as a member of the Western bloc during the Cold War. It further illustrates the social and political transformation of Japanese settlers into a "model minority" in Brazilian society in the context of Japan's rise as an economic powerhouse. The past and present of the Japanese Brazilian community became a central site for Japanese and American social scientists such as Izumi Sei'ichi, Robert Smith, and

John Cornell to conduct ethnographic research. Their scholarship served as the prelude for the discourse known as Nihonjinron, the theory about the Japanese. This discourse, which became popular in the 1970s, focused on the unique character of Japanese cultural identity as the key to Japanese ethnic and national success. It continues to influence how Japanese history and culture are understood around the world today.

PART I

THE ORIGINS,
NINETEENTH CENTURY–1908

1

The U.S. Frontier and the Making
of Two Migration States

At noon on December 15, 1869, in the castle of Goryōkaku near contemporary Hakodate, followers of the Tokugawa regime who fled to Hokkaido after losing their ground in Honshū during the Boshin War proclaimed the formation of the Republic of Ezo. These samurais held an allegedly democratic election and invited the Ainu tribe leaders to attend as observers. They voted Enomoto Takeaki, admiral of the Tokugawa Navy, president of the new government. Having studied in the Netherlands and trained in Western diplomacy, Enomoto proposed a ceasefire and an alliance with the Meiji forces. He asked the latter to allow the Tokugawa loyalists to colonize Hokkaido and turn this "barren island" into a "land of prosperity," and they would, in return, help defend the Japanese empire from Russian threats.[1] With its military ascendancy, the Meiji regime rejected the proposal and managed to completely defeat Enomoto and his followers within half a year. The Republic of Ezo, accordingly, quickly came to an end, and the newly formed Meiji empire officially annexed Hokkaido as its own territory.

Twenty years later, on the other side of the globe, in a military coup in Rio de Janeiro on November 15, 1889, Marshal Deodoro da Fonseca deposed Emperor Dom Pedro II and established a federal republic, which was officially titled the United States of Brazil. Fonseca also became the first president of the republic. Unlike its very short-lived Japanese counterpart, the United States of Brazil, also known as the First Republic, was remarkably successful. Faithful believers of "order and progress," its leaders managed to consolidate the new regime and maintain its solidarity for several decades.[2] It only came to an end following another coup d'état in 1930, succeeded by the long-lasting dictatorship of Getúlio Vargas.

With profoundly different paths, nevertheless, both republics were regimes of modern settler colonialism. Their formation marked a turning point in the settler colonial expansion of Japan and Brazil, respectively. The efforts of the Tokugawa diehards to establish an independent government in Hokkaido during the Boshin War were the culmination of a long-term and gradual expansion of the Tokugawa regime into Ainu land.[3] But as political democracy and polity served as the republic's central point of legitimacy, its birth also marked a radical departure from the past and symbolized the beginning of modern Japanese settler colonialism under the impact of the West. Meiji Japan's annexation of Hokkaido was immediately followed by the nascent empire's systematic colonization of the island, marked by the immigration of Japanese settlers, the institutional dispossession of the Ainu people's ancestral lands, and the massive extraction of natural resources.

Similarly, the formation of the First Republic was by no means the beginning of Brazil's colonial history, which could be traced to Portuguese expansion into Latin America in the sixteenth century. The history of modern settler colonialism in Brazil started in the early nineteenth century, together with the proclamation of the Empire of Brazil's independence from Portugal. The liberal-leaning elites in the era of the empire had already connected the racial exclusion of Black people, racial whitening through immigration, and the dispossession of Indigenous land in their political agendas.[4] However, the unprecedented usurpation of Indigenous land in Brazilian history, made possible by the massive influx of foreign immigrants, only started due to the new policies on land and immigration launched by the First Republic.

These two regimes, established by colonial expansion and legitimized by the claims of democracy and republicanism on opposite sides of the globe, both revealed the profound imprint of Anglo-American settler colonialism. While the fate of the two republics turned out to be very different, the historical paths of modern Japan and Brazil converged in their reproduction of Anglo-American expansion. As the following pages explain, the rise of modern Japan and Brazil as civilized nations and empires would require migration and colonial expansion at the same time. Elites in Tokyo and Rio de Janeiro alike justified such expansion by adopting the three logics of Anglo-American settler colonialism, namely, demography, race, and capitalism. Leaders of Meiji Japan saw emigration as a central means to expand the Japanese empire, through which the Japanese, people of a superior and expanding race, would claim their rightful share of power, wealth, and land in the world. Brazilian elites, on the other hand, believed that the immigration of superior ethnic groups was crucial not only for improving the existing racial composition of Brazilian society but also for claiming and utilizing the country's vast unoccupied land.

This chapter discusses the surprising parallel in the histories of Meiji Japan and independent Brazil in the nineteenth century, in which the ideas and practices of migration and colonial expansion entwine. In particular, their imitation of and interaction with U.S. westward expansion led to a series of changes in the 1880s in both countries that escalated their processes of settler colonial expansion. These changes led to the birth of migration states in Japan and Brazil, which eventually brought Japanese and Brazilian diplomats in touch with each other to start the negotiation for Japanese emigration to Brazil.

THE U.S. FRONTIER
AND JAPANESE SETTLER COLONIALISM

Thrust into the world of modern empires in the middle of the nineteenth century, Japan's rapid transformation into a modern empire took place around the same time that U.S. westward expansion and British colonial expansion shifted into high gear. Commodore Matthew Perry arrived in the Edo Bay in 1853, only five years after the conclusion of the Mexican-American War in which Perry himself fought as a navy commander. A few years later, the Government of India Act of 1858 put India under the direct control of the British Crown. The Homestead Act of 1862 stimulated an epic wave of mass migration from the eastern side of the Mississippi to the American West. In the same decade, the introduction of the Selection Act by British colonial authorities in New South Wales, Victoria, Queensland, and South Australia propelled a similar process of mass immigration and dispossession of Indigenous land in Australia. Around the same time, Tokugawa society also underwent a series of political and cultural upheavals that culminated in the formation of the Meiji empire.

The nascent Japanese empire was quick to secure its ground. Within a decade after its inception, the Meiji regime had already conducted a series of territorial expansions, including the annexation of Hokkaido and Okinawa and a military expedition to Taiwan, all of which were justified as measures of self-defense.[5] At the same time, Japan also emerged as a source of cheap labor in global capitalism's supply chain. As territorial expansion and outgoing migration had developed hand in hand, Japan's empire builders, like their counterparts in the United States, saw migration as a primary means of colonial expansion.[6]

The Meiji reproduction of U.S. settler colonialism showcased all the central logics of the latter, including the logics of demography, race, and capitalism. First, emigration-centered settler colonialism was initially put into practice during Japan's expansion in Hokkaido at the beginning of the Meiji era, when the modern discourse of overpopulation emerged in the Japanese archipelago as a rationalization. Mirroring the demographic logic of American westward migration, a governmental document in 1869 contrasted an overpopulated Japan proper with an empty Hokkaido and concluded that the unbalanced distribution of Japanese population had led to regional poverty.[7] The solution, accordingly, was to relocate the surplus people to underpopulated Hokkaido.[8] By exporting the "surplus people" as trailblazers of an expanding empire, Meiji Japan would not only alleviate its domestic population pressure but also expand its power and acquire additional wealth. In the same year, the imperial government established the Hokkaido

Development Agency (Kaitakushi) to oversee the colonization of Hokkaido. The agency quickly launched a series of migration campaigns that showed the clear imprint of Anglo-American expansion in the recent past. The *Hokkaido Development Journal* (*Hokkaido kaitaku zasshi*), the mouthpiece of the agency, compared the Japanese migrants in Hokkaido to the *Mayflower* pilgrims. It urged the first Japanese migrants to overcome all obstacles to clear a path for future empire builders in the northern frontier, just as the Americans' ancestors had done in the New World.[9]

Second, like its Western counterparts, the Japanese discourse of overpopulation emerged together with a celebration of the overall increase in the Japanese population, which served as evidence for Japanese racial superiority. Sugi Kōji, commonly known as the founder of modern Japanese demography, used modern statistical methods to illustrate the comparability of Japan's population growth rate with that of the European powers.[10] For the educated Japanese, Japan's world-class rate of population growth was a clear sign of its racial superiority and the government's political success. While they imagined the Japanese migrants in Hokkaido as Japan's own *Mayflower* settlers, the Ainu, native residents on the island, were cast in the role of the Native Americans. Horace Capron, American chief adviser of the Development Agency, came with a resume in colonial expansion: during Millard Fillmore's presidency, Capron had overseen the removal and resettlement of several Native American tribes after the Mexican-American War.[11] While investigating the land of Hokkaido, Capron perceived clear parallels between the primitive Ainu and the unenlightened Native Americans.[12] The description of the Ainu by Meiji leaders and Capron as an uncivilized people served as a justification for the Meiji government's appropriation of their ancestral land. Tsuda Sen, editor of the *Hokkaido Development Journal*, argued that the Ainu lacked both the drive and the ability to develop their land. Rather than let the land sit wasted, it was only natural for the civilized Japanese to take over the land and use it for better purposes.[13]

This racial hierarchy was codified in laws and regulations that empowered the Japanese government to deprive the Ainu of their land. The Land Tax Reform (*Chiso Kaisei*) of 1873 defined the Hokkaido land that sustained the Ainu's livelihood as wasteland and allowed the government to grant landownership to the Japanese settlers. In 1876, the Meiji government also outlawed the Ainu way of fishing and hunting.[14] In the name of spreading civilization, this series of policies deprived the Ainu of their land, materials, and cultures, leading to a sharp decline in the Ainu population. The educated Japanese, once again, looked to American history for an explanation. They described the Ainu as a vanishing race (*horobi-yuku minzoku*), like the Native Americans in North America. They believed that the demographic decline of the Ainu, though unfortunate, was both natural and unavoidable: in a Social Darwinist world, the backward Ainu could not hope to successfully compete with the superior races.[15]

Last but not least, Meiji leaders also legitimized settler migration and land acquisition in Hokkaido by the logic of modern capitalism. In the mind of Tsuda Sen, once in the hands of the Japanese, Hokkaido could be transformed into a land of formidable wealth where the Japanese settlers could farm, hunt, and engage in commerce.[16] It would become a precious source of ever-growing wealth, because its earth, river, mineral deposits, and flora and fauna were all potential resources for Japan's nascent capitalist economy. In this respect too, American westward migration served as a guide. Even though Japan could not yet compete with the United States in terms of wealth, power, and progress in democracy and education, Tsuda argued, the soil of Hokkaido was as rich as that of North America, and its climate was equally suitable for farming. He declared that an "America" would soon emerge from the Japanese archipelago, because as Japan's colonial project continued to develop, material production in Hokkaido would match that in the United States. In particular, he likened the position of Hokkaido to that of California. In his mind, California had been no more than an empty land until it became a U.S. territory, yet within two decades of American settlement, blessed with the discovery of gold and tremendous improvement in agricultural technology, California's population and material products had grown exponentially. Tsuda placed his hope in Hokkaido because he found it comparable to California in terms of both latitude and natural resources; and he envisioned that as Japanese settlers continued to make progress in land exploration, the Ezo of yesterday would become the California of tomorrow. A transformed Hokkaido would become Japan's own cornucopia; its output would both sustain Japan's economic growth at home and bring in wealth from abroad through exportation.[17]

THE AMERICAN WEST AND COLONIALISM
IN THE EMPIRE OF BRAZIL

Where Meiji leaders viewed U.S. westward expansion as a model for emigration-driven settler colonialism in Hokkaido, Brazilian elites also studied the U.S. experience closely as they designed their own blueprints for expansion in the Southern Cone. Brazil's history as a colonial territory of the Portuguese Empire could be traced to the sixteenth century. It did not emerge as an independent geopolitical power until the early nineteenth century. Due to immigration restrictions during the centuries-long colonial period, the settler population in Brazil remained relatively small, mainly residing on the east coast.[18] The settlers had made efforts to expand into the hinterland since the very beginning of the colonial era. The most noteworthy campaign of their inland exploration was the Bandeirante Movement in the seventeenth and eighteenth centuries that began with slave hunting and ended with mining.[19] In general, these activities did not seek to occupy the land itself. However, the Brazilian elites' ambition for land colonization in the interior grew rapidly after Brazil declared its independence, especially after Pedro II came to power in 1840.[20] They began to see colonization of the hinterland as a critical step in the dual process of nation making and empire building for the newly independent Brazil.[21] The ongoing U.S. westward expansion served as a successful example that they could borrow a page from.[22] Like their Japanese counterparts, the Brazilian elites strove to imitate the U.S. frontier experience by following the logics of demography, race, and capitalism.

First, the Brazilian elites saw population growth as the cornerstone of Brazil's rise as a modern nation. Similar to the United States in the nineteenth century, Brazil had a large territory and a small settler population. Impressed by the role that immigrants played in land exploration in the American West, Rio had an urgent demand for immigrants as the engine of colonization. Brazilian leaders expected immigrants to assist the government as the state moved to claim its sovereignty over the vast Indigenous land it had inherited from the Portuguese Crown. As a result, migration, colonization, and peopling were often conflated in the minds of Brazilian elites at the time.[23]

In Brazilian elites' blueprints of empire, race also played a central role. They were convinced by the history of immigration in the United States that only white people could create progress. Henrique J. Rebbello's 1836 book, *The Treatise of the Population in Brazil*, for example, stressed the urgency to increase Brazil's population through immigration but also made it clear that only migrants from "civilized" Europe were welcome.[24] As subscribers to modern racism, educated Brazilians concluded that the nation's current backwardness was due to the inferiority of its racial stock, a product of miscegenation between the Portuguese, the Indigenous peoples, and African slaves.[25] They believed that the only way for Brazil to catch up with the United States was to "whiten" Brazilians through immigration.[26]

Meanwhile, Brazilian leaders also believed that immigration-centered colonization was crucial for Brazil's economic development and cultural progress. For those who endorsed the abolition of slavery, immigration was essential to agricultural development. They wanted to model Brazil's agricultural structure after the United States, preferring small farms to big plantations. As abolition appeared increasingly inevitable, the planters themselves were also warming up to the idea of lenient immigration policies. Though having little interest in turning immigrants into settlers, they believed that immigration could fill the eventual labor vacuum on plantations.[27]

The Brazilian elites' desire for non-Portuguese white immigrants was evident in the Imperial Constitution promulgated in 1824. One article of the constitution permitted people of all religions to worship privately in this formally Roman Catholic nation. Another article offered Brazilian citizenship to all born in its territory and to women who married Brazilian men.[28] While this new constitution opened Brazil's doors to immigrants, 1850 marked a decisive moment in the convergence of immigration and settler colonialism. The Queiroz Law, enacted in that year, cut off the major source of slave labor by ending Brazil's participation in the international slave trade. As the labor demand on plantations continued to grow along with Brazil's coffee exports, the ban on the international slave trade made the inflow of free immigrants an economic necessity.

Passed in the same year, the Land Law (Lei de Terras) would allow the government to legally deprive Indigenous peoples of their land by defining it as publicly owned. The Land Law also banned private acquisitions of such land except through purchase, enabling the government to monopolize ownership of the land and its distribution. Due to the overall weakness of state power at the time, large planters often ignored this law by claiming new land near their plantations through de facto occupation. Nevertheless, the law established a legal basis for the Brazilian government to appropriate Indigenous land. Together with the law, the central government created a bureaucratic service, the Repartição Geral das Terras Públicas, in charge of managing public land and promoting colonization.[29] Immigrants were among the main beneficiaries of public land. They were invited into the country and then transported to the inland region, occupying and farming the land there in the decades to come. In essence, they functioned as colonial settlers.[30]

These two important laws represented a turning point in Brazilian history during the mid-nineteenth century, a time when Rio de Janeiro was adopting an increasingly favorable view of immigration. The reasons for this attitude shift included the modernization of Brazil's transportation system and the rise of a generation of liberal-leaning intellectuals and politicians who were amazed by American achievements in modernization and territorial expansion. They believed that immigrants, like their counterparts in the United States, could serve as agents of progress and civilization for Brazil. To make the country more attractive for immigration, they called for a more liberal, open, and democratic Brazil by emphasizing local and provincial power, slavery abolition, and free trade.

In 1866, a group of politicians, journalists, and intellectuals formed the Sociedade Internacional de Imigração (SII; International Immigration Society), a symbol of the Brazilian liberals' collective effort to promote immigration. The founders of the SII believed that immigration was a crucial tool to bring about structural changes in Brazil. They argued that immigrants were an essential source for non-slave labor and agents of civilization and progress.[31] However, Brazil's conservative institutions made the country an undesirable destination for migrants. The society's mission, as its members envisioned, was to facilitate immigration through political liberalization in the form of slavery abolition, greater religious freedom, and revision of existing laws on land and taxation. In addition to calling for these institutional reforms, society members tried to attract more immigrants through a variety of avenues. Some tried to promote the image of Brazil as a wonderful migration destination, others urged the government to improve transportation logistics for newly arrived immigrants, and still others became migrant recruiters.[32] Though the society itself only lasted a year because of a lack of governmental support and resources, the words and deeds of its founding members deserve close examination because they represented the aspirations of the liberal-leaning elites, the same group that successfully turned Brazil into a republic by deposing Dom Pedro II. Once in power, the republican government immediately carried out the liberals' agenda and ushered in the era of mass immigration.

A particularly noteworthy figure was Aureliano Cândido Tavares Bastos, an influential politician and journalist. He was one of the core leaders of the SII who had drafted its manifesto. An admirer of the United States, Tavares Bastos believed that the U.S. immigration-driven model of nation building was the one that Brazil should imitate. A set of far-reaching liberal reforms, including the establishment of a federal system, free trade, the opening of the Amazon, and the gradual abolition of slavery, was necessary to attract immigrants.[33] However, not all foreigners were suitable for Brazil's grand task. Tavares Bastos's admiration of the United States made him particularly interested in recruiting U.S. citizens.[34] The fact that the SII was founded in 1866, only one year after the end of the U.S. Civil War, reflected the Brazilian elites' intention to recruit Confederate supporters.[35]

American westward expansion also profoundly shaped the migration recruiting activities of William Scully, another core member of the society, whose primary targets were Europeans. An admirer of the success of Anglo-American settler colonialism in general, Scully believed that the English and the Irish, two major immigrant groups in the United States, were the most desirable for Brazil.[36] To attract Anglophone immigrants, he named the newspaper that he founded for migration recruitment purposes *Anglo-Brazilian Times*. The newspaper was published in English and circulated in both Brazil and Europe. Its central message was straightforward: like the United States, Brazil was a land of promise for agricultural settlers. It was similarly endowed with vast terrain, fertile soil, and a pleasant climate; there ordinary men could easily acquire land and farming tools and prosper through honest labor.[37]

In addition to attracting the British, the Portuguese, and former U.S. Confederates, Brazilian leaders explored other migration sources. Between 1820 and 1875, they conducted several campaigns to attract immigrants from central and northern Europe as well as Qing China. While none of these campaigns succeeded as planned, the government did manage to bring in 330,000 immigrants overall.[38] With free land granted by the government, some immigrants indeed became frontier settlers. However, this number was dwarfed by the nine million immigrants who entered the United States during roughly the same period. Moreover, over half of the immigrants who arrived in Brazil during this period were Portuguese, the majority of whom resided in coastal cities instead of the interior.[39] Although the last fifteen years of the empire saw the arrival of some additional 330,000 immigrants, compared to the massive influx of immigrants during the First Republic, the immigration policies of this period were far from effective.[40] Nevertheless, neither the idea nor the practice of taking Indigenous land through immigration was new in the era of the First Republic. Settler colonialism, as both a political structure and an ideology, had already been firmly established during the imperial era.

THE RISE OF MIGRATION STATES IN BRAZIL AND JAPAN IN THE 1880S

The decade of the 1880s saw both Brazil and Japan making a substantial leap forward in their practice of settler colonialism, a development that was driven by political and economic changes at both global and local levels. In the Southern Cone, the State of São Paulo's coffee economy continued to expand. This led to not only further encroachment of Indigenous land, but also a series of institutional changes that resulted in a mass influx of immigrants. Meanwhile, in East Asia, the Meiji government made policy changes that opened the gate for Japan's emigration-driven expansion overseas. These developments symbolized the formation of the migration states in Japan and Brazil that jointly brought the diplomats of the two settler colonial regimes to the same table to discuss Japanese migration to Brazil.

Commercial coffee cultivation in Rio de Janeiro first started in the late eighteenth century, and the beans quickly became a major source of wealth in Brazil's export-centered economy. By the 1850s, half of the country's export revenue came from coffee. In the 1860s, thanks to the sale of coffee, the Brazilian empire finally achieved a positive trade balance.[41] The expansion of coffee cultivation also brought about monumental economic and political changes. During the first half of the nineteenth century, Rio de Janeiro remained the central state for coffee cultivation, and the city of Rio continued to be the central port for coffee exportation. By midcentury, however, coffee cultivation had expanded southward to São Paulo and Minas Gerais. By the century's end, the state of São Paulo had overtaken Rio de Janeiro and became the new coffee center. The rise of São Paulo in the coffee economy was accompanied by the emergence of a new mode of coffee production. Traditional coffee *fazendas* (plantations), represented by those in Rio, were supported almost exclusively by slave labor. However, because the abolitionist movement increasingly gained momentum, new coffee planters in São Paulo turned to immigrants as an alternative source of labor. As coffee cultivation in the state of São Paulo expanded westward into the inland region, the reliance on immigrant labor only increased.

The westward expansion of coffee cultivation was made possible by the construction of railways in the state. Since the formation of the São Paulo Railway Company at the turn of the 1860s, several railway lines had begun to link the state's interior with the city of São Paulo and then to the Port of Santos.[42] New railway lines kept pushing the frontier of the coffee economy westward and northward, making possible the transportation of coffee and goods between the eastern coast and inland. In the name of law, more and more Indigenous land was taken by

FIGURE 3. The front cover of an 1882 issue of *Revista Illustrada*, an independent cartoon magazine based in the capital, Rio de Janeiro. The magazine was one of the most influential humor
periodicals focusing on contemporary politics in Brazil at the end of the nineteenth century.
The image shows that the speeches and debates in the imperial parliament of the day only led to
the further deterioration of the living conditions of Indigenous people. The caption reads, "Poor
thing!" Source: *Revista Illustrada*, no. 301 (1882).

coffee growers. The rapid appropriation of Indigenous land can be measured by
the increase in coffee trees in the state: in 1870, there were 70 million coffee trees;
in 1880, 106 million; in 1890, 200 million; and in 1900, 600 million.[43]

The coffee boom in São Paulo hastened the political rise of the liberal-leaning
Brazilian elites. Seeing the United States as a role model of nation building, they
were advocates for both slavery abolition and mass immigration. Two organizations for immigration promotion emerged in the 1880s as a result of their efforts.
Of the two, the Sociedade Central de Imigração (SCI; Central Immigration

FIGURE 4. The back cover of an 1877 issue of *Revista Illustrada*. It shows how Quintino Bocaiúva, a leading anti-monarchy journalist and politician in Imperial Brazil, envisioned the United States as a model for Brazil's future nation. Bocaiúva served as Brazil's foreign minister after the republican revolution. Source: *Revista Ilustrada*, no. 63 (April 1877).

Society) called for an increase in government subsidies to attract immigrants, hoping that increased immigration would foster the growth of the small farm economy.[44] The large coffee plantation owners and their supporters formed the Sociedade Promotora de Imigração (SPI; Immigration Promotion Society). Its members opposed government subsidies for immigration and believed that only private funds should be used for this purpose. While these two societies represented the divergent interests of two very different social groups, both functioned as key organizations sponsored by the government to recruit immigrants and promote immigration. In addition to seeing immigration as the primary labor source for the booming coffee economy, members of both societies believed that immigration was essential to claim and occupy the vast land in the interior and to whiten the Brazilian racial stock.[45]

With military support, the liberal-leaning faction brought the empire, already exhausted by the Paraguayan War, to an end in 1889. Brazil's transition to a republic, along with the abolition of slavery, marked the political ascendancy of its southern coffee elites, especially those from the state of São Paulo. The establishment of the First Republic was the culmination of policy and institutional changes within the government aimed at fostering immigration—a process that was already underway in the final years of the empire. This regime change, therefore, marked the formation of the migration state in Brazil. As the SPI and the SCI continued to function toward the end of the century, funds to subsidize immigration, drawn from both the public and private sectors, grew steadily.[46] As a result, the republic would receive 2.6 million immigrants within the next three decades. The Japanese were initially deemed undesirable. Merely a year after its formation, the new regime banned the immigration of Africans and Asians, as its leaders considered these two groups racially inferior and believed they would only degrade Brazil's racial stock.[47] Yet the republic soon reopened its doors to Asian immigrants in 1893 due to a pressing demand for coffee labor. In response to the Meiji empire's overall successful Westernization and expansion in East Asia, Rio turned to the Japanese as a more palatable alternative to the heavily maligned Chinese.[48]

Meanwhile, on the other side of the globe, Japanese expansionists had begun to look beyond Hokkaido to search for migration destinations overseas. The rampant inflation triggered by the Satsuma Rebellion forced Meiji leaders to adopt a restrained fiscal policy known as the Matsukata Deflation. Amid steep budget cuts, Tokyo suspended government-sponsored migration to Hokkaido and lifted the ban on overseas emigration. Thus, Japan's emigration-centered migration state took shape. Just as the Japanese were initially unwelcome in Brazil due to its policy of racial whitening, Brazil was not the first choice for Meiji leaders, who sought to reposition the Japanese within the global racial hierarchy through emigration-driven expansion.

While the Meiji government had first sponsored Japanese labor migration to the Kingdom of Hawai'i in 1885, American westward expansion had inspired Japanese expansionists to view the American West itself as the first ideal destination for Japanese emigration. In the mind of Fukuzawa Yukichi, one of the most influential intellectuals in Meiji Japan, what made the United States especially attractive was not its material wealth but its recent experience of westward expansion. Fukuzawa described the United States as an expanding nation that kept opening up new land through frontier conquest and migration. He believed that the Japanese should follow the example of the Europeans by migrating to this land of promise and participate in U.S. frontier expansion as colonial settlers. One day, he envisioned, the offspring of Japanese immigrants would gain political rights in the United States and sway American politics. Starting from the United States, Japan's overseas migrants—and their descendants—would establish ten or even twenty settler nations, which he called "new Japans" (*shin nihon*), around the world.[49]

Fukuzawa put his ideas into action. He did not achieve much success with his campaigns to relocate Japanese subjects to the U.S. West Coast, but a number of students from his Keiō School did manage to land in San Francisco. In 1888, they formed the San Francisco chapter of the Keiō Alumni Association with thirty-five members.[50] During the 1880s and 1890s, many educated youth, like these Keiō students, had reached the U.S. West Coast along with Meiji Japan's political dissidents. Together, they constituted the bulk of the elite circle of the Japanese American community of the day.[51] Although holding divergent political views, they all saw the United States as both a land of promise for individual success and a frontier for Japanese expansion.

The Japanese settlers' experience at the frontier of American westward expansion confirmed the intrinsic ties between migration and colonial expansion in their minds. However, those who hoped to pursue a colonial dream in the American West were soon disillusioned by rampant racism against Asian immigrants on the West Coast. Some took the institutionalized Chinese exclusion and the rise of anti-Japanese sentiment in the United States at the end of the nineteenth century as an announcement that white settlers had monopolized the land of North America. As a result, the United States was no longer an ideal target of expansion for Japan. Instead, the Japanese should make haste to occupy the supposedly unmarked and unowned territories in the South Seas and Latin America; once they staked their claims to ownership, they could exclude other races, just like white Americans were now doing.[52] Of course, in the minds of Meiji expansionists, only the "civilized" races were qualified to compete for landownership. Indigenous peoples such as Native Americans and Pacific Islanders were, like the Ainu in Hokkaido, uncivilized races who had no right to the land they were wasting. It was at this time that Brazil caught the interest of Meiji expansionists.

FROM MEXICO TO BRAZIL

The central figure behind the ideas and practices of Japanese expansion to Latin America was Enomoto Takeaki. After serving as a high-ranking official during the colonization of Hokkaido in the 1870s, Enomoto rose to a series of key cabinet positions in the Meiji government by heading the Ministries of Communications (1885–89), Education (1889–90), Foreign Affairs (1891–92), and, finally, Agriculture and Commerce (1894–97).[53] Believing that national strength could only be achieved by frontier conquest and colonial expansion, Enomoto made a few unsuccessful attempts to purchase the Mariana Islands, the Palau Islands, and Borneo as early as the mid-1870s.[54] To promote studies on the Pacific Rim with colonial ambitions in mind, he helped establish the Tokyo Geographical Society (Tokyo Chigaku Kyōkai) in 1879, modeled after the Royal Geographical Society in London.[55]

A decisive step that Enomoto made in his promotion of Japanese expansion in Latin America was the formation of the Colonial Society (Shokumin Kyōkai) in 1893, the same year that Brazil's First Republic reopened its doors to Asian immigration.

As Japan's first nationwide organization to facilitate overseas expansion, its members and donors came from a variety of social backgrounds and political causes. Their ranks included politicians and bureaucrats, owners and employees of migration companies, journalists and business elites. However, they were unified in their acceptance of the convergence of emigration and settler colonialism, and they shared a belief in the urgent need for Japan to participate in the scramble for land and resources through overseas migration.[56] The society diligently disseminated information and ideas for overseas expansion by hosting public lectures and publishing its official journal, *Reports of the Colonial Society* (*Shokumin Kyōkai hōkoku*). It also sponsored investigative trips and expeditions around the Pacific Rim. Facilitating Japanese migration to Mexico was among the society's first missions.

In 1891, two years before the formation of the Colonial Society, Enomoto had already begun exploring the possibilities of Japanese expansion to Mexico by taking advantage of the Mexican government's policies to attract immigrants and international investment.[57] In the same year, under his leadership, the Ministry of Foreign Affairs established the Japanese consulate in Mexico City, which collected local information in order to facilitate migration planning. Fujita Toshirō, Japanese consul in Mexico, investigated Sonora, Sinaloa, and Chiapas to evaluate their suitability for Japanese migration.[58] Fujita hired D. W. Jones, an American expert, as a translator and adviser for this project. Jones convinced Fujita that Mexico was endowed with fertile land and limitless natural resources. He reasoned that because the majority of existing residents were Native Americans who were backward and inferior, Mexican land could be considered empty and open. Jones suggested that Japanese settlers should purchase land along the Mexican west coast, where they would settle and prosper.[59] In his report to Tokyo, Fujita also pointed out the importance of coffee cultivation as a promising business for potential Japanese colonies in Mexico.[60]

In 1893, the Colonial Society dispatched its secretary, Nemoto Tadashi, to southern Mexico to conduct another survey, and Nemoto pointed to Chiapas as the best region to establish Japan's first colony in Mexico. After a few more inspections and years of negotiation, Enomoto and the Colonial Society eventually garnered sufficient financial and political support to complete a land purchase with a fifteen-year loan from the Mexican government. They established the first Japanese settler community, known as Enomoto Colony, in southern Chiapas in 1897. This colonial project intended to relocate Japanese subjects to Mexico as agricultural settlers who would make a living by cultivating coffee and other tropical crops.

Though Enomoto Colony quickly ran into trouble and collapsed because of a lack of financial backup and a labor shortage, the efforts of Enomoto and his followers marked the starting point of Japanese expansion in Latin America.[61] During his trip to Mexico in 1893, Nemoto also investigated Peru as another potential destination for Japanese migration.[62] The next year, following the first meeting between Japanese and Brazilian diplomats in San Francisco, Tokyo dispatched Nemoto to investigate Brazil. Nemoto reached Rio de Janeiro in September 1894

FIGURE 5. This is a picture of a European settler community called Nova Europa in São Paulo that Fujita Toshirō attached to his report to Tokyo in 1908. Japanese policy makers referred to European immigration and land acquisition in Brazil as a model for Japanese migration since its very beginning. Source: Fujita Toshirō, Box 1, Access No. 2017c47–14. 36, Hoover Institution Archives.

and, in the next few weeks, toured Brazilian coastal states such as Pernambuco, Bahía, Minas Gerais, and São Paulo. Unsurprisingly, he was most impressed with São Paulo. There he was not only warmly welcomed by the governor but also amazed by the developed transportation system and the facilities to accommodate immigrants in the Port of Santos.

In his report to Tokyo, Nemoto concluded that the Brazilian East was a perfect alternative to the American West as a destination for Japanese migration. Just like the United States, he reasoned, Brazil was endowed with vast and rich land. Among its most prosperous states along the east coast, São Paulo was particularly promising. Its climate was as pleasant as San Francisco's, and its vast land had boundless potential to accommodate Japanese migrants, who could easily settle down and expand their community.[63] Encouraged by Nemoto's report, the Meiji government and Japanese migration companies began to earnestly explore the possibility of migration to Brazil. Their Brazilian counterparts, including government officials, planters, and migration recruiters, were likewise awash with enthusiasm. Thus began the negotiations. After a few failed attempts, the first official group of Japanese migrants eventually reached the shore of São Paulo in 1908 via the *Kasato Maru*, one year after the United States shut its doors to Japanese labor migrants in the Gentlemen's Agreement.

The settler colonial nature of Japanese migration can be attested further by the sailing of the *Kasato Maru* itself. This first group of immigrants appeared to be no more than contract laborers who simply filled the labor vacuum in Brazil's coffee plantations created by the abolition of slavery. Among the 793 migrants on board, all but 12 had signed labor contracts with São Paulo's coffee planters.[64] However, the initial agreement actually required the government of São Paulo to establish colonies for these Japanese migrants along the state's central railway line so that they could purchase land at a low price. This was because the Japanese government, which had actively supported the *Kasato Maru* migration campaign, expected these migrants to eventually settle down in Brazil as landowning farmers once their labor contracts ended.[65]

. . .

This chapter explains how American westward expansion inspired settler colonialism in both Meiji Japan and post-independence Brazil. These two countries' paths to settler colonialism eventually crossed when their diplomats made contact in 1893 regarding Japanese emigration to Brazil. The convergence of Meiji Japan and post-independence Brazil in their nineteenth-century expansion deepens our understanding of the history of Japanese migration to Brazil in two ways. First, it demonstrates that both the intellectual and political origins of the migration should be traced to the nineteenth century, decades before the sailing of the *Kasato Maru*, hitherto the commonly accepted starting point of the migration. Second, the migration itself, from its inception, should be understood in the context of both Japanese and Brazilian settler colonial expansion.

Meiji leaders believed that the Japanese, people of a civilized race like the Anglo-Saxons, had their own manifest destiny to fulfill. The empire's expansion started with the colonization of Hokkaido through the migration of Japanese settlers to its northern frontier. During the 1880s, it turned to the American West and later Latin America as destinations for Japanese emigrants. In the Southern Cone, Brazilian elites saw immigration-driven colonization as a primary means for Brazil's own project of nation building. For the liberals who established the First Republic in 1889, immigration meant much more than simply meeting the growing labor demand in coffee plantations. An influx of racially superior people, they believed, would not only improve the existing Brazilian racial stock but also turn Brazil's hinterland into a source of wealth and power for the expanding nation.

From both the sending side and the receiving side, leaders of Meiji Japan and post-independence Brazil saw migrants as agents of colonialism. Both regimes had embarked on the processes to institutionally dispossess Indigenous peoples of their ancestral land through migration. These processes were marked by the promulgation of the Land Law of 1850 in Brazil and the Land Regulation Ordinance of 1872 in Japan. Both laws defined the land owned by Indigenous peoples as wasteland and allowed the government to legally appropriate and redistribute it to migrants.

In addition to the formation of migration states in both Brazil and Japan in the late nineteenth century, a comparison of the migration organizations established in the Empire of Brazil and Meiji Japan reveals yet another surprising parallel between these two colonial powers on opposite sides of the globe. Established by Brazilian elites at different times in the nineteenth century, organizations that promoted immigration, such as the SII, SCI, and SPI, all aimed to attract white immigrants to Brazil as agents of civilization and land colonization. The Colonial Society, established in Tokyo in 1893, on the other hand, took upon itself the mission of facilitating Japan's emigration-driven expansion overseas. In both Japan and Brazil, the sociopolitical elites who made up the membership of these migration societies revealed the link between migration and colonial expansion in their minds. The next chapter examines more closely the contexts of the sailing of the *Kasato Maru*, the commonly accepted starting point of Japanese immigration to Brazil.

2

———

Before the Sailing of the *Kasato Maru*

In 1904, four years before the *Kasato Maru* reached the shores of São Paulo, the United States hosted another World's Fair after the World's Columbian Exposition in Chicago. Known as the last great international exposition before World War I, the World's Fair of 1904 took place in St. Louis, Missouri. The completion of westward continental expansion, the victory in the Mexican-American War, and the annexation of Hawai'i had turned the United States into a rising leader of modern empires; at the same time, the focus of international colonial competition had begun shifting to the Pacific Rim. The fair, designed to showcase U.S. greatness to the world, highlighted American achievements in material wealth, cultural progress, and cutting-edge technologies. Then U.S. president Theodore Roosevelt's multivolume epic, *The Winning of the West*, well documented the spirit of the moment. Completed at the beginning of the twentieth century, the book celebrated U.S. westward expansion as part of the dispersion of the English-speaking people across the "waste spaces" around the globe as the "most striking feature in world history" of the past few centuries.[1] This settler colonial logic was undergirded by a rigid global racial hierarchy that placed white Americans and Europeans at the top and Indigenous peoples at the bottom, justifying Anglo-American settler colonial expansion in the name of human progress. This concept is illustrated on the front cover of the fifth volume of the official guide to the St. Louis World's Fair.

Policy makers in both Japan and Brazil saw the World's Fair as an opportunity to demonstrate the progress their own nations had made on the way to becoming civilized powers by emulating Anglo-American settler colonialism. Both Tokyo and Rio dispatched delegations. To emphasize this progress, a main task of both delegations was to present the primitivity of their respective Indigenous peoples. With the assistance of Frederick Starr, a professor of anthropology at the

42

FIGURE 6. Titled *Types and Development of Man*, this picture served as the front cover for volume 5 of the official guide to the St. Louis World's Fair. It ranked human races based on a hierarchy of civilization. Its description read: "The photogravure herewith is from an excellent specially prepared drawing which very accurately illustrates, as nearly as the science of ethnology is able to do, the characteristic types of mankind in a progressive order of development from primitive or prehistoric man to the highest example of modern civilization. The two central figures are symbolical, representing Intelligence, with the torch of Enlightenment and book of Wisdom, invading the darksome cave in which Ignorance skulks in companionship with a bird of evil omen and superstition. It is aspiration lighting the dungeon of savagery and directing the race to better conditions, moral, intellectual, and social."

FIGURE 7. Photos of the Ainu people of Japan on display at the St. Louis World's Fair of 1904. Source: *Louisiana and the Fair: An Exposition of the World, Its People and Their Achievements*, vol. 5 (1904), 1705.

University of Chicago, the Japanese delegates brought a group of Ainu people to be exhibited at the fair, together with Native peoples from North and South America, Africa, and the Philippines in the Pavilion of Anthropology.[2] By contrasting the "savageness" of the Hokkaido natives, the Japanese delegation aimed to underscore the stunning progress the Japanese had made to become civilized people themselves.[3] Likewise, Hermann von Ihering, director of the State Museum of São Paulo, wrote an essay for the fair that described Brazil's Indigenous people as hopelessly backward.[4] As they were incapable of making any contribution to Brazil's progress in land colonization, Ihering argued, they were doomed to extinction.[5] The parallel in the Japanese and Brazilian delegations' presentation of their countries' Indigenous peoples at the fair revealed their continuing reproduction of Anglo-American settler colonialism.

This chapter discusses the significance of the *Kasato Maru*, which transported the first official group of Japanese immigrants to Brazil in 1908, in this historical context. It should be noted that migration-related diplomatic contact between Japan and Brazil began as early as 1893, but fifteen years passed before any plans materialized. This chapter examines how a confluence of events during these years in Japan and Brazil, as well as other parts of the world, eventually led to the sailing of the *Kasato Maru*. It also explains why it took fifteen years for bilateral negotiations between the two migration states to come to fruition. A careful examination of these related events not only elucidates the historical contexts and political and intellectual origins of Japanese migration to Brazil but also sheds light on the close ties it had with the settler colonialism of both the Japanese empire and the First Republic.

The turn of the twentieth century was a critical phase in the history of Japan's migration-driven expansion. During these years, Japanese expansionists gradually reached a consensus that farmer migration and agricultural settlement would be a desirable form of overseas migration. This intellectual change determined the character of Japanese migration to Brazil from the start. While the vast majority of Japanese migrants carried by the *Kasato Maru* to Brazil were under labor contracts with coffee plantations in São Paulo, the intention of their recruiter, Mizuno Ryū, was to turn them into farming settlers who would establish the first Japanese colonies in Brazil.[6] In fact, the establishment of Japanese agricultural colonies was also the primary motivator for Tokyo to approve and support Mizuno's initiative.[7] How farmer migration and agriculture-centered colonialism became the dominant discourse of Japanese expansion at the turn of the twentieth century, accordingly, is another question this chapter seeks to answer.

This chapter locates its analysis in four geographic sites across the globe: the Japanese archipelago, southeastern Brazil, and the Pacific coast and Texas Gulf coast of the continental United States. First, it analyzes the fundamental changes in social relations and the political terrain in the Japanese archipelago between the First Sino-Japanese War and the Russo-Japanese War. It discusses the social changes in domestic Japan that led to the rise of agrarianism and the discourse of farmer migration. It then examines Japanese migration to Hawai'i, the U.S. West Coast, and Texas during this period. It explores the important ways these experiences had transformed Japanese settler colonialism and stimulated Japanese migration to Brazil. Finally, the chapter examines the important changes that took place in southeastern Brazil, including the rapid development of the coffee economy and the rise of the state of São Paulo as Brazil's new economic and political center, which made it the most suitable destination for Japanese migrants.

FROM LABORERS TO FARMERS:
THE TRANSFORMATION OF JAPAN'S
MIGRATION-DRIVEN EXPANSION

The meeting between Japanese and Brazilian diplomats in San Francisco in 1893 seemingly heralded a bright future for Japanese emigration to Brazil. Four years later, the two governments established a formal diplomatic relationship, and it was none other than Chinda Sutemi, the Japanese consul in San Francisco, who arrived in Rio de Janeiro as the first Japanese minister plenipotentiary to Brazil.[8] One of his main tasks was to seal the emigration deal and oversee the process of Japanese migration and settlement in South America. Between 1893 and the sailing of the *Kasato Maru* in 1908, policy makers and migration companies in both Brazil and Japan made several attempts to bring Japanese migrants to Brazil, yet none succeeded.

The main reason for these failures was that neither side was the other's first choice. For the leaders of the First Republic, European immigrants were both plentiful and preferable to Japanese laborers. Starting in the late 1880s, the abolition of slavery and a series of new government policies ushered in the era of mass migration in Brazil. In the last decade of the nineteenth century alone, about 1.1 million European immigrants arrived in Brazil, nearly tripling the number of immigrants arriving in the previous decade.[9] This new wave of immigration was marked by a rapid increase in Italian immigrants, who made up about 60 percent of all immigrants to Brazil between 1890 and 1902.[10] As European immigrants poured into the republic in the 1890s, the Brazilian elites did not consider Japan as a source of immigrants with any sense of urgency. With the goal of whitening the nation's racial stock in mind, they saw Europeans as Brazil's top choice for immigration, and Brazilian migrant recruiters were not eager to offer attractive conditions to Japanese laborers. At times, they did not take their Japanese counterparts seriously, a prime example of which can be seen in the abrogation of the migration contract between Yoshisa Emigration Company of Japan and Prado Jordão & Company of Brazil.

The contract in question was the second one between the two companies. The first contract, signed only one year after the first meeting between Japanese and Brazilian diplomats in San Francisco, became void because a new regulation promulgated by the Japanese government that year banned the migration of Japanese subjects to countries without formal diplomatic relations with Japan. Anticipating that Japanese-Brazilian diplomatic relations would be established in 1897, the two companies made a second deal that sought to transport 1,500 to 2,000 Japanese subjects to the state of São Paulo that year. The Japanese were supposed to work as laborers on local coffee plantations for five years. While Prado Jordão & Company was responsible for the migrants' round-trip transportation, the planters would offer them lodging, food, clothing, and other necessities, in addition to wages. However, Prado Jordão & Company backed out of this agreement four days before the migrants' scheduled departure, leaving its Japanese partner and the migrants themselves to deal with the fallout.[11]

There were a number of reasons for the unfortunate fate of this agreement. For one, the price of Brazilian coffee plummeted on the international market in 1897, losing more than a half of its value from the previous year; this meant that planters were unmotivated and financially ill prepared to recruit new laborers. At the same time, the First Republic was only able to suppress the Canudos Rebellion in Bahia after years of armed conflict. Known as the deadliest civil war in Brazilian history, it left the federal government less capable of providing financial support to immigration.[12] Race also played a role. The fact that Prado Jordão & Company only gave its Japanese partner last-minute notice demonstrated how insignificant the Japanese immigrants were in the minds of the Brazilian agents when European immigrants were easy to recruit.

Meanwhile, for leaders of imperial Japan, Brazil was far from an ideal destination of Japanese emigration. A few weeks after the cancellation of the above-mentioned contract, Chinda Sutemi took office as Japan's first minister to Brazil. He quickly became pessimistic about the prospects of Japanese migration because the racism he observed in Brazil echoed his experiences in North America. Moreover, he realized that life on the Brazilian coffee plantations would be extremely challenging for Japanese migrants. Not only would they have to work in poor conditions with low wages for several years in order to pay off their debts to the planters, but there was also the matter of adjusting to a foreign culture, religion, and language.[13]

In a report to Tokyo in 1898, Chinda opined that the current plan for Japanese labor migration would have no future in Brazil. The only viable path, he argued, would be for the Japanese to follow the example of German immigrants in southern Brazil. That is, instead of working on coffee plantations as laborers, they should become independent farmers and build settler colonies. To do so would require a Japanese company to purchase land in Brazil and build self-sufficient settler colonies on it. In other words, the way to Japanese success in Brazil was to back up the migration with capital investment and create settler colonies, not to simply export plantation laborers.[14]

Chinda resigned in the same year due to illness but not before calling off two migration plans. One was a labor migration contract between the Japanese Emigration Company (Nihon Imin Gaisha) in Kobe and Fiorita & Company in Rio de Janeiro, and another was the Oriental Emigration Company's (Tōyō Imin

Gaisha's) plan to bring Japanese laborers to the Amazon Basin.[15] Ōkoshi Nari-nori, Chinda's successor, who took office in 1899, held a similar opinion. He also warned Tokyo and the prefectural governments against granting migration per-mits to Japanese subjects tempted by Brazilian recruiters' empty promises. This led to the cancellation of two more contracts signed by Japanese and Brazilian migration companies.[16]

An immediate reason for Chinda and Ōkoshi's opposition to labor migration to Brazil was the austere living and working conditions on the coffee plantations coupled with paltry benefits for the laborers. In a broader context, their pessimism also stemmed from the events that took place in Hawai'i and the U.S. mainland at the turn of the twentieth century. From the late 1880s to the end of the 1900s, these two locations were the most popular destinations for Japanese emigrants outside of Asia. Most of the migrants were the rural poor who decided to leave the archi-pelago in order to lift themselves out of poverty. To them, the U.S. mainland was particularly attractive due to its plentiful opportunities and relatively high wages for migrant laborers. As the number of Japanese labor migrants to the United States grew steadily, exporting migrants to Brazil where the working and living conditions were not as good appeared unnecessary.

The Japanese government's pessimism about Brazil-bound migration also reflected an ongoing intellectual shift in the debate surrounding colonial expan-sion within the empire. At the turn of the twentieth century, an increasing num-ber of Japan's empire builders began to favor the emigration of farmers to that of laborers as a means of expansion. In their minds, farming was a better way to secure Japanese subjects' ownership of foreign land. In fact, Chinda's and Ōkoshi's calls for land acquisition and colonization in Brazil were echoed by their colleagues on the Korean Peninsula around the same time. Katō Masuo, Japanese minister to the Kingdom of Korea, made a similar proposal in 1901. Complaining that Japanese migrants in the United States and Hawai'i were noth-ing more than temporary laborers, Katō urged his fellow countrymen to focus their efforts on Northeast Asia instead. He argued that the Kingdom of Korea was the most ideal destination for Japanese migration because of its rich and abundant land, its obedient natives, and the colonial privileges that the Japanese enjoyed there. While Japanese migrants faced numerous difficulties in many locales around the world, on the Korean Peninsula they could easily acquire land and settle down as owner-farmers.[17]

Though Chinda and Ōkoshi would certainly disagree with Katō on where the Japanese subjects should migrate, all three singled out farming as the preferred occupation for the emigrants and envisioned land acquisition as the latter's ultimate mission. These diplomats' ideas were echoed by other Japanese expan-sionists both in and outside the government. As I explain below, their overall preference for farmer migration over laborer migration and the call for a shift to the former was a result of the rise of agrarianism in Japan around the turn of the twentieth century. In the meantime, this change was also a direct response to white racism directed against Japanese migrant laborers on the U.S. mainland and in Hawai'i.

THE RISE OF JAPANESE AGRARIANISM

A direct reason for the boom of Japanese migration to the United States during the 1890s was the poverty that plagued the Japanese countryside. Agriculture did not occupy a central place in the Meiji leaders' blueprints for the empire. For both "enriching the nation and strengthening the army" (*fukoku kyōhei*) and "developing industry and trade" (*shokusan kōgyō*), two policy agendas central to Japan's rise during the Meiji period, agriculture was expected to be a contributor rather than a beneficiary. As a major sector of the national economy, agriculture served as the biggest source of government revenue during most of the Meiji era, yet the bulk of the government's budget was allocated to industrialization and military buildup.

In addition to the government's relative negligence toward agriculture, there was a rapid concentration of farmland ownership in the Japanese countryside following the promulgation of the Land Tax Law of 1873, which legitimized private landownership. This process substantially accelerated during the Matsukata Deflation, when 70 to 80 percent of Japanese farming households ran into debt due to a steep drop in the prices of silk and rice. As many small landowners were forced to sell their land to pay off debts, the population of owner-farmers declined sharply, while the number of tenant farmers as well as tenant disputes skyrocketed.

The First Sino-Japanese War in 1894–95 dealt yet another blow to Japanese agriculture. The war led to a boom in urban industries, which lured an increasing segment of the rural population out of the countryside. As a result, food production in the archipelago could no longer meet the demand of a rapidly expanding urban society. Rice, a staple food of the Japanese, began to flow into the archipelago from Taiwan and later the Korean Peninsula; by the late 1890s, Japan had turned from a rice exporter into a rice importer.

In response to the significant decline of the farming population and Japan's loss of self-sufficiency in rice, Japanese intellectuals embraced a new school of thinking known as agrarianism (*nōhonshugi*). It emphasized the central role of agriculture in Japan's dual process of nation and empire building; moreover, it called on the government to protect farmers and facilitate economic growth in the countryside. The most influential advocate for agrarianism at the turn of the twentieth century was Nitobe Inazō, who was best known for his leadership in establishing and developing the discipline of Japanese colonial policy studies (*shokumin seisaku kenkyū*). Nitobe published a book-length study in 1898, aiming to analyze the predicament of agriculture in the Japanese empire and provide a solution. Titled *Agriculture as the Foundation* (*Nōgyō honron*), the book portrayed agriculture as the very basis of Japanese society. Like most Meiji policy makers at the time, Nitobe had no doubt that Japan was destined to follow the path of the West and become an industrialized empire. However, he criticized the Meiji government's strategy of promoting industry at the expense of agriculture. A strong and self-sufficient agricultural sector, he argued, was essential for Japan's cultural progress, public health, industrialization, and urbanization.[18]

Nitobe's advocacy of agrarianism also demonstrated the profound connection between agriculture and colonialism and that between farming and expansion in Japanese colonial thinking. His interest in agriculture stemmed from his study at Sapporo Agricultural College in Hokkaido and his personal connection with Tsuda Sen, founder and editor of the *Hokkaido Development Journal*. Tsuda, an admirer of the U.S. model of expansion, was already calling for modernizing Japan's agriculture at the very beginning of the Meiji era. To this end, he established the Association for Studying Agriculture (Gakunōsha) to encourage and train the declassed samurai to become new farmers (*shinnō*) of the empire through Western learning. Modernized agriculture was also central to Tsuda's design for the Japanese colonization of Hokkaido, which would effectively extract natural wealth from the island.[19]

Having studied at the Agricultural School affiliated with Tsuda's Association for Studying Agriculture, Nitobe believed that the backbone of Japan's future empire was owner-farmers. Those who farmed, according to him, had superior physical conditions, which made them better soldiers. Farmers also had higher fertility rates and longer life spans, further making them ideal subjects of the empire. As the primary suppliers for food and manpower and the best source of soldiers, Nitobe contended, farmers should be protected by the government from losing their land, for otherwise they would fall into poverty and lose their vigor and strength due to excessive labor.[20]

Nitobe's thesis was well received among his peers. *Agriculture as the Foundation* was reprinted five times within ten years of its publication. In 1902, four years after the book's initial publication, Hiraoka Hikotarō published *Placing Agriculture at the Center in Japan* (*Nihon nōpon ron*). This book not only embraced Nitobe's main argument, which emphasized the centrality of agriculture in the national economy, but also delineated the connections between agriculture and colonial expansion. This 1902 book suggested several ways for policy makers to rescue the agricultural sector, including tax relief, protective tariffs, and the modernization of farming equipment and techniques.[21] More importantly, Hiraoka identified overpopulation as a reason for the decline in productivity and land shortage in Japanese agriculture. He believed that exporting and settling a certain number of farmers overseas would increase Japan's agricultural productivity, as it would free up farmland and accelerate the process of agricultural mechanization. The expansion of Japanese overseas communities would further benefit Japan's agriculture by stimulating the exportation of Japanese farm goods.[22]

ANTI-JAPANESE CAMPAIGNS ON THE U.S. WEST COAST

As agrarianism became a popular political discourse in Japan and grew intertwined with overseas migration at the turn of the twentieth century, the Japanese community on the U.S. West Coast also went through a fundamental change. The rural poor replaced students and political dissidents as the main source of Japanese migrants to the United States. Most of them made a living through labor, and they soon became the targets of anti-Japanese campaigns on the West Coast. White exclusionists repeated their accusations against Chinese immigrants by labeling Japanese newcomers as lacking in social manners and education, greedy, and having no intention to contribute to the host society. Their campaigns were spurred by Japan's victory in the Russo-Japanese War. In the exclusionists' rhetoric, the image of the Japanese as an uncivilized and inferior race overlapped with that of Japan as an aggressive empire, legitimizing their demand to keep the Japanese out of the white men's domain.

The anti-Japanese campaigns gained momentum in 1906, when the Board of Education in San Francisco ordered the exclusion of Japanese pupils from the city's public schools. The sentiment against the Japanese on the West Coast also received support from the national media. In September 1907, the *New York Times* published a lengthy article that described Japanese migration to the United States as "Japan's invasion to the White Man's World." The article pointed to the idea of overpopulation, the same one used by the Japanese leaders to justify the empire's expansion and emigration, to argue against allowing further Japanese immigration.[23] Having failed to export its surplus people to Hokkaido, Taiwan, the Korean Peninsula, and Manchuria, the article warned, the Japanese were now raiding the United States, the territory of the "White Man." The Russo-Japanese War, it also argued, was damning evidence that the Japanese were not only inassimilable but also dangerous, and Japanese migrants were the vanguards of this aggressive empire.[24]

Such anti-Japanese sentiments became institutionalized by the Gentlemen's Agreement reached by the governments of Japan and the United States. In 1908, Tokyo stopped issuing passports to Japanese subjects who intended to migrate to the United States as laborers. In return, the United States reopened public schools in San Francisco to Japanese children and promised not to impose official restrictions on Japanese immigration.[25] The Gentlemen's Agreement marked a watershed in the history of Japanese migration to the United States by bringing an end to labor migration. Based on the agreement, Tokyo enacted a strict ban on migration to the United States, the only exceptions being remigrants, family members of existing migrants, and U.S.-approved agricultural settlers.

The rise of anti-Japanese sentiments on the U.S. West Coast led to contrasting reactions in Japan. While hostility and anger were the general response in the mass media, Western-trained intellectuals sought to reconcile what was happening in the United States with their perception of the country as a righteous empire and a guide for Japan's own path. This was particularly true for students of Nitobe Inazō and his colleagues in Japanese colonial policy studies. Their intellectual origins can be traced to Sapporo Agricultural College, which was established by William Smith Clark and modeled after the Massachusetts Agricultural College. They faithfully accepted the logic of the U.S. exclusionists and saw labor migration as a failed model of Japanese expansion. They also connected the failure of Japanese labor migration to the United States with rising agrarianism in Japan and embraced farmer migration as a better model of expansion. For them, the migration of farmers overseas would serve as a perfect solution to the rapidly escalating tensions in Japan's countryside and as a way to pivot agriculture back to the center of Japan's national economy.

Two academic works on colonialism, both strongly influenced by Nitobe Inazō, came out in Japan at this time. One was *On Japanese Emigration* (*Nihon imin ron*), by Ōkawadaira Takamitsu, published in 1905; the other was *On Japanese Colonial Migration* (*Nihon shokumin ron*), by Tōgō Minoru, published in 1906. For both authors, anti-Japanese campaigns in the United States pointed to an urgent need for Japan to change its existing model of migration. The new model, they argued, should be agrarian: unlike the migration of laborers that would only stir up ill feelings against the Japanese due to the laborers' sojourning mind-set and refusal to assimilate, the migration of farmers would bring permanent benefits to the empire.

Tōgō divided the practices of expansion in human history into two categories, the nonproductive and the productive. The former was conducted via military conquest, while the latter was accomplished by the migration of farmers. Tōgō quoted the German historian Theodor Mommsen in the book's preface to explain the difference between the two: "That which is gained by war may be wrested from the grasp by war again, but it is not so with conquests made by the plough."[26] Military conquest may bring temporary profits, but only agricultural settlers could put down the roots of the empire in the newly acquired land. For Tōgō, this point was self-evident when one compared the different trajectories of Latin and Anglo-Saxon expansion in the Americas. As he argued, the Portuguese and Spanish colonizers only cared about how to obtain treasures from the new land, a mentality that ultimately led to the collapse of their transatlantic empires. The Anglo-Saxons, on the other hand, came with plows and pruning hooks and farmed the new land as their own.[27] Their success could be seen in the prosperity of the United States today.

Ōkawadaira shared Tōgō's view and saw the emigration of farmers as a must for the empire. Both works demonstrated the convergence between agrarianism and settler colonialism for Japanese expansionists around the time of the Russo-Japanese War. It should be noted that for both Tōgō and Ōkawadaira, farmer migration was not only a means of successful expansion but also a solution to Japan's rural depression. They believed that the exportation of surplus population from the overcrowded countryside would increase the productivity of Japan's agriculture.[28]

On the other hand, Tōgō and Ōkawadaira did not agree on the ideal emigration destinations. Tōgō believed that the Korean Peninsula and southern Manchuria were the answer, as both regions were newly brought into Japan's sphere of influence as a result of the Russo-Japanese War. Ōkawadaira, however, urged Japanese farmers to venture beyond overpopulated Asia and secure their future in South America.[29] Both Tōgō and Ōkawadaira had supporters in policy-making circles; their agendas of expansion materialized between the second half of the 1900s and the early 1910s with the support of the government. Tōgō's proposal was carried out by the formation of the Oriental Colonial Company and its programs of farmer migration to the Korean Peninsula. Meanwhile, Ōkawadaira's call for South America–bound farmer migration was realized by the establishment of the Tokyo Syndicate and its land purchase in Brazil. However, it was in the U.S. state of Texas that the Japanese expansionists first experimented with farmer migration before replicating the experience in Northeast Asia and South America.

FARMER MIGRATION TO TEXAS AND THE ROOTS OF THE JAPANESE FARMING COMMUNITY IN BRAZIL

Though both Ōkawadaira and Tōgō were pessimistic about the future of Japanese migration to the United States, the experience of Japanese American immigrants continued to serve as a guide for the expansionists in Tokyo as the latter sought to turn the idea of farmer migration into reality. The Japanese community along the U.S. West Coast experienced rapid demographic growth at the turn of the twentieth century as waves of Japanese rural poor arrived in the area. Initially they simply filled the labor vacuum created by the Chinese Exclusion Act, but some gradually climbed up the ladder to become owner-farmers and even landlords.[30] By 1909, Japanese immigrants owned about twenty thousand acres in California.[31]

While Japanese immigrants' farming success further agitated the anti-Japanese sentiment that had already been swelling on the West Coast, their accomplishments also inspired Japanese expansionists to establish a Japanese farming presence elsewhere in the United States. Around the same time that Japanese diplomats in Brazil and Korea were envisioning Japanese farmer migration, their colleague Uchida Sadatsuchi, Japanese consul in New York, made a pitch to Tokyo in 1902 about exporting Japanese farmers to Texas. During an investigative trip to the American South, Uchida met with agricultural leaders in Texas who expressed interest in attracting Japanese farmers to develop rice cultivation in the state. Uchida believed that an invitation from Texas would open a new path for the Japanese community in the United States by avoiding the racial hatred from white Americans on the West Coast.[32]

Uchida's report, widely circulated in the mass media, inspired hundreds of Japanese expansionists to migrate to Texas as rice farmers between 1903 and 1908. Compared to the rural poor who constituted the bulk of Japanese migrants on the West Coast, the majority of the initial settlers in Texas were relatively wealthy and educated. They purchased sizable plots of land, ranging from two hundred to six hundred acres, and started farming right away. These owner-farmers recruited help from both Japan and the existing Japanese migrants on the West Coast.

Some of these Japanese farming settlers held global visions and linked their efforts in Texas to the empire's expansion in Asia and Latin America. A noteworthy example of this was Yoshimura Daijirō, who was among the first to answer Uchida's call. Only one year after Uchida's report was published, Yoshimura formed the Society of Friends of Overseas Enterprises (Kaigai Kigyō Dōshikai) in Osaka to facilitate farmer migration to Texas. With financial contributions from its members, the society was able to purchase 160 acres in League City next to the Gulf of Mexico, where it established a rice farm in 1904.[33]

Yoshimura was also a prolific writer and passionate advocate for expansion. His words and experience illustrated the confluence of agrarianism and expansionism and, more specifically, the connection between Japanese migration to Texas and Japanese expansion in Asia and South America. For Yoshimura, relocating Japanese farmers to Texas would not only rescue Japanese agriculture but also demonstrate to white Americans the superior aptitude of the Japanese for farming: while white Americans were good at commerce and industry, the Japanese, being world champions in agriculture, deserved a place in the land of the White Man.[34]

Yoshimura also considered the history of Texas itself as especially instructive to the Japanese because it demonstrated how migration to the land of another sovereign country could turn into territorial expansion. As he observed, the land of Texas had changed hands numerous times, first from Native Americans to Spanish colonists, then to Mexicans, and eventually to Anglo-Americans. This process revealed the fact that military conquest, exemplified by the Spanish Empire, was now being replaced by the new and peaceful way of expansion centered on migration, spearheaded by the United States. White Americans had initially moved to the Mexican land as farming settlers without military or governmental support back home, but through diligence and resolution, Yoshimura argued, they eventually made this foreign land their own.[35]

If the colonial history of Texas was a lesson for Japanese empire builders, the Japanese farmers' settlement in Texas, for Yoshimura, was a critical step in Japanese settler colonial expansion around the world. He envisioned that the success of Japanese rice farming in Texas would allow Japanese settlers to monopolize rice production in the United States, thereby dominating a critical sector of its national economy. In Yoshimura's imagination, besting the White Man in agriculture would herald the success of Japanese expansion in Asia and South America in the following decades, where the Japanese would also need to compete with white colonists.[36]

However, by the end of the first decade of the twentieth century, the fever of Japanese farmer migration to Texas had subsided. Most Japanese farms, including one owned by Yoshimura, had fallen into bankruptcy, and only a handful of them continued to operate. While the sudden drop in the global rice price was the direct reason for their failure, the crisis of the Japanese rice farmers was also a result of the shortage of Japanese laborers caused by the Gentlemen's Agreement.[37] Saibara Seitō's farm was among the small number of survivors. During the peak of the boom, it was one of the most successful farms, and Saibara was widely celebrated in Japanese mass media as a role model of the Japanese migrant farmer in Texas.[38] A former president of Doshisha University in Kyoto, Saibara came to the United States to study in 1902 but was persuaded by Uchida to start his farming career the next year. After purchasing three hundred acres in Webster, Texas, and establishing his own farm that year, he convinced his family members in Japan to migrate to Texas with him. Later he also recruited farmers from Kōchi, his native prefecture in Japan, to work on his farm.[39]

While Yoshimura articulated the intellectual link between Texas and Japan's colonial ambitions in Asia and South America, Saibara embodied this link by his deeds. Disappointed by institutionalized racism against the Japanese in the United States, Saibara entrusted his farm to his son and migrated to Brazil in 1918 and started a farm in the state of São Paulo. In 1928, he was employed by the then newly formed Japanese South American Colonization Company (Nanbei Takushoku Gaisha) and moved north to Pará to manage an experimental farm in the Amazon Basin.[40]

THE RISE OF SÃO PAULO AND A NEW MODE OF COFFEE ECONOMY

Saibara's re-migration was made possible by the prosperity of the Japanese community in Brazil. The initial formation and development of the Japanese community in Brazil took place in the context of a paradigm shift in Brazil's coffee economy and the rise of São Paulo as the new center of coffee cultivation. Since its first commercial cultivation in Rio de Janeiro in the late eighteenth century, coffee quickly became a major source of wealth for Brazil's export-centered economy. By the 1850s, coffee constituted half of Brazil's export income. Thanks to the sale of coffee, the Brazilian empire, for the first time since its independence, exported more than it imported in 1860.[41] The expansion of coffee cultivation also led to critical economic and political transformations in Brazil. For the first half of the nineteenth century, Rio de Janeiro remained the center for coffee cultivation and the city of Rio was the primary port for coffee exportation. However, as coffee cultivation expanded southward into São Paulo and Minas Gerais, by the end of the nineteenth century the state of São Paulo became the new center of the coffee economy.

The rise of São Paulo in the coffee economy was accompanied by a new mode of coffee production. Rio's traditional coffee fazendas, like the sugar plantations before them, relied almost exclusively on slave labor. With the full abolition of slavery in Brazil gradually becoming a certainty, the newly formed coffee planters in São Paulo had to turn to immigration as an alternative source of labor. The development of this immigration-centered mode of coffee production was marked by the expansion of coffee cultivation in the state of São Paulo from its eastern coast into the western inland areas, which was made possible by the advancement of railways. After the formation of the São Paulo Railway Company in 1859, railroads began to link the state's western areas with the city of São Paulo and then to the Port of Santos, making possible the transportation of coffee and goods between the east coast and inland.[42]

The transition of Brazil from an empire into a republic in 1889 signaled the political ascendancy of the new coffee elites in southeastern Brazil. In the following several decades, all but two civilian presidents of the First Republic would come from the bastions of the new coffee elites: São Paulo, Rio de Janeiro, and Minas Gerais.[43] As the coffee industry became central to national policy making, this regime change was accompanied by an immigration boom. To compete with other Latin American countries such as Argentina and with the United States, the Brazilian government, at both the central and state levels, began to provide financial subsidies to attract immigrants.[44]

As Brazilian elites saw immigration as a crucial means to whiten the Brazilian racial stock, they had a clear preference for Europeans. In the 1890s, the decade that immediately followed the formation of the First Republic, over half of the immigrants that entered Brazil were Italians. Most of the rest were from Portugal, Spain, and Germany.[45] Though Brazil reopened its doors to Asian immigrants in 1893 due to a temporary shortage of European immigrants, for the most part, the Brazilian leaders saw Asian immigration as neither desirable nor necessary.

However, at the beginning of the twentieth century when Japanese migration to Texas was gaining momentum, the prospects of Japanese migration to Brazil began to improve. The Italian government, in response to numerous reports about the terrible treatment of Italian laborers at Brazilian coffee plantations, issued the Prinetti Decree of 1902 that banned subsidized Italian migration to Brazil. This led to a precipitous drop in the number of Italian immigrants, forcing Brazilian elites to seek alternative sources of immigrants. Japan, once again, emerged as an alternative migrant supplier. The empire's victory in the Russo-Japanese War three years later further consolidated the image of the Japanese as the "white people

FIGURE 8. This image illustrates the settler colonial nature of the pro-immigration republican regime by showing how it managed its internal power balance while standing on the body of an Indigenous person. Source: *Revista Illustrada*, no. 564, 1889.

in Asia" in the minds of Brazilian policy makers. Federal Deputy Nestor Ascoli went as far as to argue that the result of the Russo-Japanese War demonstrated that the Japanese were now a better agent of progress and modernization than the Europeans. The introduction of Japanese blood into the Brazilian racial stock, Ascoli reasoned, would be a better choice than the immigration of any other non-white people.[46] The logic of white racism behind the Brazilian preference for the

Japanese is attested by the 1912 book, *Samurais e mandarins*, by the Brazilian diplomat Guimaráes Filho. Filho argued for the "whiteness" of the Japanese by contrasting them with the Chinese, whom he believed would only lead to the degeneration of Brazilians due to their racial and cultural inferiority. The Japanese, he asserted instead, were progressive and civilized and would help whiten the Brazilian race.[47] After Brazilian leaders came to view the Japanese race in a more favorable light, they quickly removed legal barriers for the federal and state governments to subsidize immigration from Japan.

"HAPPY HOME AND BLESSED LAND":
THE START OF JAPANESE BRAZILIAN MIGRATION

At around this time, Sugimura Fukashi arrived in Brazil as the new top diplomat. At their first official meeting, Brazilian president Francisco de Paula Rodrigues Alves, a native of São Paulo, asked for Sugimura's help jumpstarting Japanese migration to Brazil. Brazil's finance minister, Leopoldo Bulhões, also reached out to Sugimura, requesting Tokyo's help to populate Brazil's territories and establish colonies through immigration. Shortly afterward, Sugimura embarked on a tour in São Paulo in the company of Brazilian officials. In his report to Tokyo right after the tour, Sugimura concluded that the state of São Paulo was a "happy home and blessed land" (*rakkyō fukudo*) given to the Japanese by the heavens, where Japanese migration was bound to succeed.[48]

Sugimura's positive outlook, a marked turnaround from his predecessors such as Chinda and Ōkoshi, was not only due to solicitous gestures from the Brazilian side. He understood that Brazil's newfound enthusiasm for Japanese immigration was a direct result of the decline in Italian immigration. Compared to the passion of the Brazilian leaders, he was more interested in what São Paulo could actually offer to the Japanese migrants: generous state government subsidies to fund their trips from Japan to Brazil, a pleasant climate for living and farming, developed transportation facilities, and a booming economy. However, what Sugimura considered more attractive still was the possibility for Japanese immigrants to settle down and become landowning farmers in São Paulo.[49]

Sugimura's report was soon released to the Japanese public and immediately inspired a number of individuals to migrate to Brazil.[50] The report also caught the eye of Mizuno Ryū, president of the Imperial Colonial Migration Company.[51] Between 1905 and 1908, Mizuno traveled back and forth between Tokyo and São Paulo several times to negotiate a migration contract. Though Sugimura died suddenly in 1906, the next Japanese minister to Brazil, Uchida Sadatsuchi, also supported Mizuno's cause. Uchida, the architect of Japanese farmer migration to Texas, believed that São Paulo was another perfect migration destination for Japanese farmers.[52]

The result of these negotiations was a contract that allowed Mizuno to success-fully bring the first official group of Japanese labor migrants to the Port of Santos in 1908. Based on these contracts, 60 percent of their steamship fares were jointly paid by the state of São Paulo and coffee planters in the form of a loan. The immi-grants shouldered the remaining 40 percent themselves, an amount that exceeded an average Japanese farmer's three years' worth of income.[53] They were expected to repay their debts via wage deduction during their contract periods. The sailing of the *Kasato Maru* is widely known as the starting point of Japanese labor migra-tion to Brazil, but what has been usually overlooked is the fact that the contract required the state government of São Paulo to establish a number of colonies for the Japanese migrants to settle after their contract terms ended. These colonies were expected to be located along the central railway lines, where the Japanese subjects would be able to purchase land at a low price.[54]

On June 18, the *Kasato Maru* reached the Port of Santos after sailing across the Indian and Atlantic Oceans for fifty-one days. The migrants onboard were brought to Hospedaria de Imigrantes in the city of São Paulo the next day, and there they confirmed their specific contracts with coffee planters. Shortly after-ward, 772 migrants were transported by train to six coffee plantations in the state of São Paulo and started working as contract laborers.[55] Mizuno Ryū, Uchida Sadatuschi, and others behind the sailing of the *Kasato Maru* had envisioned that these migrants would put down permanent roots for the Japanese empire in Bra-zil. However, the majority were simply hoping for a way out of poverty. This gap between the expectations of the Japanese elites and those of the migrants them-selves were further enlarged by misleading advertising that the Imperial Colo-nial Migration Company used: to recruit enough migrants to meet the contract's requirement, the company promised to give every recruit a generous subsidy to cover the cost of migration right after they arrived in Brazil, but it later failed to fulfill its promise.[56] During the recruitment, the company also idealized Brazil as a country where the Japanese migrants could make quick and easy money, yet the *Kasato Maru* migrants found themselves ill-prepared for the challenges waiting for them in Brazil; more than half of them eventually broke their contracts and left their initial plantations.[57] The failure of the *Kasato Maru* migrants led to the bankruptcy of the Imperial Colonial Migration Company.

· · ·

This chapter explains how the sailing of the *Kasato Maru* was made possible in the contexts of both Japan's and Brazil's settler colonial expansion at the turn of the twentieth century. With the rise of agrarianism at home and the intensification of anti-Japanese campaigns in the United States, Japanese expansionists began to favor farmer migration over labor migration. At around the same time, the state of São Paulo emerged as the new center of the coffee economy and the primary destination of immigrants in Brazil. The campaign of Japanese migration to Texas, though short-lived, not only marked the beginning of Japanese farmer migration overseas but also paved the way for the sailing of the *Kasato Maru*. Two central figures in the Texas campaign, Uchida Sadatsuchi and Saibara Seitō, became ardent supporters of and participants in Japanese collaborative settler colonialism in Brazil.

The chapter also highlights an important but often overlooked fact about the *Kasato Maru* migrants: though most of them arrived as contract laborers, both the recruiters and the Japanese government expected them to eventually become farming settlers who would put down their roots in South America permanently. It was no mere coincidence that two supervisors onboard the ship, Uetsuka Shūhei and Kōyama Rokurō, became the arms and mouthpieces of Japanese settlers in São Paulo in the following decades. Uetsuka founded one of the earliest Japanese settler colonies in São Paulo and became an influential leader of the Japanese immigrants in the state in the 1910s and 1920s. Kōyama established and edited *Seishū shinpō*, one of the three most widely circulated newspapers in the Japanese Brazilian community before World War II, which played a central role in fostering the formation of a collective identity among Japanese settlers in Brazil.[58]

Though disappointed by the outcome of the *Kasato Maru* migration, the Paulista government could not afford to suspend Japanese immigration given the shortage of coffee labor. It negotiated a new contract with Mizuno, who partnered with the Takemura Emigration Company (Takemura Imin Gaisha) to continue recruiting Japanese migrants and transporting them to São Paulo. With better preparation and more stable financial resources, the Japanese migrants who arrived in 1910 on the *Ryojun Maru* were more successful overall.[59] Unlike the *Kasato Maru* migrants, over half of whom broke their initial contracts within six months after arrival, 75 percent of the *Ryojun Maru* migrants remained in their contracts after nine months of stay.[60] However, the Paulista government's new contract reduced its subsidies for Japanese immigrants and withdrew its commitment to establish Japanese colonies.[61]

The waning of Brazilian support necessitated further involvement by the Japanese government and social groups in support of farmer migration to Brazil. The next chapter explains how the first Japanese settler colonies came into being in São Paulo in the 1910s as a result of the collaborative efforts of the Japanese government, business elites, and migration companies. It also discusses how these settler colonies developed and expanded in the context of the great social changes in both Japan and Brazil brought on by World War I.

PART II

THE FORMATION OF SETTLER COMMUNITIES, 1908–1930s

3

Seizing the Land

Coffee, Railroad, and Settler Community Making

In 1907, a group of Japanese political and business elites led by Minister of Agriculture and Commerce Ōura Kanetake gathered in Tokyo. In response to the suspension of Japanese labor migration to the United States due to the Gentlemen's Agreement, the participants sought to promote Japanese overseas expansion by altering the general nature of emigration. Echoing the growing calls for farmer migration among Japanese empire builders as a solution to the rural depression in the archipelago, they vowed to replace temporary labor migrants with permanent agricultural settlers.[1] The next year, they jointly established the Tokyo Syndicate, a business cooperative dedicated to facilitating the emigration of Japanese farming settlers. Aoyagi Ikutarō, head of the Tokyo Syndicate, embarked on an investigative trip to Brazil in 1910. Two years later, he obtained a land grant contract from the state government of São Paulo that allowed the Tokyo Syndicate to establish a few Japanese settler villages that were collectively known as the Iguape colony, the first official Japanese colony in Brazil.

Iguape was quickly followed by the formation and development of more Japanese settler villages of different sizes and types in São Paulo and nearby states. The rise of these villages marked the beginning of a new stage in the history of Japanese migration to Brazil: Japanese immigrants' transition from plantation laborers to landholding farmers. This transition and the continuation and further development of Japanese migration to Brazil during this period took place hand in hand with the Japanese expansionists' efforts to export farming settlers to Northeast Asia and the South Seas.

As this chapter explains, the Japanese exclusion campaigns in the United States that culminated in the Gentlemen's Agreement ushered in a new era in the development of the Japanese migration state. Concluding that the Gentlemen's

Agreement signified the failure of labor migration as a means of expansion, Tokyo in the 1910s and 1920s not only explored alternative destinations of migration but also sought to replace temporary laborers with farming settlers as the backbone of Japanese emigration. Compared to the organized campaigns of farmer migration to Northeast Asia and the South Seas, Japanese farmer migration to southeastern Brazil proved most successful in terms of the number of farmers relocated.

The birth and growth of Japanese settler villages was also made possible by the new development of Brazil's own migration state. Along with Brazil's territorial expansion in South America through diplomatic maneuverings, the government at the central and especially the state level escalated its efforts to build railways that connected the coast with the inland regions. As exemplified by the developments in the state of São Paulo, these penetrating railway lines not only expanded coffee cultivation but also accelerated the process of Indigenous dispossession by redistributing the land near the new railway lines to immigrants.

This chapter details the origin, development, and expansion of Japanese settler villages in southeastern Brazil. It explains this success by placing it in three distinct but interconnected contexts, namely, new developments in Japanese migration-driven expansion, railway expansion and new land distribution policies in the state of São Paulo, and global changes in politics and the economy as a result of World War I. Tokyo's success with Japanese farming villages in Brazil boosted enthusiasm for expansion in Brazil throughout the Japanese empire. More importantly, the growth of Japanese farming villages also convinced Japanese empire builders to view farmer migration as the most effective means of colonial expansion in the decades to come.

THE GENTLEMEN'S AGREEMENT
AND NEW DIRECTIONS OF JAPANESE EXPANSION

In 1908, the same year the Gentlemen's Agreement took effect, a novel titled *Two Dragons on the Pacific Ocean* (*Taiheiyōjō no sōryū*) was published in Japan. The story began with a honeymoon period between Japan and the United States starting from Perry's arrival in the Japanese archipelago to the American acclamation of Japan's victory in the Russo-Japanese War. However, the bilateral relationship started to deteriorate due to American expansionism in the Pacific region and growing racism in the United States marked by the annexation of Hawai'i and the Philippines, the Chinese Exclusion Act, and anti-Japanese campaigns on the U.S. West Coast. The story climaxed in a war that took place in 1918, an event triggered by the massacre of fifteen hundred Japanese immigrants amid intensified anti-Japanese campaigns in the United States. The war began with Japan's swift seizure of the Philippines, Hawai'i, and Alaska, with the Japanese navy completely wiping out the American fleet. While Japan did not attack the U.S. mainland, it imposed a devastating embargo on the latter. Meanwhile, the United States suffered from

FIGURE 9. The front cover of *Tokyo Puck's Issue of Anger Toward the United States* (*Taibei happungō*). Titled *A Medical Examination*, the image shows how "Dr. Taft," representing then U.S. secretary of war William Taft, is astonished by the fast-beating pulse of "Miss Rising Sun," representing an angry Japan. Source: *Tokyo Puck* 3, no. 17 (1907).

domestic rebellions launched by African American soldiers and Native Americans. Eventually it was forced to accept a peace treaty with Japan with France as the mediator. As a result, in addition to a large amount of indemnity, the United States had to cede Hawai'i, the Philippines, and Alaska to Japan.[2]

Likely the first fiction imagining a war between Japan and the United States with the former's victory, *Two Dragons on the Pacific Ocean* was serialized in *Amerika*, a Japanese journal designed to promote U.S.-bound emigration.[3] It reflected the ire of Japanese intellectuals toward the United States as a result of the anti-Japanese campaigns that reached a peak at the time of the Gentlemen's Agreement. *Tokyo*

Puck, a popular satirical magazine, voiced similar anger a year earlier in a special issue not too subtly titled, "The Issue of Anger toward the United States" (*Taibei happungō*). It criticized the hypocrisy of white Americans, who failed to live up to their self-professed principles of freedom and democracy by cruelly discriminating against peoples of color in both domestic politics and immigration policies.[4]

Despite these public expressions of anger, Tokyo's overall diplomatic strategy toward the United States in the two decades following the enactment of the Gentlemen's Agreement remained one of reconciliation and cooperation. This was signaled by the signing of the Root-Takahira Agreement in 1908, the same year the Gentlemen's Agreement took effect. Sealed by U.S. Secretary of State Elihu Root and the Japanese ambassador to the United States, Takahira Kakugorō, this agreement confirmed the two countries' acknowledgment of their respective colonial acquisitions and interests. Japan recognized U.S. annexation of the Kingdom of Hawai'i and the Philippines and vowed to defend the American "Open Door" policy in China. In exchange, the United States acknowledged Japan's right to annex Korea and its newly gained colonial privileges in southern Manchuria following the Russo-Japanese War.

The context of Tokyo's pro-U.S. diplomacy was the steady growth of Japan's geopolitical influence in the first two decades of the twentieth century. The Japanese empire not only entrenched its market monopoly and commercial advantages in China thanks to the outbreak of World War I but also became one of the four permanent members of the League of Nations Executive Council. Along with Japan's ascendancy as a world power, its politicians and intellectuals continued to be captivated by the even more successful ongoing process of empire building of the United States. The United States was quickly expanding its geopolitical and economic influences around the world, and Japan saw it as both a model to imitate and a partner to work with.

The consistency of the Japanese elites in pursuing Japan's expansion by cooperating with the rising American power in the 1910s and 1920s can be seen in the establishment and activities of two associations: the Great Japan Civilization Association (Dainihon Bunmei Kyōkai) and the Emigration Association (Imin Kyōkai). While the former aimed to foster the appreciation of modern Western knowledge and culture among the Japanese public, the latter focused on promoting migration-centered Japanese expansion by reconciling it with the existing world order. Both associations were led by political and business elites of the day; their activities demonstrated a synergistic partnership between the imperial government and civil society in the venture of emigration.

Formed in 1908 under the auspices of Ōkuma Shigenobu, the Great Japan Civilization Association was the wellspring of the Civilization Movement (Bunmei Undō) in Japan. Centered on Ōkuma and his associates both in and outside the government, the goal of this cultural movement was to prepare Japanese subjects to become qualified citizens as the Japanese empire was quickly emerging as a global leader. The intellectual core of the Civilization Movement was Ōkuma's idea of reconciliation between Eastern and Western civilizations (*Tōzai bunmei chōwa*). Ōkuma and his followers believed that the Japanese empire, due to its history, functioned as a bridge between the East and the West; therefore, it was destined to play a unique and leading role in guiding the world toward a better future.[5] The actual activities of the association, however, demonstrated that Japan's role as a bridge was rather one-sided in the design of Ōkuma and his followers. The association was mainly dedicated to diffusing Western knowledge in the social sciences to the Japanese public by writing and translating books and holding public lectures; it urged its audience to embrace the Anglo-American world order by finding Japan's place in it.[6] The association's influence substantially expanded after Ōkuma became prime minister in 1914.

Also in 1914, the newly minted Prime Minister Ōkuma became the founding president of the Emigration Association. Similar to the Great Japan Civilization Association, the Emigration Association sought to expand the wealth and power of the Japanese empire in the Anglo-American order. Members of the Emigration Association saw the emigration of Japanese subjects overseas as the most desirable means to this end. In Ōkuma's imagination, the fate of Japanese migration to the United States had a particularly significant meaning. The American acceptance of Japanese immigration, he believed, would prove that the Japanese were the ideal candidates to integrate the essences of the East and the West.[7] The Emigration Association, therefore, made cultural and diplomatic efforts with the goal of reopening U.S. doors to Japanese immigrants. This was to be achieved by disciplining the bodies and minds of Japanese American immigrants, on the one hand, and improving the image of Japan and the Japanese in the United States, on the other.[8]

A careful examination of the activities of these two associations further reveals that Japanese expansionists were also exploring migration destinations outside of North America, including Northeast Asia, the South Seas, and South America. In 1916, the Great Japan Civilization Association published a major book, *The Overseas Development of the Japanese* (*Nihonjin no kaigai hatten*). With an enthusiastic preface by Nitobe Inazō, the book enumerated the previous activities of Japanese emigrants in different locations around the Pacific Rim, such as southern Manchuria, the Philippines, Hawai'i, the United States, Canada, Australia, Mexico, and Brazil. It urged its readers to take on the mission of expansion by migrating overseas.[9] The Emigration Association too published books and hosted lectures to encourage ordinary Japanese to see a number of destinations around the Pacific Rim as their future homes.[10]

These two associations' efforts in exploring alternative migration destinations were echoed by *The Sun* (*Taiyō*), one of the major popular magazines of the day. In 1910 and 1914, the magazine published two special issues to popularize the debates among Japanese expansionists on where and how the empire should expand: "The

Expansion of the Japanese Nation" (*Nihon minzoku no bōchō*) and "Expanding to the South or to the North?" (*Nanshin ya, hokushin ya?*).[11] The contributors to the two issues—policy makers, military officers, diplomats, university professors, and journalists—were united in their belief in Japan's destiny of overseas expansion. However, the contributors also advanced their own agendas on the directions and strategies of this endeavor. These calls for empire building followed the same guiding principle of the Emigration Association and the Great Japan Civilization Association: to pursue Japan's expansion by cooperating with the United States and the United Kingdom. This principle was best presented by Takekoshi Yosaburō in his article published in *Taiyō*'s 1910 special issue, "The Expansion of the Japanese People." Though Japan was late in joining the civilized world, Takekoshi argued, it was now ready to partake in carrying the "White Man's Burden" (*Hakujin no omoni*) and bringing civilization to the unenlightened corners of the world.[12]

Guided by the principle of cooperating with Euro-American powers, Japan's expansion in the 1910s and 1920s took three general directions: Northeast Asia, the South Seas, and Latin America. Campaigns of Japanese expansion along these three paths were closely connected by shared ideologies, institutions, and enduring human networks. For all three routes, farmer migration stood out as the optimal means of expansion, and most efforts to promote farmer migration started between 1908 and 1913, during Prime Minister Katsura Tarō's second term.

One of the most vocal supporters of expansion in Northeast Asia was Komura Jutarō. As minister of foreign affairs in the second Katsura cabinet, he famously proposed the agenda of "concentrating on Manchuria and the Korean Peninsula" (Man Kan shūchū) to the Diet in 1909 as Japan's grand strategy of empire building. His primary goal was to minimize the empire's conflicts with Anglo-American powers by limiting Japanese expansion in Northeast Asia. A year earlier, Tokyo had put this strategy into practice through the formation of the Oriental Development Company. With the government's financial aid, the company aimed to acquire farmland in the Korean Peninsula by taking advantage of the colonial privileges the Japanese enjoyed there and redistributing the land to the recruited Japanese farmers.[13] Kanbe Masao, a professor of law at Kyoto Imperial University, supplied justification for their land acquisition and migration campaign. In his book, *On Agricultural Migration to Korea* (*Chōsen nōgyō imin ron*), Kanbe promoted the migration of Japanese rural residents to the Korean Peninsula as a way to bring the blessings of civilization to Koreans.[14]

The empire's annexation of Korea in 1910 and the substantial growth of Japanese political and economic influence in China during World War I, however, did not bring success to Japanese farmer migration in Northeast Asia. Despite its consistent efforts, the Oriental Development Company managed to relocate fewer than four thousand Japanese farming households to colonial Korea by 1924. About eight thousand Japanese farmers settled in Japanese-controlled southern Manchuria by 1931.[15] These lackluster results were mainly due to the Japanese farmers' inability to compete economically with local Korean and Chinese farmers, who had a much lower cost of living than the occupiers did.[16]

In terms of governmental policy, Japan's efforts to export farming settlers to the South Seas dates to Katsura Tarō's tenure as governor general of Taiwan in 1896, when he envisioned Taiwan as a base for the empire's expansion into the South Seas.[17] Katsura also served as the founding president of the Taiwan Association (Taiwan Kyōkai) in 1898, a semigovernmental organization that supported Japanese colonization of Taiwan by promoting Japanese migration and business expansion on the island.[18] Japan's government-sponsored farmer migration to the South Seas indeed began with Taiwan in 1910. That year, the Japanese colonial administration on the island established the Department of Migration and began to attract farming settlers from Japan by distributing local land to them.[19] Yet, because of the higher living costs of the Japanese compared to those of the local farmers, the migration scheme in Taiwan, like its counterpart in the Korean Peninsula, proved unsuccessful.[20]

The end of World War I brought another wave of Japanese expansion to the South Seas. The victorious empire not only annexed German Micronesia but, as an ally of the United Kingdom and France, also gained further access to their Southeast Asian colonial markets and resources. In 1915, Inoue Masaji and Uchida Kakichi, both employed by the Japanese colonial government in Taiwan, established the South Seas Association (Nan'yō Kyōkai), an organization that had financial support from both Tokyo and Taipei. Like the Taiwan Association, it was a semigovernmental organization that sought to aid Japanese expansion in Southeast Asia and the South Pacific by facilitating investigations in these regions and educating the public about them as potential migration destinations.[21] The primary target of this wave of expansion was Micronesia, migration to which began soon after World War I. Yet commerce, rather than migration, proved more successful in this endeavor.[22]

The third target of Japanese expansion was Latin America, particularly southeastern Brazil. Japanese farmer migration to Brazil, first launched by Aoyagi Ikutarō in 1908, was closely connected to the contemporaneous campaigns in Northeast Asia and the South Seas. Like its counterparts in the Asia-Pacific region, Aoyagi's project was made possible by political support from Katsura Tarō during his second term as prime minister. On a more practical front, the Aoyagi project mirrored the other two by acquiring local lands, relocating Japanese farmers there, and then distributing the lands to them. Between the 1910s and the mid-1930s, southeastern Brazil was where Japanese farmer migration proved to be the most successful. In 1920, among the 28,000 Japanese settlers in Brazil, 94.8 percent earned their livelihood by farming in one way or another.[23] Until the early 1930s, along with the steady inflow of Japanese migrants, the number of Japanese farming settlers continued to grow annually. The success of Japanese farming settlers in São Paulo, as the following paragraphs explain, was not possible without the political and economic transformations taking place within the state as well as in Brazil in general during the early twentieth century.

THE UNITED STATES, RAILWAYS, AND A NEW
PATTERN OF SETTLER COLONIALISM IN SÃO PAULO

At the turn of the twentieth century, a parallel developed between Japan and Brazil as both countries successfully pursued territorial expansion. From 1895 to 1910, Meiji Japan quickly emerged as a regional hegemon in Northeast Asia after the First Sino-Japanese War and the Russo-Japanese War, turning Taiwan, southern Manchuria, and the Korean Peninsula into its colonies. At the same time, the First Republic substantially expanded its territory in Latin America through diplomacy. Through stunningly successful negotiations, Brazilian diplomats led by José Paranhos, Baron of Rio Branco, settled Brazil's historical territorial disputes with Argentina, Peru, British Guiana, French Guiana, Colombia, and Bolivia. As a result, Brazilian territory expanded substantially both in the Amazon region in the north and the La Plata River Basin in the south. This series of land acquisition and border settlement concluded the centuries-long Luso-Brazilian territorial expansion from the Atlantic coast toward the Andes. During this period, Brazil added 342,000 square miles, an area bigger than that of France, to its territory. It was now the fifth largest country in the world.[24]

In addition to territorial expansion, Rio sought to assert the republic's leadership in Latin America. In the first decade of the twentieth century, Brazil not only became the first Latin American country to have a cardinal assigned by Rome, but it also played a central role as mediator in a number of diplomatic disputes among Latin American countries. Brazil became the only Latin American country to actively participate in World War I, and, like its fellow victor, Japan, it profited from the war by cementing its status as a major power of the world. Though it was unable to become a permanent member of the League's Executive Council like Japan, Brazil was reelected repeatedly to the council from 1920 to 1926.[25]

Comparable to Japan's quest for empire by maintaining friendly relations with the United States, Brazil's quick rise as a regional power was only possible through its close alliance with the United States.[26] Its transition from an empire to a republic at the end of the nineteenth century decisively shifted the anchor of Brazilian diplomacy from Europe to Washington, DC. Founders of the First Republic not only modeled its 1891 Constitution after that of the United States but also saw the latter as the best example they could follow.[27] Rio welcomed the ongoing expansion of the United States, both in the Americas and across the Pacific, and strived to pursue Brazil's own wealth and power under the umbrella of growing American hegemony.

In 1905, Brazil became the first South American country to exchange ambassadors with the United States. Joaquim Nabuco, one of Brazil's most vocal and influential pro-U.S. elites, arrived in Washington as the republic's first ambassador to the United States. He worked closely with Elihu Root, U.S. secretary of state, to

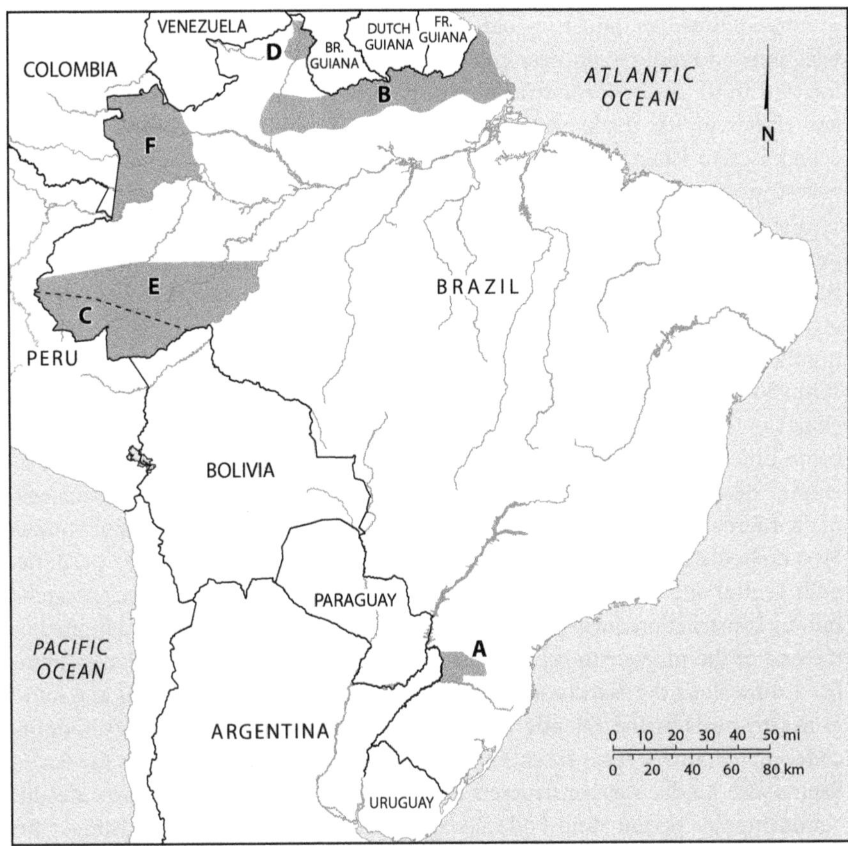

MAP 1. This map shows the territories that Brazil acquired from its neighbors through diplomacy from 1895 to 1928. Source: E. Bradford Burns, *A History of Brazi* (New York: Columbia University Press, 1993), 279. A. Acquired from Argentina in 1895; B. Acquired from Swiss Federal Council in 1900; C. Acquired from Bolivia in 1903; D. Acquired from Italy in 1904; E. Acquired from Peru in 1909; F. Acquired from Colombia in 1928.

promote Pan-Americanism. With the endorsement of Washington, Rio hosted the third Pan-American Conference the next year, consolidating its role as an ally and proxy of the United States in Latin America. The United States, in return, stood firmly behind Brazil's demands at Versailles as a victor of World War I and its broader quest for increased influence in the postwar world.[28]

The political closeness between the First Republic and the United States developed in tandem with the rapid growth of American economic interests in Brazil. After World War I, the United States replaced Great Britain as the biggest investor in the Brazilian economy. With British presence waning, the United States not only became Brazil's most important trade partner but also supplied it with the biggest amount of investment. American merchants established monopolies in a number of Brazilian industries, old and new, ranging from shipping, meatpacking, telegraph, and radio to popular entertainment.[29] This was also when Brazil strode forward in its process of industrialization and urbanization. Much of the capital and resources was made available by the continuing development of the coffee economy. São Paulo, the new center of Brazil's coffee economy, also became the fastest-growing industrial region in the country.[30]

The Brazil-U.S. intimacy, Brazil's rise as a regional power, and São Paulo's prosperity in the coffee economy and success in industrialization jointly turned the state into the cradle of a new form of settler colonialism, one that was centered on immigrant farmers. São Paulo became a frontrunner among Brazilian states in immigration-based land exploration and redistribution. One of the most immediate stimulations was the rapid construction of railroads in the state, which reached its climax in the 1910s. The Brazilian leaders' desire to expand railway lines to improve communication and reduce the cost of transportation dated to the early days of the empire. Because of the lack of capital, at the end of the imperial period, the majority of the railroads were still built—and owned—by foreign companies mainly funded by shareholders in London. Though the Imperial Railroad Law of 1873 permitted both central and local governments to use land grants to attract foreign capital, railway construction during the imperial period was generally slow and limited. At the end of the nineteenth century, railway lines remained concentrated in populated areas along the east coast, conveniently linking the big plantations and mines to nearby ports by the Atlantic Ocean.[31] The state of São Paulo, with its booming coffee plantations, was no exception. Since 1860, when a line to connect the Port of Santos with Jundiai was constructed, the railway network in the state grew steadily. Yet during this period almost all railway tracks were located in the existing coffee zones in the Old West, including the Central, Mogiana, and Paulista regions.

This pattern of railway construction began to change at the turn of the twentieth century, when the First Republic began to buy back the foreign-owned railroads. By 1914, the central and state governments owned up to 61 percent of the railway lines in the country. In the meantime, they were also building their own railways, though still with the support of foreign capital. Unlike those built in the nineteenth century, these new railways were not located in the existing coffee zones. Instead, they penetrated the remote interior, linking it to the east coast. São Paulo exemplified this new pattern as the state where most of the new railway tracks in the nation were being laid.[32] One of the most representative railway lines of this period was the Estada de Ferro do Noroeste, or Northwest Railroad, whose construction began in 1905 with the express goal to tighten the Brazilian state's military control over its western borders. During the first phase of construction, Noroeste linked the city of Bauru with Araçatuba in 1908, where an inland city was established in the same year. When the entire line was completed in 1914, it reached the border of Bolivia.[33] This wave of railway construction came to an end in the last half of the 1910s, when the outbreak of World War I led to a sharp drop in foreign capital.[34]

The Noroeste line, like many others laid during this period, not only strengthened the republic's military presence along its borders but also substantially accelerated the state governments' appropriation of Indigenous land. The Kaingang people, known for their resilience and combat skills, had withstood the invasion of white settlers for generations. However, violent clashes began as soon as railroad construction started. The Kaingang retaliated against the railroad workers by killing some, which led to brutal reprisals from the workers. A 1908 newspaper even described the massacre of the Kaingang as if it were a sport for the workers. In a particularly heinous incident, a man named João Pedro led an attack on a Kaingang village at night, killing more than a hundred people. Despite their reputation as formidable warriors, the Kaingang were overpowered by the unexpected assault and the superior weaponry of the attackers.[35]

As railway networks now linked the interior with port cities, the output of the land—coffee as well as other crops—could be transported to industrial centers and the coast at low cost. As a result, more and more Indigenous forests in the interior became potential coffee fields. Once again, as the center of the coffee economy in the country, the state of São Paulo served as an example of this process. As late as 1907, when the state had already become the top coffee producer of Brazil, more than half of its land, mainly in the northern and western interior, remained unfarmed. Yet by the early 1920s, the Noroeste line, together with the Alta Sorocabana line and the extension of the Mogiana line, had pushed the coffee frontier to the state's western and northern borders.[36] These new coffee zones, including the New West and the Upper Mogiana, quickly became the main coffee suppliers of São Paulo within a decade; by the early 1930s, they made up more than 60 percent of the total coffee output in the state.[37]

This wave of railway-driven expansion of coffee farming developed in tandem with a fundamental change in the practice of property rights. The Land Law of 1850 empowered the central government to appropriate Indigenous land in the interior by defining it as publicly owned. However, because of a lack of political resources and limitations in transportation, the imperial regime was incapable of exerting de facto control over the interior. As a result, landlords and individual farmers alike continued to claim new land by squatting. The transition of Brazil into a republic and the promulgation of the 1891 Constitution shifted the authority to define and enforce property rights from the central government to individual states. However, this did little to strengthen the state's power to impose control and only led to a diversification of land policies throughout the country.

It was not until the wave of inland-bound railway construction that state governments could finally exercise a firm grip on what they defined as public land through a revolutionary mode of land distribution.[38] Known as *loteamento*, this model of land distribution aimed to create small owner-farmers. A typical practice was that the state government granted a portion of what it defined as public land in the interior to a land development or railway company. The latter would then divide the land into small units, usually over twenty hectares each, and sell them to individual farmers. In order to make its land attractive, the company would lay roads and build cities and related facilities, turning the land into a community of small farmers.[39] Since the individual buyers shouldered the responsibility of turning forests into coffee fields, the land was sold at low prices. Soon the land of interior São Paulo became a magnet for individual farmers, who were the backbone of land exploration and coffee cultivation. As a result, a number of new coffee zones emerged in western and northern São Paulo that were fundamentally different from the traditional coffee zones in the Paraíba Valley: the former was mainly made up of small farms; the latter, of large plantations.

Loteamento made it easier for immigrants, both Europeans and Japanese, to become independent landowners.[40] A 1920 proclamation by Washington Luís, governor of São Paulo, emphasized the state government's commitment to facilitating immigrant-centered, small farm–driven land colonization. "Retain those [immigrants] who live here, welcome those who come, colonize, settle," he claimed, "that is our desideratum." He promised to promote further public land distribution under the loteamento system in a manner similar to what was done along the Noroeste and Sorocabana railway lines: conducting further land surveys, building new towns along the frontier-bound railways, and offering conducive policies in tax and finance.[41]

In this wave of immigrant-driven colonization made possible by the new railways and expansionist state policies, the Indigenous people were not the only ones affected. While previously the state governments had claimed the land without modern titles as publicly owned, they were often unable to assert actual control in the interior regions due to the lack of resources and transportation restrictions. As a result, both caboclo farmers and big plantations continued to claim new land on their own by squatting. Plantations usually gave sharecroppers usufruct rights to the land they farmed in return for their services.[42] Now, with government presence established, these independent squatters and sharecroppers had to purchase the title from the state in order to retain their land. Those who could not afford the title often abandoned their plot and moved inland, further encroaching on Indigenous land. They also fought back against the state through lawsuits as well as rebellions. The Contestado Rebellion in southern Brazil in 1912–16 was an example of how the new infringement on the existing residents' rights to their land during this period led to land disputes and armed conflicts.[43]

DIVERGENCE AND CONVERGENCE
OF JAPANESE SETTLERS

São Paulo, the center of coffee production and railway expansion, was the forerunner in this new wave of settler colonialism in Brazil. It was not a coincidence that the state was also where the first dozens of Japanese Brazilian farming colonies emerged in the 1910s. Almost all of the Japanese colonies were located along railway lines beyond Paraíba Valley, home of the old coffee zones. Most of their

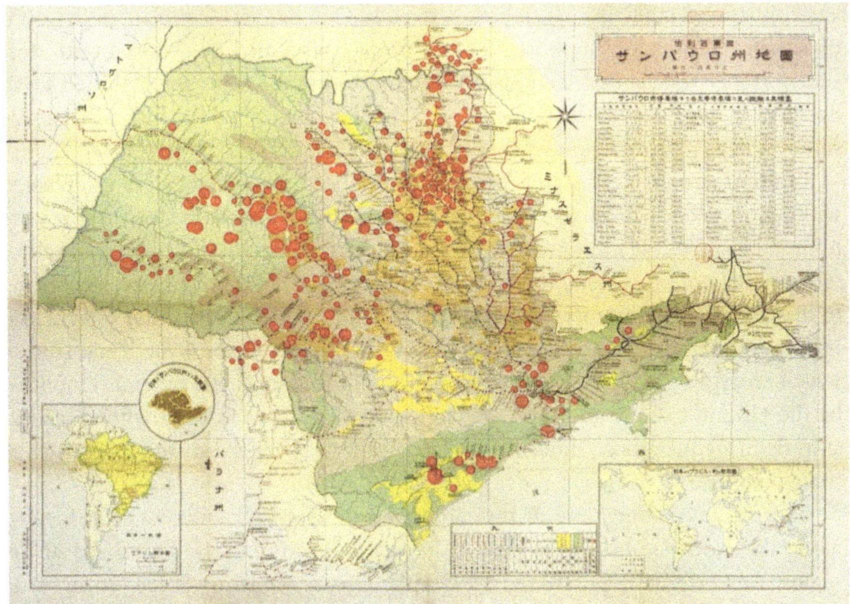

MAP 2. The locations of Japanese settler communities in the state of São Paulo in the early 1930s. The vast majority of the communities were located along the railway lines in the new coffee zones in the west and north. Source: Gaikō Shiryōkan, *Honpon imin toriatsukainin kankei zakken, Kaigai Kōgyō Kabushiki Gaisha*, vol. 10, J.1.2.0. J 3–1.

inhabitants were Japanese immigrants who arrived in Brazil initially as contract laborers on coffee plantations. According to how they were formed and financed, these settler colonies can be classified as two general types: top-down and bottom-up. The former were established directly by the joint forces of the imperial government, business elites, and migration promoters in Japan. The latter were organized by immigrants who were already in Brazil. Villages of these two types differed significantly but also shared many features.

The Iguape project, spearheaded by Aoyagi Ikutarō, represented the top-down type.[44] Both its founders and its financial resources came directly from Tokyo. In 1913, with the support of then prime minister Katsura Tarō, a group of political and entrepreneurial elites established the Brazil Colonization Company. This venture was led by the business tycoon Shibusawa Ei'ichi, who aimed to profit from the acquisition and development of Brazilian land by Japanese migrants. With an initial investment of one million yen, the Brazil Colonization Company took over the Brazilian government's land grant from the Tokyo Syndicate and carried out the project of settler community building under Aoyagi's leadership.[45]

The first portion of land, 1,400 hectares, that the Brazil Colonization Company obtained from the Iguape municipal council was on the left bank of the Ribeira River in the Gipuvura region. The company promised to settle thirty Japanese families within five years. Aoyagi and the first group of residents, including a few agriculture and medicine specialists, arrived in October 1913 from Japan. In honor of Katsura Tarō, a key supporter of this project who died the same month, this settler village was named the Katsura Colony.[46] Soon the company obtained 9,300 hectares in Registro, up the Iguape River. There it established the second Japanese settler village in Iguape, known as the Registro Colony.[47]

In contrast, Japanese settler villages of the bottom-up type were established without direct financial and political support from Tokyo. Instead, they were founded by Japanese immigrants who were already in Brazil. Most Japanese settler villages that emerged along the Noroeste railway fell into this category. According to the ways the community leadership took shape, they can be further categorized into two subtypes. One was represented by the Birigui Colony, the leadership of which emerged gradually after the formation of the colony. The other, exemplified by the Hirano Colony and the Uetsuka Colony, already had well-defined leadership from its inception; indeed, that leadership was crucial to the formation of these colonies.

The Birigui Colony, one of the largest Japanese settler colonies, was located along the Noroeste line, southeast of Araçatuba station.[48] The forestland of the region was originally purchased by Cia de Terras, Medeiras & Colonização de São Paulo, a land developer funded by British and Brazilian capital. The company divided its 125,000 hectares into units of 25 hectares and started selling them to small farmers in 1913 via three-year loans. In order to attract farming settlers, it not only paved roads but also offered its residents free train tickets on the Noroeste line.[49] The red clay soil (*terra rosa*) in the area proved to be highly fertile. Within a few years, Birigui had already attracted a few thousand immigrant settlers, including Italians, Spanish, and Portuguese.[50]

The first thirteen Japanese families arrived in Birigui in 1915, and the number of Japanese settlers grew steadily after. Its community leadership began to take shape in 1916, when the company employed Miyazaki Hachirō as its agent in charge of recruiting Japanese settlers and managing their community.[51] Under Miyazaki's leadership, Japanese settlers began working together to build public facilities and provide services for themselves. In 1923, when the Japanese Association of Birigui was established with Miyazaki as its first president, the Japanese settlers in the region expanded to Araçatuba station and areas farther west.[52]

In 1915, the same year Japanese immigrants arrived in Birigui, Hirano Unpei established the Hirano Colony. A graduate of Tokyo University of Foreign Studies, Hirano came to Brazil as one of the five interpreters on the *Kasato Maru* and was assigned to the Guatapara plantation in Mogiana. Because of his leadership and language skills, he was soon promoted to assistant director of the plantation to manage affairs related to Japanese coffee laborers. With the goal of establishing a village of independent Japanese farmers, Hirano left his plantation job and purchased 3,920 hectares of forestland northeast of Cafelândia station (now Presidente Penna station), about 125 kilometers from Bauru station on the Noroeste

line. His influence among Japanese immigrants attracted eighty-two settler families to his colony during the first year.[53]

Three years later, another *Kasato Maru* migrant, Uetsuka Shūhei, purchased
3,388 hectares near Heitor Legru station (now Promissão station) along the Noroeste line, between the Birigui and Hirano Colonies. Uetsuka had initially worked
as a migration agent of the Imperial Colonization Company and an assistant to
Mizuno Ryū. Following Hirano's example, he took advantage of São Paulo's public land sale amid the wave of railway expansion and established the First Uetsuka Colony (also called the Promissão Colony). He founded the Second Uetsuka
Colony in 1922.[54]

Though bearing significant differences in the ways they were established and
managed, these two types of settler villages were similar to one another in no less
important ways. Both types exemplified Japanese collaborative settler colonialism
in Brazil. On the one hand, the formation of these settler villages marked a new and
successful chapter in the history of Japanese migration-driven overseas expansion
that was centered on agriculture, permanent settlement, and land acquisition. On
the other hand, the emerging Japanese villages in southeastern Brazil, like many
other farming villages established in the same region by European immigrants
such as the Italians, Spaniards, and Portuguese, became the arms of the Brazilian
state to claim and colonize the land in the country's interior.

First, the formation of Japanese settler villages of both types in São Paulo was
the Japanese expansionists' response to anti-Japanese sentiment in the United
States. They sought alternative destinations for Japanese migration and emphasized land acquisition and agricultural settlement in their destinations. Aoyagi
Ikutaro's project, which saw the purchase of land in Iguape and the establishment
of Japanese farming villages there, was closely linked to Tokyo-sponsored programs of farmer migration to Northeast Asia and the South Seas. This was not
only because Katsura Tarō, then prime minister of Japan, played an important
role in their conception. All three migration campaigns, though oriented in different directions, mirrored one another in their ideologies. Stimulated by intensified anti-Japanese sentiment in North America, these campaigns aimed to find
alternatives to the United States as new destinations of Japanese migration. More
importantly, the planners and leaders of all these campaigns deemed labor migration undesirable and instead saw farmer migration and the acquisition of land
overseas as the most desirable means of expansion.

The settler villages of the bottom-up type in the state of São Paulo were not
directly associated with the campaigns of farmer migration to Northeast Asia
and the South Seas. However, their founders and leaders considered themselves
Japan's empire builders in South America. The leaders of the most representative Japanese villages along the Noroeste line, such as Hirano Unpei, Uetsuka
Shūhei, and Miyazaki Hachirō, all shared the goal of pursuing Japanese expansion
through migration and settler colonialism with those who spearheaded Japanese

emigration campaigns on the other side of the Pacific.[55] For the same reason, villages of the bottom-up type often welcomed financial aid from Tokyo and were, therefore, subject to its political and cultural influence. From the very beginning, Hirano Unpei's endeavor to acquire land and create a Japanese settler village was inspired and guided by Matsumura Sadao, then Japanese consul general in São Paulo. Matsumura also swiftly provided aid to Hirano when some of the latter's employees fell ill with yellow fever.[56] A more direct example of this was Uetsuka Shūhei, who, like Hirano, was supported and guided by the Japanese consul in São Paulo in his efforts to establish two farming villages along the Noroeste line.[57] He also led Japanese farmers along the Noroeste line to collectively submit an appeal to Tokyo, which successfully obtained a ten-year low-interest loan from the Japanese government to Japanese coffee growers in São Paulo; this helped the latter survive a historic drought in the 1920s.[58]

Second and no less significant, Japanese settler villages of both types were agents and beneficiaries of Brazil's own settler colonialism. The dramatic proliferation of railway lines in the first two decades of the twentieth century substantially increased the state governments' capacity to assert control over the interior lands. The state governments sold them to land investment companies, which in turn distributed the land to individual farmers in small portions. With railways now connecting these once-remote areas to the eastern coast and urban centers, interior land became attractive to immigrants desiring land of their own. The loteamento mode of distribution and the multiyear installment financial scheme made it possible for individuals who had little wealth to afford the land. The economic boom and the rapid urbanization triggered by the outbreak of World War I further provided a growing demand for agricultural products, which ensured that the newly formed farmer-centered settler villages in the interior could stay afloat financially.

These individual settlers who became owner-farmers in the interior, in turn, served as the trailblazers of state-sponsored settler colonialism. In the state of São Paulo, the Japanese settlers, like those from Europe, were indispensable arms of the Paulista government in its land colonization. The Noroeste railway, which quickly became a hub of Japanese settler villages, was put into use while the state government was at war with the Indigenous peoples along the line. By defining Indigenous land and the land occupied by squatters as state owned, the government sold land wherever railways were constructed.[59] The establishment of the Birigui, Uetsuka, and Hirano Colonies and other Japanese colonies along the Noroeste line was an integral part of this process of land appropriation. Japanese settlers in Iguape, located in the Gipuvura region of the state's south coast, also served as agents of the Paulista government to claim its ownership of the local land.[60]

When Japanese settlers found their feet in southeastern Brazil, contract laborers from Japan continued to populate the coffee fazendas in the same region. Except during the first two years of World War I, when the numbers of Japanese immigrants dropped sharply due to a downturn in the global coffee market, about 2,700 Japanese laborers entered Brazil's coffee plantations every year during the 1910s. This stable flow of Japanese labor immigrants to southeastern Brazil was crucial for the emergence and growth of Japanese settler villages in the interior, as the majority of the farming settlers were former contract laborers who had either completed or terminated their contracts.

Although the Brazil Colonization Company spared no efforts to recruit farmers from the Japanese archipelago to Iguape, few answered its call. The top-down type of Japanese settler villages in Brazil encountered difficulty recruiting farmers from Japan, a phenomenon that mirrored the domestic expansionists' failure to relocate sufficient numbers of farmers to Northeast Asia and the South Seas. As a result, the growth of Japanese villages in Iguape was primarily due to its ability to attract Japanese immigrants who initially arrived as contract laborers. Similarly, residents of the bottom-up type villages were almost exclusively immigrant laborers who had previously worked in coffee plantations.

Though most of the Japanese settler villages emerged in the state of São Paulo during this era, it was not the only state where Japanese settlers claimed land. Yamagata Yosaburō, a merchant from the Hizen domain (now Saga Prefecture), purchased 5,000 hectares in Rio de Janeiro and established a farm for rice and sugarcane cultivation.[61] Yamagata's life demonstrated the connection between Japanese settler community building in Brazil and Japan's colonial expansion in the Asia-Pacific region in the first two decades of the twentieth century. He started his career by moving to Hokkaido and investing in a local fishery and soon expanded his business into mining and livestock husbandry. He also made an unsuccessful attempt to expand his commercial network into southern Manchuria during the Russo-Japanese War. In 1908, after his business in Japan ran into a crisis, Yamagata migrated to Rio de Janeiro in search of a fresh start.[62] Like many Japanese community leaders in São Paulo, Yamagata consciously associated his endeavor of migration and land acquisition with the goal of putting down the roots of the Japanese empire in South America.[63]

. . .

The first two decades of the twentieth century marked an important period for the development of both Japanese and Brazilian colonialism. As the United States rose steadily as a global power and substantially expanded its political and economic influence, empire builders in Japan and Brazil continued to see the United States as the ideal model of settler colonialism. They sought to pursue their own expansion by accommodating and collaborating with the global rise of American power. By participating in World War I, both Japan and Brazil increased their global and regional influence at the beginning of the American century.

Through the Russo-Japanese War and World War I, Japan secured its grasp of swaths of Northeast Asia and Micronesia. While anti-Japanese sentiment in the United States pushed Japanese expansionists to seek alternative migration destinations, it also convinced them that agricultural settlement and land acquisition was a more desirable migration model than that of contract labor. South America, especially southeastern Brazil, became one of the three destinations of state-sponsored Japanese expansion, together with Northeast Asia and the South Seas. Brazil's First Republic, on the other hand, had achieved stunning success in territorial expansion through diplomacy with support from the United States, which stimulated a new wave of railway construction in southeastern Brazil that linked the economic and population centers along the east coast to the interior. These railways decisively increased the state's power to appropriate Indigenous and communal land.

It was in these global and regional contexts that the first group of Japanese settler villages emerged in the state of São Paulo along its main railway lines. Jointly facilitated by the migration states of Japan and Brazil, these settler villages served as instruments of Japanese expansion in South America and of Brazil's settler colonialism in its own interior. They continued to grow and expand by attracting Japanese immigrant laborers from coffee plantations. The end of World War I led to new changes in the economy, social structure, and political ideologies in both the Japanese empire and the First Republic, and the next chapter examines how these changes on both sides of the Pacific led to the heyday of Japanese collaborative settler colonialism in Brazil.

4

"Making the World Our Home"

The Heyday of Collaborative Settler Colonialism

To bring the empire to a better future, the Japanese should "make the world our home" (*sekai wo ie toshite*), claimed Inoue Masaji, head of the Overseas Development Company, in the keynote speech he delivered at the Conference for Overseas Colonial Migration (Kaigai Shokumin Taikai) in Tokyo in 1930. He encouraged Japanese young people to take on the mission to migrate overseas and explore the land and resources abroad (*kaigai kaitaku*). The Japanese subjects' worldwide expansion (*sekai shinshutsu*), he argued, would not only increase the wealth and power of the Japanese empire but also bring genuine peace and happiness to the world.[1] Inoue's claim represented a common understanding of Japan's expansion held by mainstream Japanese empire builders of the day. As Tokyo embraced the new imperial order after World War I and accepted the new colonial language of pacifism and international cooperation, Japanese leaders considered overseas emigration a crucial means of expansion during the interwar era.

Seeing Brazil as the most promising destination for Japanese migrants, Tokyo began to pour financial and political resources into the promotion of Brazil-bound emigration. To maximize its capacity to promote, oversee, and coordinate campaigns of Brazilian migration, Japan's migration state underwent a series of additional structural changes, signifying its progression into a mature phase. This new version of the migration state strengthened its supervision of and cooperation with various social interest groups, such as migration companies, business elites and industrial entrepreneurs, and public media, to foster migration to Brazil. The Overseas Development Company (Kaikō), led by Inoue Masaji, was one of the main partners of the Japanese government to this end. Accordingly, the history of Japanese migration to Brazil entered its golden era. During the years from 1921, when the government started providing subsidies to Brazil-bound Japanese migrants through Kaikō, to 1934, when the Brazilian government imposed a quota restriction on Japanese immigration, nearly ten thousand Japanese subjects reached the Brazilian shores annually. The substantial growth of Brazil-bound migration also led to the rise of Kobe as a major port for emigration in Japan in the 1920s.

This chapter explains how these new structural changes by the Japanese government took place in the global and regional contexts brought by the end of World War I to maximize its ability to promote and manage emigration to Brazil. As the chapter shows, this new version of the migration state operated using two different models, where central and local governments worked closely with industrial capital, migration companies, and various social groups. Together they managed to enlist an unprecedented number of Japanese subjects from different social strata into the march of Japanese collaborative settler colonialism in Brazil. From rural masses to business elites, from desperate job seekers to ambitious investors, Japanese emigrants were hailed by the migration state as trailblazers who would put down the roots of the Japanese empire in the coffee fields of São Paulo and civilize the Amazon jungle. The same migration state, together with some of its collaborative social groups, continued to serve as engines of Japanese expansion in Manchuria and Southeast Asia from the 1930s to the end of World War II. The boom of Brazil-bound emigration, as well as the growth of trade between Japan and South America, also fostered the rise of Kobe as a central port for emigration and commerce.

EMBRACING PEACEFUL EXPANSION: COOPERATION, TRADE, AND EMIGRATION

As a winning nation of World War I, Japan rose quickly to become one of the few world powers that held a voice in the construction of the postwar global order. It not only harvested German Micronesia and expanded its territory into the South Pacific but also joined the United Kingdom, France, and Italy as one of the four permanent members of the Executive Council, the core policy-making body of the League of Nations. However, these stunning diplomatic achievements did not come without a cost, as the empire encountered a variety of new limitations in its path of expansion. Although the United States stood outside the League of Nations, its central role in the construction of the new world order was manifested at the Washington Conference of 1921. The conference reaffirmed the American agenda on the new order proclaimed by President Woodrow Wilson's Fourteen Points, emphasizing both disarmament and open trade. The conference terminated Japan's wartime monopoly on Chinese politics and markets and tied Japan into the Five Power Treaty (with the United Kingdom, the United States, France, and Italy) that limited the construction of naval forces by the signatories.

Nevertheless, right after the war, mainstream Japanese politicians and intellectuals embraced the new world order with great enthusiasm. The opinion leaders of a variety of social interest groups ranging from mass media to military strategists recognized the need for Japan to accept the principles of the new order, such as international cooperation, pacifism, and liberalism, in order to continue its pursuit of expansion.[2] Japanese leaders embraced the idea of "peaceful expansion" as their new principle of empire building. Prime Minister Takahashi Korekiyo's New Year's message in 1922 illustrated this concept well. It was no longer possible to expand one's territory through force, Takahashi argued, because of the fundamental changes that the Great War had brought to the world. Yet, he continued, great powers never stopped expanding. They would no longer do so through military and territorial invasion but through trade and economic competition.[3]

For Japanese empire builders of the day, the peaceful expansion had three major components: trade, international cooperation, and emigration. As the United States served as a reliable market that consumed 40 percent of Japanese exports throughout the 1920s, the overseas expansion of trade and investment naturally remained one of the top priorities of the empire's diplomacy in this new Anglo-American order. Japanese diplomats managed to reduce tariff obstacles in China for Japanese exports and created more opportunities for Japanese traders in Southeast Asia and the Middle East.[4] Japanese investment also poured into the South Seas and South America. Represented by the ideas and activities of Shidehara Kijūrō, who served as the foreign minister of Japan from 1924 to 1927, Tokyo's dedication to economic expansion followed the same economic liberalism that buttressed the Open Door policy of the United States. "Shidehara Diplomacy" was firmly supported by the growing business elites of the Taishō era who called for broadening political participation at home and exploring new markets abroad.[5]

Japan's economic expansion was guided by the principle of international cooperation. In addition to playing a key role in the League of Nations' deliberations as a permanent member of its Executive Council, Japan was widely involved in a variety of other internal organizations such as the International Labor Organization, the International Court of Justice, and the Advisory Committee on Traffic in Opium and Other Dangerous Drugs.[6] Nitobe Inazō, a prominent Japanese intellectual who served as undersecretary general of the League of Nations for seven years, urged Japanese subjects to think beyond the archipelago, become the "citizens of the world," and dedicate themselves to the service of all humankind.[7]

In this new design of the empire, emigration played a central role. For many Japanese leaders of the day, the emigration of Japanese farmers and their permanent settlement overseas would not only be a peaceful means of national expansion but also increase trade opportunities between Japan and the host societies. By the 1920s, various experiments in Japanese farmer migration to the territories in Asia and the Pacific covered by Japan's spheres of influence, including Manchuria, the Korean Peninsula, and Micronesia, proved unsuccessful. The United States

TABLE 2 Japanese emigrants subsidized by the migration state, 1923–1937

		Kaikō Model	Aliança Model					Other
	Total Number	Kaikō	Shinano Kaigai Kyōkai	Kumamoto Kaigai Kyōkai	Tottoriken Kaigai Kyōkai	Tōyamaken Kaigai Kyōkai	Kaigai Ijū Kumiai Rengōkai	
1923	110	110						
1924	3,167	3,167						
1925	4,917	4,867	50					
1926	6,054	5,854	200					
1927	8,878	8,328	243	135	106	66		
1928	9,604	9,180	235	44	13	127		5
1929	14,923	13,611					843	469
1930	8,292	7,358					554	380
1931	6,746	5,999					192	555
1932	20,277	18,589					1,148	540
1933	21,006	19,479					878	649
1934	21,025	19,251					1,488	286
1935	2,887	1,772					948	167
1936	5,836	4,366					1,334	136
1937	5,089	4,385					684	20

SOURCE: Data from Iikubo Hideki, "Burajiru imin kara Manshū imin e no kessetsuten," in *Ajia to keiei: shijō, gijutsu, soshiki*, ed. Ihara Motoi, Kikkawa Takeo, and Kubo Fumikatsu, vol. 2 (Tokyo: Tokyo Daigaku Shakai Kagaku Kenkyūjo, 2002), 109.

also shut its doors to Japanese immigrants entirely in 1924. In contrast, those of Brazil were wide open to Japanese immigration, and the Japanese farming population in the state of São Paulo had been growing at a stunning speed.

The success of Japanese Brazilian migration and community building, in turn, stimulated an unprecedented expansion in the Japanese government's involvement in emigration promotion and management, ushering in a new version of the migration state with substantially enhanced capacity. This form of migration state was marked by two new features that came into being in the 1920s. First, through a series of new legislation and structural changes, the imperial government at both the central and local levels assumed direct responsibility for planning, subsidizing, and controlling overseas emigration. Second, in a manner similar to what Sheldon Garon calls "social management," the government began to collaborate closely with different social groups and managed to involve people from a variety of social strata, from the rural masses to business elites, in the empire's emigration-driven expansion.[8]

The following paragraphs examine more closely the two main models of Japan's new migration state, which supervised most Brazil-bound Japanese emigrants. The first was the Kaikō model, in which the Ministry of Home Affairs formed a partnership with Kaikō and offered various forms of financial assistance to Japanese subjects who would migrate to southeastern Brazil and work there initially as contract laborers on coffee plantations. The second was the Aliança model, exemplified by the Aliança Colony established by expansionists in Nagano Prefecture. Under this model, the Japanese government fostered the formation of Overseas Migration Cooperatives in individual prefectures as state agents to manage emigration at the local level. Working within their respective prefectures, each of these cooperatives functioned as both a migration recruiting organization and a credit union. In addition to receiving financial aid from Tokyo, they collected small funds from individual members to make land purchases in southeastern Brazil and relocated their members there as farming settlers. The two models differed in the ways that the government was involved. While Tokyo functioned as an external partner that provided financial aid and policy support in the Kaikō model, in the Aliança model the state itself was a part of the administrative structure of the Overseas Migration Cooperatives and had more direct control. Both models of emigration were marked by the synergy of state power and private capital.

THE MIGRATION STATE IN THE KAIKŌ MODEL

Kaikō's government-sponsored migration program targeted impoverished Japanese subjects struggling with their livelihood at the bottom rung of society.[9] Providing them with financial aid through Kaikō, the imperial government encouraged the masses to move to Brazil and start a new life there. The program was not only part of the government's effort to use emigration to alleviate social poverty but also a means for Tokyo to escalate Japanese settler colonial expansion in Brazil. This is because the government's ultimate expectation was for these emigrants to become independent landowners after their labor contracts ended and settle in Brazil permanently.[10] Kaikō itself also took over the management of the Iguape colony in São Paulo previously established by the Tokyo Syndicate, securing its recruits' smooth transition from contract laborers to independent farmers.

This government-sponsored migration program was made possible by the end of World War I. The empire's economic monopoly on the Chinese market during World War I stimulated a short-term economic boom and a record-breaking wave of urbanization in the archipelago.[11] The wealth increase in the archipelago, however, came with a growing social gap. The quick emergence of the nouveau riche (Narikin) was accompanied by the rise of economic tensions in both urban and rural areas in the form of labor and tenant disputes. The end of World War I brought the termination of Japan's economic monopoly in Asia, which led to an immediate economic downturn in the archipelago and only exacerbated existing social tensions. In 1918, the inflation of food prices triggered the biggest rice riots in Japanese history. These grassroots disturbances not only ushered in the birth of the first democratic regime in Tokyo but also marked the birth of what Michael Lewis calls the "mass awakening." The urban and rural poor began to adopt more organized means of political protests, forming various unions and civil associations at the national and local levels.[12]

The rise of the masses as a major political force compelled the imperial government to take more responsibility for social welfare by providing poverty relief and basic foods to its subjects. Embracing the increasingly popular claim that overpopulation was the root of all social ills that plagued the archipelago, policy makers began to use emigration as a solution to social problems. The first institutional change in the government was the formation of the Bureau of Social Affairs (Shakaikyoku) in the Ministry of Home Affairs in 1920, which began to promote emigration to Brazil as a solution to poverty.[13] Kaikō was the primary partner of the Bureau of Social Affairs. In 1921, the bureau started providing funds to Kaikō to aid the company in promoting emigration, recruiting and training emigrants, and conducting physical exams and vaccinations for emigrants.[14]

Kaikō was established in 1917 under the imperial government's auspices to unify migration-related businesses in and outside of the Japanese empire.[15] It came into being based on the merging of four different migration companies focused on Japanese migration to Asia, the South Seas, and Latin America.[16] After annexing the Morioka Emigration Company (Morioka Imin Gaisha) in 1919, Kaikō was able to monopolize all authorized Japanese business-related emigration to Brazil for several years. In addition to Brazilian emigration, Kaikō organized emigration to Peru, the Philippines, and Australia and held investments in trade and agriculture in the Japanese empire and beyond.[17]

The first few years of the Bureau of Social Affairs' financial assistance for Brazil-bound emigration through Kaikō, however, proved unfruitful. The average number of Japanese subjects bound for Brazil between 1921 and 1923 remained less than 880, showing a decrease rather than an increase from the yearly average in the 1910s.[18] The number only began to climb in 1924, after the bureau started providing direct subsidies to individual emigrants recruited by Kaikō. Since 1923, it had begun to offer a compensation fund of 35 yen per person to up to 2,000 Kaikō-recruited emigrants, fully covering their registration fees. The next year, the bureau started providing a more substantial stipend of 200 yen to each of the Kaikō recruits to cover their steamship trip to Brazil. The number of emigrants who received the government's compensation and stipend grew to over 7,500 by 1928, right before the newly formed Ministry of Colonial Affairs (Takumūshō) took over management of migration-related affairs from the bureau.[19]

This dramatic increase in the government's financial aid was the result of two related factors. First, the state of São Paulo, where the majority of the Japanese immigrants settled, fully stopped its subsidies to Japanese immigration in 1922.[20]

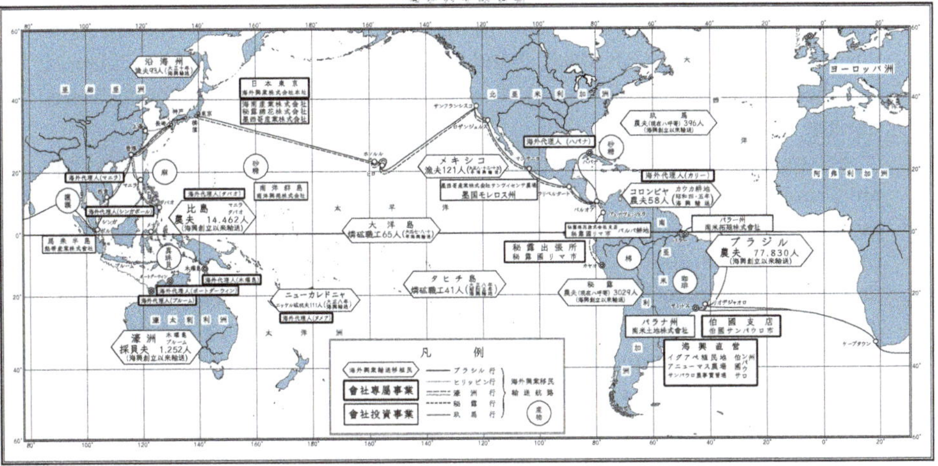

MAP 3. Redrawing of an original map showing the locations of Kaikō's branches and businesses across the Pacific in 1931. Source: Kaigai Kōgyō Kabushiki Gaisha, *Kaigai Kōgyō Kabushiki Gaisha gensei yōran* (Tokyo: Kaigai Kōgyō Kabushiki Gaisha, 1932). Redrawing by Mario Norton, Fondren Library, Rice University.

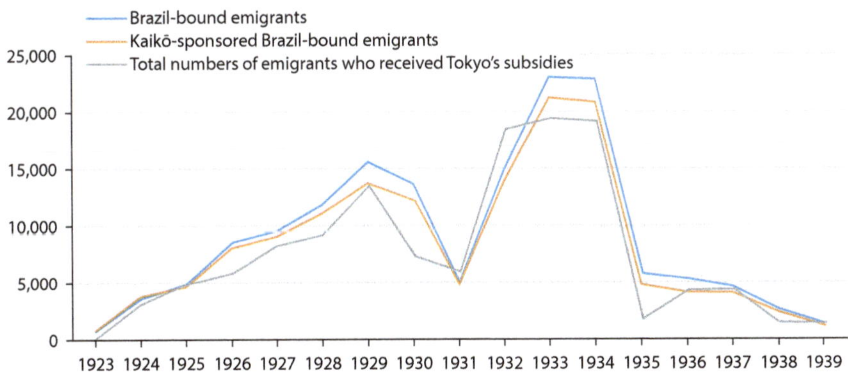

FIGURE 10. Japanese emigrants from 1923 to 1939. This chart illustrates the annual numbers of all Japanese emigrants to Brazil, those who were specifically sponsored by Kaikō, and the total number of emigrants who received Tokyo's subsidies. Tokyo's subsidies were essential for the rapid increase of Japanese emigrants to Brazil since the mid-1920s, and the majority of the Brazil-bound emigrants who received Tokyo's subsidies were emigrants recruited by Kaikō. The chart is based on data in Iikubo Hideki, "1920 nendai ni okeru naimushō shakaikyoku no kaigai imin shōreisaku," *Rekishi to keizai* 46, no. 1 (2003): 40.

The end of World War I brought hordes of European immigrants to southeastern Brazil seeking a livelihood, sufficiently meeting the local demand for coffee laborers. As the Japanese had been commonly seen by the Paulista elites as less desirable substitutes for European immigrants, they were no longer attractive when the supply of the latter was abundant. The termination of Brazilian financial aid, therefore, pushed Tokyo to increase its own financial responsibility to maintain the migration flow.

Second, two events intensified the anxiety about overpopulation in the Japanese archipelago. On the one hand, the deadly Great Kantō Earthquake that struck Tokyo and Yokohama in 1923 immediately created hundreds of thousands of victims demanding a basic livelihood. To prevent potential social uprisings and chaos, the government responded quickly by making Brazil-bound emigration one of its disaster relief programs.[21] On the other hand, the promulgation of the Immigration Act of 1924 in the United States completely shut the American door to Japanese immigration, further narrowing the options of Japanese migration promoters.[22] In the same year, the government hosted the Imperial Conference on the Economy (Teikoku Keizai Kaigi), where policy makers and bureaucrats specializing in social affairs, migration, and foreign affairs had reached a consensus to further expand the state-sponsored emigration program. Participants at the conference believed that the Bureau of Social Affairs, in particular, should play a central role in promoting and guiding overseas emigration as a solution to social problems related to rural depression and overpopulation. This initiative was approved by the Imperial Diet a month later, which offered an extra budget that allowed the Bureau of Social Affairs to cover the expenses of the entire trip to Brazil for all government-sponsored Kaikō emigrants.[23]

THE MIGRATION STATE IN THE ALIANÇA MODEL

The Aliança model, which allowed the government to collaborate closely with different social groups and migration promoters, was made possible by the growing passion of a variety of nongovernmental interest groups and of the general public for overseas emigration in general and Brazil-bound emigration in particular. This enthusiasm was reflected in the emergence of several well-circulated emigration-focused magazines in the 1920s, such as *Shokumin* (Colonial Review), a mouthpiece of Kaikō, *Kaigai* (Overseas), and *Burajiru: ishokumin to bōeki* (Brazil: Colonial Migration and Trade).[24] These newly founded periodicals were joined by existing mainstream magazines, like *Kingu* (King) and *Ie no hikari* (Light of Family), that started to have more coverage on topics related to emigration. This fed the public passion for emigration, stimulating the private sectors' interest in collaborating with the migration state.

The Aliança Colony, a Japanese setter colony in the state of São Paulo, was established in this context. It was made possible by the synergy between the

Nagano prefectural government and the individual expansionists who had personal ties with the prefecture. The Aliança model exemplified another aspect of the migration state at work, in which the prefectural government played a leading role in financing and managing emigration. The plan to build the Aliança Colony started with the collaboration of Nagata Shigeshi and Wako Shungorō, two Nagano natives who hoped to establish a new type of Japanese settler unit in Brazil. Both had previously migrated to the United States and worked as journalists for Japanese American media on the West Coast. After quitting their careers, Nagata returned to Japan and became president of Nippon Rikkō Kai (Japanese Striving Society), a major migration company based in Tokyo, while Wako moved to Brazil and continued working for Japanese media in São Paulo. Unsatisfied with Kaikō's contract laborer–centered migration programs, Nagata and Wako wanted to establish a new Japanese colony in Brazil that would be composed of independent farming settlers who migrated from Japan and were financially self-sufficient, free from the control of big companies like Kaikō.[25]

To this end, Nagata and Wako collaborated with the Nagano prefectural government and the Nagano Board of Education to establish the Shinano Overseas Association (Shinano Kaigai Kyōkai) in 1922. The association was jointly funded by public and private money, and its first director and vice director were the Nagano governor and the head of the prefectural diet, respectively. Functioning as a semigovernmental organization, it was in charge of promoting emigration among Nagano residents by hosting public lectures, publishing books, funding overseas investigative trips, and raising funds to support specific emigration campaigns.[26] The Aliança Colony was a major accomplishment of the association.

As a product of the migration state, the Aliança Colony differed from the government-sponsored emigration program of Kaikō in a few respects. First, unlike the Kaikō program, which recruited and transported Japanese subjects to Brazil as contract laborers, the Aliança Colony directly recruited and relocated Japanese subjects to Brazil as farming settlers. To this end, the Shinano Overseas Association completed a land purchase in São Paulo in advance and established a series of facilities, including a rice mill, a coffee refinery, a clinic, and a school, to foster the growth of the farming village.[27] The prosperity of independent and self-sufficient Japanese farmers, founders of Aliança believed, was essential for the success of Japanese expansion in Brazil. As Nagata claimed with pride, the goal of Aliança was "to cultivate people rather than coffee" (*kōhī yori hito wo tsukure*).[28]

Second, whereas the Kaikō program relied heavily on government subsidies, a substantial portion of the financial resources of the Aliança Colony came from individual migrants themselves. The recruited migrants fell into two categories: those who were able to purchase land in the colony in advance and would move to Aliança directly as independent farmers and those who would start in Aliança as contract farmers. The latter would receive loans from the Shinano Overseas Association and later become independent owner-farmers by paying off the loans. Both of these categories required the recruits to have a certain amount of money to start with.[29] Accordingly, unlike the recruits of the Kaikō program, most of whom were struggling at the bottom of society, an average participant in the Aliança project was financially closer to becoming an owner-farmer in Japan before migration.

Third, unlike the Kaikō program that recruited nationally, the Aliança Colony emphasized local identity and native ties. The processes of planning, fund-raising, and migration recruiting were limited to residents in Nagano Prefecture and those who held native ties with the prefecture. The prefectural government also supported the project by providing financial and political assistance through the Shinano Overseas Association. The Aliança Colony symbolized a new approach of the migration state, in which local governments began to engage directly with the campaigns of migration promotion and management. Inspired by the Aliança project, the Overseas Associations of Tottori, Toyama, and Kumamoto, backed by their respective prefectural governments, completed land purchases near Aliança in São Paulo. Modeled after Aliança, Tottori's colony, Aliança II, was established in 1926, and Kumamoto's Vila Nova Colony was established in 1927. In the same year, the Toyama Overseas Association and the Shinano Overseas Association jointly established Aliança III.

The Aliança model, with its prefecture-based scope, farmer-centered focus, and principle of mutual support among its members, was officially adopted by Tokyo as one of its major approaches in migration promotion and management. Also in 1927, the imperial government promulgated the Overseas Migration Cooperative Societies Law (Kaigai Ijū Kumiai Hō), which authorized each prefecture to establish an overseas migration cooperative society. Each society, backed by its own prefectural government, would recruit emigrants and raise funds to establish its own prefecture-centered settler colony in Brazil. Seven cooperative societies were established in the same year and jointly formed the Federation of Overseas Migration Cooperative Societies (Kaigai Ijū Kumiai Rengōkai). As the headquarters of all the prefectural cooperative societies, the federation had forty-four members by the mid-1930s. On its formation, the federation immediately received a loan of 1.7 million yen from the imperial government, allowing it to facilitate and unify the migration and land acquisition campaigns of individual societies in Brazil.[30]

The federation's first executive director was Umetani Mitsusada, Nagano governor and a central backer of the Aliança project, and he soon arrived in Brazil to conduct land investigation. The federation established the Sociedade Colonizadora do Brazil Limitada (Brazilian Colonization Company Limited / Burajiru Takushoku Kumiai, or Burataku) to serve as its agent in Brazil to carry out land purchases and Japanese community building. By the end of the 1930s, when Burataku stopped its operation in Brazil, it had established three Japanese settler colonies, including Bastos along the Sorocabana railway, Tietê along the Noroeste railway in São Paulo, and Tres Barras in northern Paraná. In addition to managing these three Japanese colonies, it also took over the administration of all four colonies associated with Aliança along the Noroesete railway, Aliança I, II, III, and Vila Nova. In total, Burataku acquired and managed 537,668 acres and 18,317 Japanese settlers, most of whom were owner-farmers.[31]

In addition to Kaikō and Burataku, several other Japanese companies emerged as agents of the migration state in Brazil by receiving support from Tokyo in one way or another. In 1922, Manabe Akira, a cotton specialist in the Ministry of Agriculture and Commerce, led a business delegation to Brazil and attended the World Cotton Conference held at Rio de Janeiro. On his return, Manabe gave a series of lectures to Japanese business leaders emphasizing the importance of encouraging Japanese emigrants to cultivate cotton in Brazil and explaining its benefits for the empire. Many answered his call. Suzuki Iwazō, head of the Kansai-based Suzuki Trading Company (Suzuki Shōten), envisioned that Brazil would become an alternative to the United States as a primary supplier of raw cotton for the empire.[32] Iwasaki Hisaya, former president of the Mitsubishi Corporation and founder of the Tozan Nōji Kabushiki Gaisha (Tozan Agriculture Corporation), was another follower. Under his leadership, the Tokyo-based Tozan Agriculture Corporation had established a series of branches in the Korean Peninsula, Taiwan, the Malay Peninsula, and Brazil. Inspired by Manabe, Iwasaki dispatched two of his company's cotton specialists previously stationed in China, Yamamoto Kiyoshi and Nagahara Shunjirō, to São Paulo to conduct further investigation. Both concluded that cotton cultivation was promising for the company's branch farm in Brazil, Caza Tozan, which became one of the earliest Japanese settler farms to experiment with cotton cultivation.[33]

The combination of state power and private capital was also responsible for the start of several Japanese enterprises in the same decade in the Amazon region. They included Amazon Kōgyō Kabushiki Gaisha (Amazonia Business Corporation) and Amazon Sangyō Kenkyūjo (Amazonia Industrial Research Center) in the state of Amazonas and Nanbei Takushoku Kabushiki Gaisha (South America Colonization Company Limited) and Nanbei Kigyō Kumiai (South America Cooperative) in the state of Pará.[34] Their primary goals were to build Japanese settler colonies in the region and to extract raw materials from the environment.[35] Like their peers in southeastern Brazil, they exemplified the combination of capital exportation, land acquisition, and farmer migration.

THE RISE OF KOBE AND THE CRESCENDO OF BRAZIL-BOUND MIGRATION

By the end of the 1920s, the Japanese government was able to form alliances with various social groups and involve Japanese subjects from different social strata in Japan's migration-driven expansion in Brazil. The rise of Japan's migration state ushered in the heyday of Japanese collaborative settler colonialism in Brazil. Through various migration programs that were directly or indirectly supported by the government, over 130,000 Japanese subjects reached Brazilian shores between 1925 and 1934. The Japanese settler villages in Brazil also expanded both in number

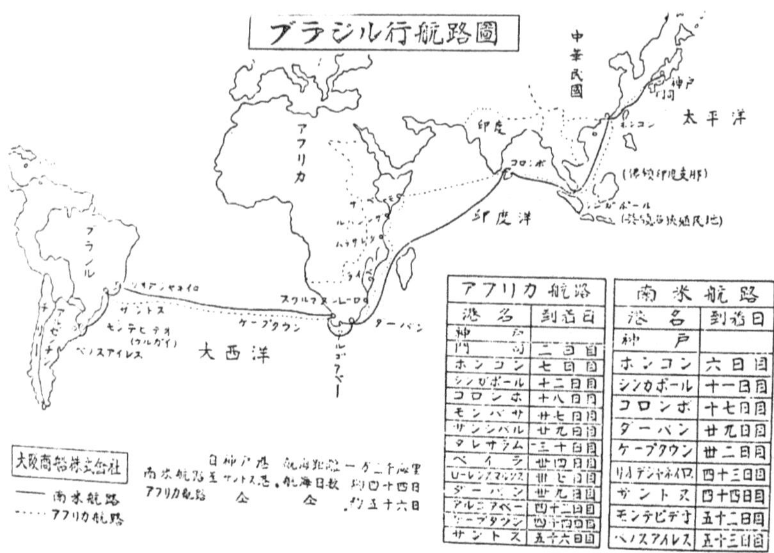

アフリカ航路

港名	到着日
神戸	
門司	二日目
ホンコン	七日目
シンガボール	十二日目
コロンボ	十八日目
モンバサ	廿七日目
ザンジバル	廿九日目
タレサラム	三十日目
ベイラ	卅四日目
ローレンツマルクス	卅七日目
ダーバン	卅九日目
アルゴアベー	四十二日目
ケープタウン	四十四日目
サントス	五十六日目

南米航路

港名	到着日
神戸	
ホンコン	六日目
シンガボール	十一日目
コロンぼ	十七日目
ダーバン	廿九日目
ケープタウン	卅二日目
リオデジャネイロ	四十三日目
サントス	四十四日目
モンテビデオ	五十二日目
ベノスアイレス	五十三日目

MAP 4. Titled *Burajiru yuki kōro zu* (Sea Route Map for Brazil-Bound Emigration), the map shows the schedule and stops of a fifty-six-day steamship trip that started at the Port of Kobe and ended at the Port of Santos. Source: *Kobe ijū kyōyōjo gaiyō* (Kobe: Kobe Ijū Kyōyōjo, 1934), ii.

and in geographic scope. While the state of São Paulo continued to be the home of most Japanese plantation laborers and farming settlers, the Amazon Basin in the north and northern Paraná in the south became new frontiers for Japanese settlers.

The boom of Japanese emigration to Brazil also led to the prosperity of the sea route between Kobe and Santos. During the golden era of Brazil-bound emigration, most Japanese subjects departed the archipelago from the Port of Kobe. Their ships would first travel west to Southeast Asia. After passing the Strait of Malacca, they would sail across the Indian Ocean to the southern tip of Africa. They would then head west across the Atlantic and reach the Port of Santos. The sea route's popularity grew hand in hand with Kobe's quick rise, along with Yokohama, as a central port for Japanese emigration. In 1928, the Japanese government established the National Kobe Emigrant Camp (Kokuritsu Kobe Imin Shūyōjo), a counterpart of the Emigration Center established previously in Yokohama during the heyday of Japanese migration to North America. As an arm of the migration state, the camp offered free eight-day accommodation and meals to Brazil-bound emigrants. These eight days were packed with mandatory orientations and trainings, as well as medical exams and vaccinations.[36] The annual number of emigrants who participated in this government-funded accommodation program increased steadily from 10,377 in 1928 to 23,579 in 1932.

TABLE 3 Daily schedule of emigrants in the National Kobe Emigrant Camp, 1934

	Morning				Afternoon		Night	
	6:30–7:00	7:00–8:30	9:00–11:30	11:30–1:00 p.m.	1:00–3:30	4:30–6:00	7:00–11:00	11:30–3:00 a.m.
1/13			Physical exam and room distribution	Lunch	Physical exam, room distribution, tips on the camp	Dinner		Bath and stool exam
1/14	National gymnastics	Breakfast	Vaccination	Lunch	Vaccination and information on dressing during the migration trip	Dinner		Bath and stool exam
1/15	National gymnastics	Breakfast	Signing documents	Lunch	Signatures on passports	Dinner	Information about Brazil	Bath and stool exam
1/16	National gymnastics	Breakfast	Checking luggage	Lunch	Checking luggage	Dinner	Information about Brazil	Bath and stool exam
1/17	National gymnastics	Breakfast	Information about migrant destinations in Brazil	Lunch	Class on Brazilian Portuguese	Dinner	Information about Brazil's national religion	Bath and stool exam
1/18	National gymnastics	Breakfast	Distributing the government's financial aid	Lunch	Information about transportation costs and workshop for women	Dinner	Recreational gathering	Bath and stool exam
1/19	Worship in a Shinto shrine	Breakfast	Information about personal hygiene	Lunch	Meeting of the heads of households	Dinner	Field trip to a church	Bath and stool exam
1/20	Checking luggage	Breakfast	Name check and distribution of passports	Bentō and departure				

SOURCE: *Kobe ijū kyōyōjo gaiyō* (Kobe: Kobe Ijū Kyōyōjo, 1934), 3.

FIGURE 11. This set of pictures on display at the Harbor Exposition contrasted the past and present of the shore of Ikuta (*Ikuta no ura*) in Port Kobe. It aimed to showcase the rapid development of the port as an industrial and commercial hub of the empire. The picture at the top shows the shore at present, the one at the lower left is the shore in 1780, and the image at the lower right is the shore in 1870. Source: *Kobe hakurankai shuppin mokuroku* (Kobe: Kobe Hakurankai Kyōkai, 1931), 15.

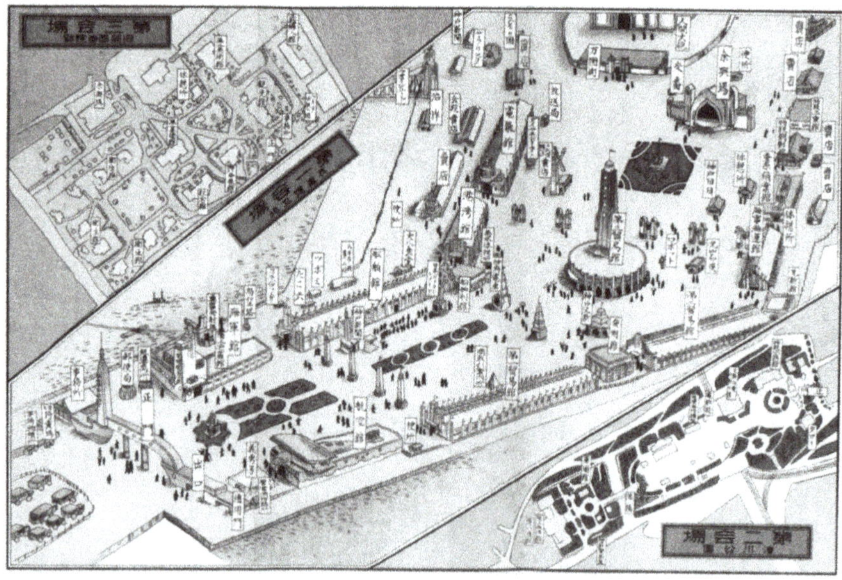

FIGURE 12. The tourist map of the Harbor Exposition. Source: *Kaikō hakuran kaishi: kankan-shiki kinen* (Kobe: Kobe Hakurankai Kyōkai, 1931), 105.

In 1930, one year before the Manchurian Incident that would pull the empire into a new stage of territorial expansion in Northeast Asia, the Kobe municipal government hosted a national event that combined the Harbor Exposition with the Fleet Review (*kankanshiki*). Attended by one and a half million people, the event highlighted Brazil-bound emigration as an integral part of the global expansion of the Japanese empire, which involved the military, trade, and emigration. It also emphasized the increasingly important role of Kobe in this expansion. The Harbor Exposition lasted from September 20 to October 31 and had three exhibition locations. Cosponsored by the Kobe Chamber of Commerce and supported by several ministries of the central government, the exposition aimed to highlight Kobe's historical rise as Japan's top harbor city and a central base of the empire's maritime expansion to the South Seas and South America.

The first location featured the Navy Pavilion, the Ship Pavilion, the Harbor Pavilion, the Aviation Pavilion, the Maritime Trade Pavilion, and three Commerce Pavilions. Through images, goods, music, and films, as well navy and air displays, it showcased the growth of Japan's transoceanic trade, the advancement of the Japanese navy and air force, and the development of the empire's maritime transportation.[37] The first location also featured the Textile Pavilion and the Korean Pavilion, which respectively showcased the empire's world-class achievement in its textile industry and its accomplishment in civilizing people in the colonies.[38] Similarly, the second location offered a display of the empire's war trophies, the Fishery Pavilion, and an aquarium, which aimed to present the empire's advancement in maritime technology.

The third location, on the other hand, focused on displaying the achievements of emigration-driven expansion. Central to this location was the Pavilion of Overseas Expansion (Kaigai Hattenkan). A highlight of the pavilion was the exhibition, *The Dream Land: Migration to Brazil: Ten Years of Hard Work* (*Burajiru Ijū: Jūnen of Funtō*). It drew a sharp contrast between a modern, civilized, but overcrowded Japan and an ancient, primitive, but resourceful and empty South America, legitimizing emigration from the former to the latter as an act of spreading human progress and sharing its benefits. The exhibition had six consecutive scenes, starting with the emigrants' departure from the Port of Kobe and ending with the emigrants harvesting the abundance of the agricultural products as farmers in Brazil. It narrated the experience of the Japanese migrants in South America as a saga of how men conquered nature. In describing a decade of hard work, including laboring on coffee plantations and exploring and taming the forest, the exhibition presented a challenging but rewarding process whereby Japanese migrants eventually became independent farmers with their own land. The exhibition encouraged others to follow in the footsteps of their countrymen to pursue their own success.[39]

In addition, the Pavilion of Overseas Expansion featured booths from a variety of organizations associated with emigration and trade in South America and the South Seas. They included primary agents of the migration state like Kaikō and

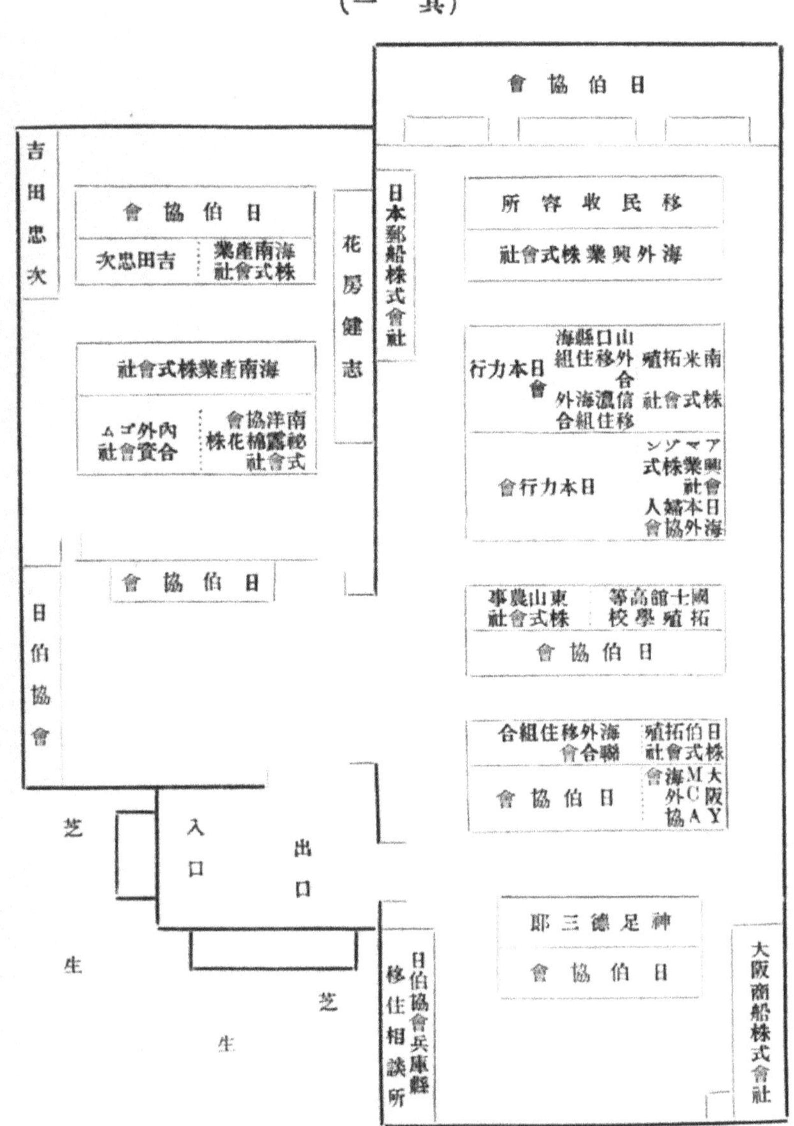

FIGURE 13. Part of the layout of the Kaigai Hattenkan (Overseas Expansion Pavilion). Source: *Kaikō hakuran kaishi: kankanshiki kinen* (Kobe: Kobe Hakurankai Kyōkai, 1931), 217.

the Federation of Overseas Emigration Cooperatives, as well as private businesses like the Japanese Striving Society, the South America Colonization Company, and the Tozan Agriculture Corporation, all of which played a role in Japanese collaborative settler colonialism in Brazil. The Hyōgo-based Japan-Brazil Association (Nippaku Kyōkai / Associação Nipo-Brasileira), which was dedicated to the promotion of Japanese industrial investment and capitalist expansion in Brazil, also had a few booths in the pavilion providing individual consultation. The Fleet Review held on October 25 and 26 marked the climax of the combined event. Attended by Emperor Hirohito and the fleet's commander in chief, Yamamoto Isoroku, the review was by far the largest one that Kobe had hosted, boasting 161 ships of the Imperial Navy. It showcased the empire's naval strength by demonstrating both its size and technological advancement.[40]

As Japanese migration to Brazil grew steadily both in number and in political and economic importance for the empire, it resulted in another profound structural change in the central government in 1929. That year, the government established the Ministry of Colonial Affairs, which took over the responsibilities of subsidizing overseas migration to Brazil and elsewhere from the Bureau of Social Affairs. It continued to provide various grants to migration companies such as Kaikō, Nantaku, and the Federation of Migration Cooperative Societies.[41] At the same time, the ministry managed affairs related to Japan's colonies in Asia by overseeing colonial administrations and colonial companies like the Southern Manchuria Railway Company (Mantetsu) and the Oriental Development Company (Tōtaku). The new ministry strengthened the grip of the migration state by unifying the governmental branches that previously oversaw migration activities in and outside the empire separately. More generally, the Ministry of Colonial Affairs symbolized the institutional convergence in the state structure of the empire between Japanese collaborative settler colonialism in Brazil and Japanese colonial expansion in Asia.[42]

In 1930, the same year the Harbor Exposition and Fleet Review celebrated Kobe's critical role in Brazil-bound emigration and the empire's southward expansion, the Overseas Colonial Migration Conference (Kaigai Shokumin Taikai) took place in Tokyo. On January 19, in Hibiya Park in downtown Tokyo, next to Kasumigaseki, where the Japanese government buildings were located, the Colonial Migration Association (Shokumin Dōshikai) hosted the conference with the cosponsorship of Tokyo Nichinichi News Agency.[43] This half-day conference, attended by over three thousand people, was intended to encourage more Japanese subjects to participate in Japan's migration-driven expansion in Latin America. It began with three keynote speeches given by the representatives of the host and cosponsor and Inoue Masaji, head of Kaikō, who made the call for Japanese youth to make the world their home. The keynotes were followed by a tribute by the minister of colonial affairs, which emphasized the empire's mission of peaceful expansion through emigration and the importance of the collaboration between the government and social forces. Next were tributes by diplomats from Brazil, Argentina, Peru, and Mexico, the main destinations of Japanese migration in Latin America, who extended warm invitations to more Japanese subjects to their land. The conference ended with the screening of two documentaries. One highlighted the accomplishment of the Japanese farming settlers in Brazil, and the other was a history of Western colonial expeditions in Africa, an example that the Japanese, the empire builders of the new era, were supposed to learn from.[44]

BETWEEN BRAZIL AND ASIA

Japanese migration to Brazil reached a crescendo when the third decade of the twentieth century was about to unfold. Meanwhile, the Manchurian Incident in September 1931 and the establishment of Manchukuo the following year ushered in a new era of Japanese expansion in Asia. Mobilizing Japanese subjects to migrate to Manchuria became a military and political necessity for the empire. Apparatuses of the migration state wasted no time rising to the occasion. Beginning in 1932, the Ministry of Colonial Affairs began to fund investigations in Manchuria and organize migration campaigns. Some individuals who spearheaded Japan's state-sponsored migration to Brazil quickly turned to Manchuria as a new frontier of Japanese expansion. Umetani Mitsusada, first director of the Federation of Overseas Migration Cooperative Societies, moved back to Asia in 1932 to head the migration department of the Kwantung Army. He proceeded to carry out a series of migration campaigns and land acquisitions in Manchuria.[45] Nagata Shigeshi, a cofounder of the Aliança Colony in São Paulo, also participated in the promotion of Manchurian migration as early as 1932. He would later serve on a government committee to draft a plan for mass migration to Manchuria.[46] In the early 1930s, institutions that had backed the establishment of the Aliança Colony (including the Shinano Overseas Association, the Shinano Board of Education, the Japanese Striving Society, and the Nagano prefectural government) committed themselves to the promotion of Manchurian migration with great enthusiasm.[47] It was Nagano that pioneered Japan's prefecture-centered model for Brazil-bound migration; thus perhaps unsurprisingly, of all the prefectures, it was Nagano that exported the largest number of migrants to Manchuria.[48]

However, before Tokyo launched its mass migration project on the eve of the Sino-Japanese War, none of its Manchurian migration campaigns was successful: government subsidies were relatively limited, and the living conditions in Manchuria were unattractive. In contrast, Japan's migration and capital exportation to Brazil continued to grow. In 1933, the annual number of Japanese who arrived in Brazil reached 24,493, the highest in history.[49] After decades of unfruitful campaigns, the anti-Japanese social forces in Brazil pushed through a quota restriction on Japanese immigration in the Constitution of 1934. However, the restriction was not strictly imposed and only had limited effects on Japanese immigration, which began to decline but continued until 1941.

As the following chapters explain, however, the decline in Japanese immigration was accompanied by a new surge in Japanese capitalist exportation in Brazil. In 1935, Tokyo dispatched an economic delegation to Brazil headed by Hirao Hachisaburō, director of the Federation of Overseas Migration Cooperative Societies, to promote bilateral trade. A major achievement of this mission was a dramatic increase in Japanese importation of raw cotton from Brazil.[50] Responding to the Commonwealth nations' boycott of Japanese textiles, the Japanese government eschewed India in favor of São Paulo as a major cotton supplier. Japanese textile companies began to pour investments into Japanese farming villages in Brazil to expand their cotton cultivation.[51] The 1930s also witnessed further expansion of Japanese presence in the Amazon Basin, a trend exemplified by the formation of the Amazonia Industrial Company (Amazonia Sangyō Kabushiki Gaisha) in 1935 based on a land concession in the state of Amazonas. The company was funded by a ten-year loan approved by the Imperial Diet, as well as several Japanese industrial corporations.[52] It managed both Japanese settler community building and agricultural cultivation.

A turning point in Japanese migration to Brazil was Japan's further expansion into China proper, which led to the outbreak of the Second Sino-Japanese War and, eventually, the Pacific War. To facilitate this total war, the imperial government elevated migration to Manchuria as a national policy (*kokusaku*) by launching an ambitious 1936 campaign with unprecedented financial and political commitments. This program called for relocating five million Japanese farmers to settle in Manchuria within the next two decades.[53] At the same time, on the other side of the Pacific, anti-Japanese sentiment continued to intensify. For example, the totalitarian regime Estado Novo, proclaimed by Getúlio Vargas in 1937, banned all Japanese-language schools in the Brazilian countryside.[54] Then, in 1941, by presidential order, Vargas banned the publication of foreign-language print media, including all Japanese newspapers and magazines.[55] The next year, after Brazil entered World War II as an Allied power, Rio confiscated all businesses owned by Japanese companies as enemy properties, including those of Kaikō, the Federation of Overseas Migration Cooperative Societies, Nantaku, and the Amazonia Industrial Company, among others.[56]

Around this time, apparatuses of Japan's migration state in Brazil were quick to shift the focus of their activities to Asia in support of the empire's further expansion in Southeast Asia. Kaikō, for example, obtained Tokyo's permission to start emigration programs to Northern Borneo.[57] With financial assistance from the imperial government, Kaikō and the Federation of Overseas Migration Cooperative Societies relocated some Japanese immigrants in Brazil to Hainan Island in China. These re-migrants from Brazil, with their farming experiences in the subtropical climate in South America, were expected to become trailblazers of the new subtropical frontier of Japan's Greater East Asia Co-Prosperity Sphere in Asia.[58] The Japanese Striving Society, led by Nagata Shigeshi, launched campaigns to relocate Japanese subjects to the Philippines and Java.[59]

. . .

The years from 1921 to 1934 were the heyday of Japanese migration to Brazil. This era was marked by the Japanese empire's embrace of the renewed Anglo-American order after World War I, as well as the historic rise of Kobe as a critical industrial and naval port of the empire. The success of Brazil-bound emigration was both a stimulation for and a result of the increasing involvement of the Japanese government in promoting and managing Brazilian migration. This chapter examines important changes in the structure of the government and the new ways it collaborated with various social groups and involved Japanese subjects of different social classes in Brazilian migration campaigns. Together, these changes led to an enhanced version of the migration state that was able to penetrate into the society to mobilize and control emigration as never before. With social groups it had collaborated with for Brazilian migration, the migration state took responsibility for relocating hundreds of thousands Japanese subjects to Asia to facilitate the empire's expansion during World War II. Japanese migration to Brazil during the interwar period, therefore, should be seen as a critical preparation period that led to Japan's state-driven mass migration to Asia during World War II.

In addition to being the heyday of Japan's Brazil-bound migration, the interwar years were marked by the formation of a collective identity among Japanese settlers in Brazil. The next chapter explains how this identity took shape in the state of São Paulo in local, national, and global contexts. It also discusses how Japanese settler elites in Brazil consciously participated in debates among Japanese empire builders in Tokyo by connecting their experience in Brazil with Japan's colonial expansion in Asia.

PART III

SETTLER IDENTITY IN CRISIS, 1920s–1940s

5

Land, Media, and the Formation
of Settler Colonial Identity

During the interwar period, both Japan and Brazil began to adopt more independent diplomacy in relation to the United States, even though U.S. economic influence grew steadily in both societies during and after World War I. Brazil was the only Latin American power that actively participated in World War I, yet the United States had reservations about supporting Brazil's aspirations to increase its naval strength and claim a seat on the Executive Council of the League of Nations. This led to a deterioration in the countries' political relations. Rio began to pursue a more independent and noncooperative policy vis-à-vis Washington, DC following the former's withdrawal from the League of Nations in 1926.[1] Brazilian elites were replacing their existing Europe-oriented racial identity centered on racial whitening with a new, indigenized racial identity based on interracial mixing.

Brazil's adoption of a new racial identity and change in its diplomatic policy during the interwar years found close parallels in East Asia. The Allies' rejection of Japan's request to include the racial equality clause in the Treaty of Versailles and the promulgation of the Immigration Act of 1924 in the United States became important factors in the rapid popularization of Pan-Asianism and nativism in Japanese society. Intellectuals and politicians alike began to embrace a new racial identity for the Japanese; instead of a white people in Asia, they now celebrated the Japanese as the champion of the yellow race and envisioned that Japan would take on the mission to liberate Asian people from the colonial rule of the West.[2] The empire's creation of Manchukuo as a purported racial paradise for East Asians in 1932 and Tokyo's withdrawal from the League of Nations in 1933 were clear examples of this transformation in both racial thinking and foreign diplomacy.

The changes taking place in Brazil, Japan, and the world at large in the 1920s and early 1930s contributed to the formation of a collective identity in the Japanese community in Brazil. The Japanese Brazilian community, concentrated in the state of São Paulo, experienced unprecedented population growth and geographic expansion as a result of increased immigration from Japan and successful agricultural development in the community. As Brazil's traditional fazenda-centered coffee production was being replaced by small farmer–centered cultivation, the coffee economy's absolute dominance was challenged by the growing production of rice, beans, vegetables, and cotton. The Japanese settler community played a major role in both of these economic changes. With a vibrant transoceanic network of information between Japan and Japanese communities across the Pacific, Japanese Brazilian elites connected southeastern Brazil's racial politics in their daily lives with the evolution of Japanese colonialist expansionism in Asia as well as Japanese exclusion in the United States.[3] In this process, these community leaders gradually established a collective identity that defined the Japanese in Brazil not as immigrants but as colonizers who were uniquely suited to civilize Brazil's primitive land.

In these settler leaders' imagination, of all the civilized peoples in the world the Japanese were the most qualified colonizers: not only were they exemplary farmers, unlike the selfish and racist Anglo-Americans who practiced discrimination and exclusion, but the Japanese were willing to be a partner of and guide for the local people and make contributions to local society. To exemplify this superior settler colonial identity, settler leaders emphasized the need for all Japanese immigrants to settle permanently and the importance of Japanese education of the next generation.

This chapter delves into the world of Japanese settlers in Brazil during the interwar period and examines how Japanese Brazilian elites created and cultivated a colonist identity for ordinary settlers. Central to this colonist identity was the strategic biculturalism that the settler elites adopted. By exploiting the fact that Japanese settlers served as agents of settler colonialism for both Japan and Brazil, community elites described Japanese settlers as both trailblazers of the Japanese empire in South America and vanguards of Brazil's own land exploration. This chapter's analysis focuses on Japanese-language print media in Brazil, the primary platform through which the settlers communicated with one another. The formation of this settler colonial identity was the formation of the Japanese settler society itself. In this process, individual settlers, men and women, first and second generation, rural and urban, began to connect with each other through an imagined collective identity as never before.

THE RISE OF SETTLER MEDIA

The rise of the migration state in Tokyo during the interwar years ushered in the golden age of Japanese migration to Brazil. As the number of Japanese who reached the shores of São Paulo grew steadily, Japanese farming villages continued to grow. By the mid-1930s, five hundred to six hundred self-identified Japanese colonies had emerged in the state.[4] In addition to the growing number of farming settlers who arrived directly from Japan, the proliferation of Japanese farming villages was due to the fact that an average Japanese plantation laborer could become a farming settler with relative speed and ease. In 1912, only 8 percent of Japanese subjects in Brazil were farmers; by 1932, this number grew to 45.5 percent, including 23.8 percent owner-farmers and 21.7 percent tenant farmers.[5]

This laborer-to-farmer transition took place in the context of the overall transition of the coffee economy in Brazil from big fazenda-centered production to small farmer–centered production. As the ratio of Japanese immigrants to total immigrants in Brazil grew substantially during the interwar years, they became a main immigrant group.[6] Like others, they benefited from the loteamento system of land distribution that was part of the Brazilian government's policy to encourage immigrant-driven land colonization and coffee cultivation.[7] As a result, Japanese immigrants played a key role in facilitating the rise of the small farmer–centered coffee economy. *Kyō hakushaku* (*A Mad Count*), one of the earliest novels to emerge from the Japanese Brazilian community, testified to this transition and highlighted the role played by Japanese immigrants. The novel was serialized in 1923 in *Burajiru jihō*, the most widely circulated newspaper in the Japanese Brazilian community before World War II. It featured a confrontation between a Japanese immigrant, Shinsaku, a revolutionary young man representing the new small farmer–centered coffee economy, and a wealthy coffee planter, Count M, a symbol of the old fazendas. Armed with socialist ideas, Shinsaku criticized Count M for exploiting the laborers on his plantation, which was eventually destroyed by flood and labor strikes. Bankrupt, desperate, and deeply ashamed, Count M went insane.[8] The character's mental collapse and the demise of his plantation symbolized the fate of fazenda-centered coffee production in general, doomed to be replaced by the new coffee economy represented by the Japanese immigrants.

A major force behind this economic transition, Japanese settler villages that emerged in the 1920s and early 1930s were mainly located in western and northern São Paulo, the new coffee zones where land was sold via the loteamento system to encourage land colonization by small farmers. Railway lines connected these villages to each other and also linked them to urban centers like São Paulo, Bauru, and the Port of Santos on the eastern coast. Along with coffee, goods, people, and information traveled on the railway; a well-connected Japanese settler society with a collective identity was taking shape. Central to the formation of this collective identity were vernacular newspapers and magazines in São Paulo that emerged in the 1910s and 1920s, which were transported and sold among Japanese villages along the railway lines. Japanese settlers subscribed to these newspapers at a substantial rate. According to a survey at the end of the 1930s, nearly 90 percent of Japanese households along the Noroeste and Paulista lines subscribed to vernacular newspapers.[9] Since all major Japanese newspapers and magazines in Brazil were based in São Paulo, an analysis of Japanese media in this state would reveal the nature of Japanese media in Brazil at large.

FIGURE 14. A Japanese settler village near a railway station in rural São Paulo. Source: Japanese Striving Society Archive. The trains carried food, crops, goods, newspapers, magazines, and letters between the cities and Japanese settler villages multiple times each week.

A close look at their origins reveals three key aspects of Japanese-language media in Brazil: their connection with land acquisition, the impact of Japanese migration to the United States, and influences from Tokyo. First, Japanese settler media in Brazil, from the very beginning, were tied with Japanese settlers' land acquisition efforts. The original impetus for the media was to facilitate the sale and purchase of land. The first newspaper created by Japanese settlers in Brazil was *Shūkan Nanbei* (*O Nambei Semanario*). It was established in 1916 by Hoshina Ken'ichirō, a Japanese landowner based along the Sorocabana line, for the purpose of selling his land to other Japanese settlers.[10] *Shūkan Nanbei* was soon followed by *Nippaku shinbun* (*Nippal-Shimbun*), founded by Kaneko Hōsaburō also in 1916; *Burajiru jihō* (*Notícias do Brazil*), founded by Kuroishi Seisaku in 1917; and *Seishū shinpō* (*Semanário de São Paulo*), founded by Kōyama Rokurō in 1921.[11] The latter three became the most influential newspapers among Japanese settlers in Brazil before the outbreak of World War II. All these newspapers functioned as key platforms for land sale among Japanese settlers, with substantial portions of their pages dedicated to property advertisements.

Second, Japanese media in Brazil carried the deep imprint of the Japanese American migration experience in previous decades, and a number of their founders were once immigrants in the United States who migrated to Brazil. Hoshina

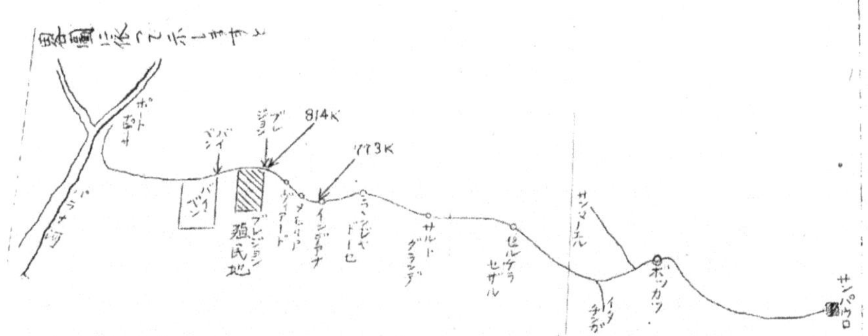

FIGURE 15. The map featured in *Shūkan Nanbei* highlighted two parcels of land for sale owned by Hoshina, demonstrating that the settler media served as a platform for land transactions among the settlers. One parcel was part of the Japanese Burejon Colony, and the other was located near the Indeana railway station. Source: *Shūkan Nanbei* 1, no. 29 (1918): 28.

Ken'ichirō, founder and editor of the *Shūkan Nanbei*, had first migrated to Hawai'i and then moved to Texas to build a rice farm before remigrating to São Paulo.[12] Both Kuroishi Seisaku, founder and editor of *Burajiru jihō*, and Wako Shungorō, a central figure behind the creation of both *Nippaku shinbun* and *Burajiru jihō*, worked as journalists for Japanese American newspapers before moving to Brazil.[13] With this background, it was natural for the past of Japanese American migration to serve as a central reference for Japanese Brazilian media in their discussions of the present and future of Japanese community in Brazil.

Third, the Japanese government exerted substantial influence on Japanese settler media in Brazil. Though not uniformly uncritical of Tokyo, all of the three largest newspapers relied on Japanese consulates in the state of São Paulo as a primary information source. These consulates regularly collected up-to-date information about Japanese settlers in the state by dispatching agents to tour along the railway lines. For this reason, all three newspapers were produced and printed in the cities where Japanese consulates were located. Both *Nippaku shinbun* and *Burajiru jihō* were based in the city of São Paulo, and *Seishū shinpō*, though founded in Bauru, later also relocated its headquarters to São Paulo. The city was also a major international destination for print media from Tokyo.[14] Through various types of booksellers in São Paulo, editors, journalists, and columnists had access to a wide range of contemporary newspapers as well as popular magazines imported from Japan, such as *Kingu* and *Shufu no tomo*.[15]

The types and locations of Japanese settler media in Brazil were diverse. Beyond the three major newspapers, there were more localized newspapers such as *Ariansā jihō* and *Hokusei minpō*, which were based and circulated in the Aliança and Birigui Colonies, respectively.[16] Another newspaper, *Nihon shinbun*, primarily targeted Okinawan readers in São Paulo.[17] There were also magazines devoted to specific topics. Two noteworthy magazines were *Nōgyō no Burajiru* and *Shokumin*

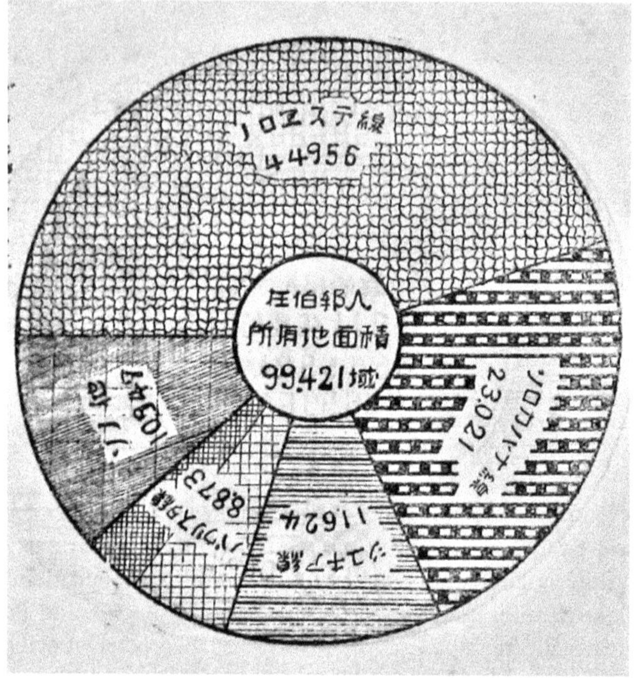

FIGURE 16. A pie chart showing the farmland owned by Japanese settlers along each major railway line in the state São Paulo in 1934. Nearly half was located along the Noroeste line. Source: Kōyama Rokurō, *Zaihaku ishokumin 25 shūnenkan* (São Paulo: Kōyama Rokurō, 1934), preface, 1.

no hikari, both aiming to guide Japanese settlers in Brazil to achieve success in farming.[18]

The three major newspapers often disagreed with one another due to the differences in their financial bases and the intellectual stances of their editors. *Burajiru jihō* was the most friendly to Tokyo, because the newspaper itself was the official mouthpiece of Kaikō, a close partner of the imperial government. *Nippaku shinbun,* on the other hand, had a markedly different stance. It often criticized Kaikō and Tokyo for their inability to protect the interests of Japanese settlers in Brazil. It also emphasized the political independence of the Japanese settler elites.[19] *Seishū shinpō* kept its distance from settler elites and the Japanese government, as its founding editor, Kōyama Rokurō, branded the newspaper as representing the ordinary Japanese settlers living along the Noroeste line. This area was home to more than half of the Japanese population in the state and was also where Japanese settler agriculture had most success. More than half of the Japanese settlers in the region had become owner-farmers by the outbreak of the Pacific War.[20]

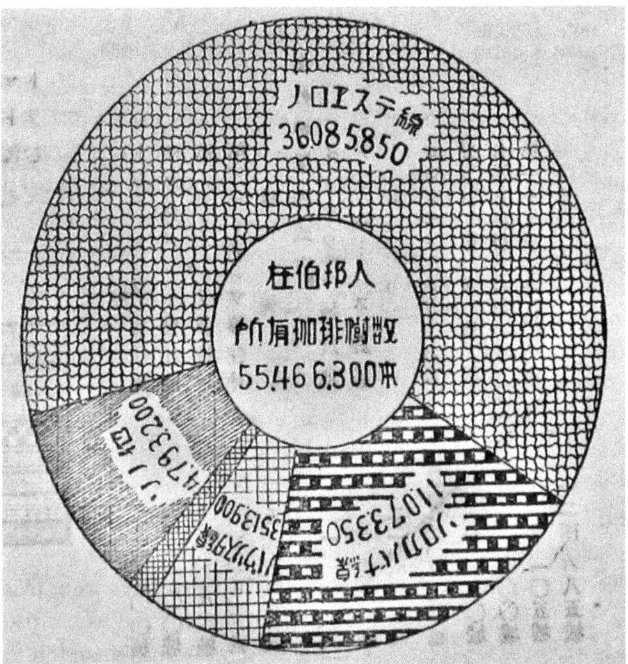

FIGURE 17. A pie chart showing the number of coffee trees owned by Japanese settlers along each major railway line in São Paulo in 1934. More than half were located along the Noroeste line. Coffee trees were the primary crop of the Japanese farming settlers at that time. Source: Kōyama Rokurō, *Zaihaku ishokumin 25 shūnenkan* (São Paulo: Kōyama Rokurō, 1934), preface, 2.

Despite these important differences, the close relationship with landownership, the impact of Japanese migration to the United States, and the influence of Tokyo loomed large as the three central factors that defined Japanese settler media in Brazil. Naturally, these factors also shaped the content that was published. Below I examine common debates in the settler media that were highly relevant to the settlers' daily lives. Not only did these debates share some dominant themes; they also interacted with changes in the sociopolitical reality on the ground. They collectively molded the minds of Japanese settlers in Brazil and ushered in a new, shared settler identity.

THE MAKING OF THE JAPANESE SETTLER MENTALITY

By the early 1930s, how Japanese immigrants would succeed in permanently settling in Brazil had become the overarching theme in the core debates of almost all Japanese settler media in São Paulo. The discussion of transforming immigrants into settlers coalesced into two major debates: how to achieve success in agriculture and how to advance settlers' children's education. Farming was key to the formation of the Japanese settler community. Therefore, it was natural that agriculture occupied a central place in the minds of the editors and writers of the settler media. As a whole, Japanese farmers in Brazil were remarkably successful when compared to their counterparts in the Japanese empire's colonies such as the Korean Peninsula, Taiwan, southern Manchuria, and Micronesia. During the 1910s and 1920s, Japanese farming settlers in São Paulo expanded dramatically both in terms of population and geography. During the interwar era, the Japanese population in Brazil had a much higher proportion of farmers than that in Japan's colonies. For this reason, Brazil became one of the most desirable destinations for Japanese emigration in the minds of Japanese empire builders.[21]

While the loteamento system of land distribution in São Paulo made it relatively easy for Japanese coffee laborers to transition into independent farmers, an immediate reason for the geographic expansion of Japanese settlers in the state was their adoption of the local method of coffee cultivation. Because of the sheer size of the coffee economy, it was natural for the majority of newly independent Japanese settlers to start out with coffee as their primary crop, and they embraced the traditional methods of coffee cultivation out of convenience. A farming cycle would begin with slash-and-burn, after which coffee trees were planted on the ashes. Because of insufficient fertilization and care, the soil would usually lose its productivity within a few years; then the farmers would abandon the land and move on to start the cycle anew.[22]

With their rapidly growing population, Japanese farming settlers in São Paulo launched the Westward Campaign (*Seishin*) in the late 1910s. In keeping with the slash-and-burn method, they collectively moved from the traditional coffee zone in the east to the west and north of the state, turning once-forested lands into new coffee zones. The development of the rail system enabled the settlers to conveniently resettle and push the coffee zones' boundaries outward. The popular Japanese-language newspapers also played critical roles in facilitating this move by promoting land sale among the settlers.

While celebrating the geographic expansion of their community, the settler media criticized their current farming practices. A turning point came in 1924, when a series of natural disasters such as frost and drought decimated the coffee trees owned by Japanese farmers along the Noroeste and Sorocabana lines, leading to a poor harvest. With the support of *Seishū shinpō* and the Japanese ambassador to Brazil, Tatsuke Shichita, the settlers collectively appealed to the Japanese government and received a low-interest loan of 850,000 yen for disaster relief.[23] Though the majority of the affected Japanese settlers managed to survive, critiques of traditional farming practices quickly emerged in the settler newspapers. The critics insisted that cultivating coffee as the only crop would leave Japanese farmers vulnerable in the long run. They also asserted that constantly moving and exploring new land would hinder the formation of long-term community.

FIGURE 18. Japanese settlers turning a forest into farmland using the slash-and-burn method. Source: Japanese Striving Society Archive.

A 1927 editorial in *Burajiru jihō*, for example, complained that Japanese settlers in Brazil had forgotten their pride and wisdom as farmers, even though Japan had over two thousand years of farming tradition. In Brazil, the article argued, Japanese immigrants adopted the inferior practice of local farmers, cultivating coffee as their only crop and giving little care to the soil. This made them vulnerable to weather and market changes. The writer urged Japanese settlers to return to traditional Japanese farming practices by diversifying their crops and cultivating cotton, potatoes, and grains in addition to coffee.[24] Another editorial, published two years later in the same newspaper, urged its readers to stop abandoning the land that they had explored with their "sweat and blood." It argued that the key to success was to maintain and protect the land they already had; it promised that with diligent cultivation and care, the farmers would always have good harvests.[25] There were also articles calling for more cooperative societies among the settlers to serve as platforms for mutual help. Others provided detailed advice on farming techniques and market analysis.[26]

Another major topic of discussion in mainstream settler newspapers was how to advance the new generation's education. Taking place in the context of anti-Japanese campaigns in North America, Japanese campaigns of migration to Brazil, from their very inception, had been family-oriented. Japan's policy makers and

FIGURE 19. Children of Japanese settlers in Brazil. Source: Japanese Striving Society Archive.

migration promoters alike were convinced that the Japanese migrants' so-called sojourner mentality (*dekasegi konsei*) was the main reason for the anti-Japanese sentiment in the United States, and they were determined to avoid the same outcome in Brazil.[27] Seeing the sojourner mentality as a result of the absence of a familial structure, they considered family migration crucial for Japanese settlement in Brazil to succeed. Both Tokyo's subsidies and the recruiting programs of migration companies were designed to encourage Japanese subjects to migrate together with their family members. Though some fabricated family relations in order to receive governmental subsidies, many indeed migrated with their spouses, children, and siblings.

As children constituted a substantial portion of the Japanese population in Brazil since the beginning of the migration, the need to educate the second generation (Nisei) emerged naturally. The first-generation Japanese immigrants (Issei) in Brazil started arranging age-appropriate education for their children almost as soon as they arrived. Formal schools in the settler community emerged in the mid-1910s.[28] Due to the lack of public education facilities in Brazil's countryside, these schools usually provided Brazilian civic education and Japanese language and culture courses.[29] In order to gain accreditation, the majority of these Japanese schools went through an authorization process and had to hire Brazilian teachers. Once authorized, they would offer civic education in Portuguese following the government's education mandate in the morning and then teach Japanese language and culture in the afternoon.[30] To meet the Japanese farming settlers' quickly growing demand for Nisei education, they were generally community funded and independent from one another. With the influx of Japanese migrants in the 1920s, more Japanese-language schools emerged together with new settler villages in São Paulo.[31] As a result of the efforts of community leaders and the Japanese government, the education programs in these schools became standardized in terms of their goals, curricula, and textbooks by the end of the decade.

Settler newspapers played a critical role in this process of standardization, as they served as the primary platforms for the discussion of the goals and strategies of Nisei education. While authors and editors held divergent opinions, most of their agendas could be categorized as belonging to one of two loosely defined camps: "Brazil First, Japan Second" (*haku-shu nichi-jū*) versus "Japan First, Brazil Second" (*ni-sshu haku-jū*). As their labels suggested, the former considered teaching the Nisei to be law-abiding Brazilian citizens the top educational priority, while the latter saw providing education in Japanese language and culture as the most important task for the Japanese schools.[32] Despite differences in their priorities, these two schools of thought shared a two-pronged approach, seeking a balance between Brazilian civic education, on the one hand, and education for Japanese subjects, on the other. For this reason, they were often not readily distinguishable from one another. A 1927 article in *Burajiru jihō* revealed this heterogeneous stance. It criticized the idea that the Nisei should be exclusively educated as Brazilian citizens. While the full assimilation of Japanese into Brazilian society could certainly be the ultimate goal, it argued, it meant that the Japanese would have to give up their native language, custom, and tradition—something that could not be achieved in a short time. For the present, the best strategy for the Nisei's education was to combine the good elements of both Japanese and Brazilian cultures.[33] The same newspaper also published an editorial that year with more concrete suggestions on how this strategy could be carried out. It called on the Nisei schools to meticulously follow the Brazilian government's education mandate and cultivate exemplary Brazilian citizens. At the same time, however, they should offer effective courses on Japanese language and cultures. To this end, the writer welcomed Tokyo's financial aid for Nisei education and suggested that the money should be used for designing standardized textbooks and raising the living standards for teachers in Nisei schools.[34]

The evolution of Nisei schools indeed followed this path. The formation of the Japanese School Parents' Association in São Paulo (Zai San Pauro Nihonjin Gakkō Fukeikai) in 1929 marked a milestone in the institutional and ideological standardization of Japanese-language schools in the state. Created under the auspices of the Japanese consul general in São Paulo, Nakashima Sei'ichirō, the association functioned as the central node of all Japanese schools in the state, standardizing their curricula and programs. Its main office was located in the consulate general building in the city of São Paulo, with branches throughout the state. The association was led by a council composed of members elected by each branch.[35] The influence of *Burajiru jihō* on the Parents' Association was evident, as Kuroishi Seisaku was named its founding vice president; the post of president was left vacant.[36]

In sum, settler media tied the Japanese population in São Paulo together and played a key role in molding the settler mentality among readers. In particular, through discussions on key issues like farming and children's education, the media strived to turn individual Japanese immigrants into self-conscious settlers. Armed with this mentality, Japanese immigrants would not only put down permanent roots in the South American soil as farmers, but also consciously associate their lives with the general course of Japanese expansion.

RACE, GENDER, AND THE ILLUSION OF THE COLONIAL IDENTITY

Though the formation of the Japanese settler mentality in Brazil was an ongoing project, it took a leap forward in the early 1930s and gave birth to the Japanese settlers' collective identity. This identity emphasized the imagined racial character of the Japanese, which made them uniquely qualified to colonize the primitive land of Brazil. The Japanese settler elites believed that unlike the white colonizers, the Japanese acted in accordance with the principle of "coexistence and co-prosperity" (*kyōzon kyōei*) while carrying out their colonial mission. By following this principle, they argued, the Japanese were not only racially superior, but more benevolent than the Anglo-Americans, as they were willing to guide the inferior locals and share the fruits of progress. It was with this collective belief that the settler elites united individual Japanese in São Paulo as members of an imagined community.

Such a collective identity came into being in the early 1930s as a result of historical changes taking place in both East Asia and Brazil. The Manchurian Incident in 1931, initiated by the Kwantung Army, led to the immediate escalation of Japanese expansion in Northeast Asia and turned Manchuria into a de facto colony. Japan occupied Manchuria by the end of 1931 and established the puppet state of Manchukuo the next year. The Kwantung Army and the imperial government wasted no time launching campaigns to relocate Japanese farmers to this new frontier of the empire. Japanese settler media in São Paulo correctly sensed that geopolitical changes in East Asia and Tokyo's new migration priorities would lead to a decrease in Tokyo's support for Brazil-bound emigration and a drop in the number of Japanese immigrants coming to Brazil. In response, they reassured their readers that Brazil continued to be the most suitable destination for Japanese migration even after the Manchurian Incident. A 1932 editorial in *Nippaku shinbun*, for example, contended that Manchuria, though huge, was a good place for capital investment, not for migration. This was because Japanese farmers could not compete against local Chinese farmers, who had a much lower standard of living.[37]

While geopolitical changes in Northeast Asia caused the Japanese settler elites in Brazil to worry about the decline in the migration flow from Japan, the intensification of Brazil's ethnic nationalism caused a crisis within the Japanese settler society itself. The global economic depression worsened preexisting conflicts between the planter elites and politicians in Brazil. The Revolution of 1930 ended Brazil's old republic and brought Getúlio Vargas to the center of political power. The rise of Brazilian ethnic nationalism during Vargas's presidency quickly led to renewed efforts to restrict Japanese immigration by a group of Brazilian politicians and social elites.

The first major wave of anti-Japanese political campaigns in Brazil can be dated to the early 1920s. The decline of European political and economic influence during and immediately after World War I coincided with a rising tide of nationalism as the nation celebrated the hundred-year anniversary of its independence from Portugal. Precisely at this moment, the cultural glorification of racial whitening, an ideology that had long dominated the nation's racial thinking, was giving way to a new, indigenized version of ethnic nationalism centered on racial mixing, a common practice that had a long tradition in Brazilian society.[38] The discourse of racial mixing, however, proved to be unfavorable to the situation of the Japanese settlers.

The first congressional campaign against Japanese immigrants was spearheaded by Fidelis Reis, a federal legislator from Minas Gerais. In 1923, he submitted what was later known as the Reis Bill to Congress that included clauses to restrict the immigration of "undesirable races," including the Japanese, by imposing quotas.[39] Reis and his supporters justified these proposals by defining the Japanese as unassimilable.[40] In addition, they cited the expansion of the Japanese empire in Asia as evidence that Japanese immigration to Brazil was a means of the empire to realize its territorial ambitions in South America.[41] The Reis Bill failed to pass because Brazilian demand for Japanese laborers and farming settlers reached an unprecedented level following World War I due to a substantial decline in European immigrants. However, anti-Japanese sentiments in Brazil continued to fester and swell at both the state and federal levels and were further inflamed after the Revolution of 1930.

In response to these deteriorating conditions, the Japanese-language settler media carefully reported the arguments of anti-Japanese politicians and elites. They also suggested various ways for their readers to pacify the anti-Japanese sentiments, such as avoiding forming Japanese-only colonies and moving from São Paulo to other states where the Japanese would be more welcome due to their small populations.[42] More importantly, as the history of Japanese immigration to Brazil was approaching its twenty-fifth year, the settler media took the initiative to legitimize Japanese immigration by defining the racial character of Japanese settlers in Brazil. At the center of this racial identity was the principle of coexistence and co-prosperity, which held up Japanese settlers in Brazil as the most competent

FIGURE 20. A cartoon in the journal *Burajiru: ishokumin to bōeki* that argued that Japanese settlers' sojourner mentality was the main cause of anti-Japanese sentiment. As the caption read: "Right after saving a small amount of money, he hurries to return to Japan with pride. This is the very cause of anti-Japanese sentiment." Source: *Burajiru: ishokumin to bōeki*, no. 6 (July 1927): 41.

colonizers because they were endowed with two key characteristics: racial superiority and benevolence. On the one hand, they were born with talent and diligence, which made them the most competent farmers to explore Brazil's primitive land; on the other, unlike the selfish Anglo-Americans who only knew how to exploit or exclude others, the Japanese were willing to cooperate and share the fruits of their work.[43]

This racial identity was articulated through a number of media events across the settler villages to commemorate the twenty-fifth anniversary of Japanese immigration to Brazil. The first was the establishment of the Colonial Literature Short Story Award (Shokumin Bungei Tanpen Shōsetsu Shō) by *Burajiru jihō* in 1932. Between 1932 and 1937, the newspaper held four contests for the award, promoting the production and appreciation of colonial literature among Japanese settlers.[44] The award committee's selection criteria explicitly favored entries that were grounded in the unique colonial experience of the Japanese in Brazil as opposed to that of the Japanese in general.[45] Most of the awardees were exactly the ones the committee were looking for: they focused on the specific experience of Japanese settlers in Brazil and contributed to the development of their collective identity. The racial identity that emphasized coexistence and co-prosperity was particularly well-illustrated by a second-place winner of the inaugural contest.

Titled "The Death of a Frontier Settler" (*Aru kaitakusha no shi*), this story by Tanabe Shigeyuki told the personal tragedy of a Japanese landowner in São Paulo, Kaneko Daisuke. Following the common path of Japanese settlers in

Brazil, Kaneko was born into a poor family in rural Japan and arrived at a São Paulo coffee plantation as a contract laborer. He was unusual, however, in his obsession with a dream of returning to Japan as a rich man. Like many other Japanese, Kaneko worked extremely hard and was able to quickly become a successful farm owner, but as he was consumed by the desire to save money for the eventual return, he had little sympathy for the less fortunate and made no commitment to the well-being of the local society. The story began with Kaneko coldly refusing to give food to a starving Black family who were trying to eke out a living on his farm; it ended with the death of Kaneko, who, on his way to return to Japan with a huge fortune, was killed by a Black man seeking vengeance. The selfish protagonist was presented in contrast to the other Japanese who worked on his farm: in the spirit of coexistence and co-prosperity, they not only welcomed the Black family but also sympathized with their plight. The story, therefore, framed Kaneko's tragedy as a cautionary tale for those who clung to the dream of going back to Japan. To avoid Kaneko's tragic fate, the story implied, settlers had to resolve to put down permanent roots in Brazil. As true Japanese settlers, they should all be willing to take the land of Brazil as their own and share their achievement with the locals.[46]

While these contests promoted a collective identity through literature, the publication of two special yearbooks by *Burajiru jihō* and *Seishū shinpō* consolidated this identity through historiography. *The Yearbook for the 25th Year Anniversary of Japanese in Brazil* (*Zaihaku ishokumin 25 shū nenkan*), by the editor of *Seishū shinpō*, Kōyama Rokurō, provided a comprehensive history of Japanese migration and settlement in Brazil. Kōyama was among the first official group of Japanese migrants who arrived on the *Kasato Maru*, and he completed his yearbook by combining the information he collected in careful research and his personal recollections.[47] The book emphasized the settlers' subjecthood to the Japanese empire by beginning with a history of Japan's diplomatic relations with Brazil and describing the settlers as Japan's representatives in South America. It provided detailed information on each Japanese settler colony in and outside the state of São Paulo, including the settlers' names, native prefectures, occupations, and sometimes the size of each settler family's land plot. The book showcased the splendid achievements of the Japanese settlers in farming and documented their contributions to the progress and prosperity of Brazilian society.

While *The Yearbook for the 25th Year Anniversary*, from a horizontal view, highlighted the Japanese settlers' contributions to Brazilian society, *The Yearbook of Brazil* (*Burajiru nenkan*), put together by the editorial board of *Burajiru jihō*, presented the story of Japanese collaborative settler colonialism through a vertical lens. It integrated Japanese immigration and community building experiences into the ongoing historical process of settler colonialism in Brazil. This yearbook contained two parts. Part 1 was a comprehensive overview of the history of Brazil, from the European "discovery" to the 1930 Revolution. It presented Brazilian

FIGURE 21. Japanese settlers with caboclos. Source: Japanese Striving Society Archive. This photo highlights the racial hierarchy between the Japanese and the caboclos; all of the former are in more relaxed poses and uniformly dressed in white shirts, while the caboclos assume more tense poses and are dressed in colorful attire. The lighter skin of the Japanese is further contrasted with the much darker complexion of the caboclos.

history as a process through which a primitive land was gradually enlightened by modern civilization. It also portrayed Brazil as a land of abundant natural resources by providing detailed information about the country's geography, agriculture, mining, and fishery. Part 2, on the other hand, focused on the twenty-five years of the Japanese settlers' experience that fit seamlessly into the historical and geographic narrative in Part 1. It narrated the history of Japanese migration as a heroic saga in which the Japanese settlers achieved great success tapping into Brazil's natural wealth by overcoming myriad difficulties. The bulk of Part 2 was devoted to detailing the information of each settler village. It presented the achievement and prosperity of the Japanese settlers not only as an indispensable part of Brazil's history of progress but also as evidence of the Japanese settlers' contribution to that progress.[48]

This self-portrait stood in contrast to the reality of Japanese settler elites' discrimination against the nonwhite locals.. Indeed, the demarcation between the Japanese and the nonwhite Brazilians was also central to the settlers' collective identity, a process in which gender played a role as important as that of race. Most of the settler elites believed that the Nisei, without proper education, would head down the path of racial degeneration due to a combination of Brazil's primitive nature and the prevalent local practice of miscegenation.[49] In their mind, proper mothering was the key to reversing this dark course. For example, a front-page article in *Seishū shinpō* in 1927 lamented that it was common for husbands to mistreat their wives; they not only forced the women to take on a full load of farmwork during the day but also burdened them with all household chores. The article urged the men to stop enslaving their wives, not because doing so was morally wrong, but because when the women were overworked to such an extent they could no longer fulfill their childcare duties. Many Japanese settler families ended up hiring caboclos, people of mixed Indigenous and European ancestry whom the Japanese deemed inferior, to look after their children. These caboclos, the article contended, only knew how to raise children as farm animals. Under such circumstances, it asked, how could the settlers still claim they were colonizers (*shokumin*)?[50]

In 1934, *Seishū shinpō*'s editor, Kōyama Rokurō, published an article in *Burajiru: ishokumin to bōeki*, a journal published in Kobe but circulated in both Japan and Japanese settler societies in Brazil, reiterating his concern for the Nisei. He lamented that though the Japanese had made impressive achievements in land exploration in Brazil, they did so at the expense of their children, who were heading down the path of racial degeneration. Hardworking as they were, Japanese settlers neglected their duty in childcare and let the caboclos raise their children instead. Kōyama was worried that the next generation of Japanese settlers would become adulterated and inferior just like the caboclos.[51]

A short story serialized in *Burajiru jihō* in the same year more bluntly revealed Japanese settlers' racism against mixed-race Brazilians. Titled "After Settling Down" (*Nyūshoku kara*), the story was told from the perspective of Shūnsaku, a new arrival from Japan at a Japanese settler farm in São Paulo. Shūnsaku described a group of mixed-blood Brazilian children as savage as monkeys or animals that "lived in the stomach of a poisonous snake." He was particularly shocked after realizing that there were a few children of his fellow Japanese settlers in this group who "had lost their Japaneseness" and spoke Portuguese as their mother tongue. The novel also referred to the caboclos as *dojin*, a derogatory Japanese word for Indigenous people.[52] The Japanese had used the same term for the Ainu in Hokkaido and Native Americans.

This discrimination was the primary reason for Japanese settler society's strict prohibition on interracial marriage. While the settler media at times published fictional stories presenting male Japanese settlers' sexual fantasies involving white Brazilian women, the settler society did not tolerate marriages between Japanese and non-Japanese.[53] Due to a lack of white Brazilian population in the countryside, the majority of such interracial marriages were between Japanese and the caboclos. The settler elites were particularly intolerant when a Japanese woman was involved in a relationship or marriage with a caboclo, seeing it as a step toward the community's racial degeneration. Women who dared to transgress this rule typically faced both stiff opposition from her own family members and complete ostracization from the entire community. The fellow residents of her colony would collectively strip her communal membership and force her to relocate.[54] Similarly, interracial marriages between Japanese and Okinawans in Brazil had no place in the settler community.[55] This gendered racial discrimination not only belied the Japanese Brazilian settlers' proclaimed commitment to interracial cooperation but also testified to the affinity between their collective identity in Brazil and Japanese colonialism in Asia.

. . .

In 1933, the Brazilian thinker Gilberto Freyre published *Casa-Grande e Senzala* after returning from the United States. Reprinted numerous times, with countless copies sold in the decades to come, *Casa-Grande*, also known by the title of its English translation, *The Masters and the Slaves*, symbolized a sea change in the evolution of racial thinking and national identity in Brazil. A direct response to Jim Crow practices that Freyre had encountered in the U.S. South, the book celebrated the tradition of racial mixing as the central strength of Brazilian civilization.[56] This practice, argued Freyre, ensured Brazilian culture's superiority over its Anglo-American counterparts; while Brazil enjoyed a balanced relationship between races, the United States was trapped in a hopeless struggle between two antagonistic halves: Black and white.[57] As the tradition of racial mixing in Brazil began to be received with increasing positivity since the end of World War I, the publication and immediate popularity of *Casa-Grande* marked the decline of the discourse of scientific racism that had dominated in elite Brazilian circles since the late nineteenth century and served as a justification for the decades-long policy of racial whitening adopted by the First Republic. *Casa-Grande* became the intellectual foundation of a new discourse of "racial democracy," one that gained momentum under the rule of Getúlio Vargas. It praised Brazil as a nation of racial harmony where people of different skin colors, unlike those who suffered the tyranny of white racism and racial segregation in the United States, enjoyed political and social equality.[58]

The rise of this new racial identity in Brazil took place at the same time that Japanese settlers in the state of São Paulo formed their own collective identity and a distinctive sense of community. This was made possible by the demographic and geographic expansion of the Japanese community in Brazil, the proliferation of print media in the community, and geopolitical changes in Northeast Asia and the Americas. Adopting a strategy of biculturalism, the Japanese settlers deemed themselves exemplifiers of the Japanese empire's ideology of coexistence and co-prosperity, as well as the most qualified colonizers of Brazilian land because of their supposed skills and benevolence.

A parallel between the Brazilian ideology of racial democracy and the Japanese settlers' discourse of coexistence and co-prosperity exists in that both presented themselves as challengers of white racism in the United States. This similarity was natural, because just as Freyre based his book on his observation of racism in the United States, the foremost architects of Japanese settlers' collective identity in Brazil were Japanese Americans who experienced racism in the United States first-hand before remigrating to Brazil. The attempts of both Japan and Brazil to pursue independent diplomacy in the 1920s and early 1930s served as the international context for this shift.

Another parallel was that both racial democracy and coexistence and co-prosperity were centered on the self-claimed principle of racial equality and fairness, yet in reality, both the Japanese and Brazilian elites practiced these ideas hand in hand with their own racial discrimination and exclusion. Japanese settlers in Brazil themselves were excluded from the class of beneficiaries of the splendid "racial democracy." Branded as members of an unassimilable race, they were victims of the institutionalized racism of Getúlio Vargas's Estado Novo, as demonstrated by its quota restriction of Japanese immigration. On the other hand, while depicting themselves as altruistic civilizers, the Japanese settlers in Brazil discriminated against locals of Indigenous and mixed origins. A modified version of the coexistence and co-prosperity discourse quickly gained popularity in Asia and became a central justification for Japanese expansion during the Asia-Pacific War.

The Indigenous people in Brazil had no place in either of these seemingly inclusive racial ideologies. The government's ban on planting new coffee trees in São Paulo in the early 1930s prompted further expansion of Japanese and other immigrant communities into northern Paraná, which was exempt from the ban. Consequently, the last independent Kaingang community in northern Paraná saw their woodlands seized by newcomers. These newcomers quickly began extensive deforestation for coffee cultivation, unaware that the soil beneath the rainforest was infertile. Therefore, the deforestation led to the destruction of native plant and animal life. Afterward, some Kaingang were given small plots of land, while others faced death.

Similar tragedies unfolded for the Kaingang in other regions. For instance, the Mangueirinha reserve, which housed the precious araucaria pine trees that sustained the Kaingang year-round, was deforested. This action not only deprived the Indigenous people of their food source but also led to a severe ecological crisis. As a result, the Kaingang living in the reserve became dependent on external food sources, as their once-lush habitat turned into overgrown fields.[59]

On the other hand, the Revolution of 1930 and the ascendency of ethnic nationalism under Estado Novo did not immediately bring Japanese migration to Brazil to an end. It continued through the end of the 1930s. However, the Japanese settlers' ambiguous identity as both Brazilian residents and Japanese subjects in the 1920s was no longer viable in the increasingly hostile environment of 1930s Brazil. How did the rising transpacific tensions before World War II affect the daily lives and the collective identity of Japanese settlers in Brazil? This is the topic of the next chapter.

6

"Orphan of the World"

The Myth and Reality of Racial Inclusion

"Japan is an orphan of the world," concluded Ishikawa Tatsuzō in his 1931 book, *Saikin Nanbei ōraiki* (On a Recent Journey to South America), after completing a trip to Brazil. Ishikawa correctly sensed the increasingly isolated international environment the Japanese empire was facing. In his book, he claimed that global leadership was in transition, implying that the Japanese would replace the Anglo-Americans as the dominant race (*chikyū wo shihaisuru jinshu*).[1] To substantiate this point, the book devoted a full chapter to a long message given by Carvalho Barbosa, a bureaucrat of the Brazilian federal government who was in charge of agriculture in São Paulo. The civilization of the northern hemisphere, claimed Barbosa, was doomed to decline and to be replaced by that of the southern hemisphere. The future of the world would hinge on the partnership of two nations: Brazil and Japan. While Brazil would emerge as the leader of the southern hemisphere, the Japanese, a superior race and the best farmers in the world, were essential contributors through immigration. The synergy between Brazil's rich resources and Japan's excellent farmers would usher in the global ascendancy of the southern hemisphere.[2]

As the word *orphan* implied, the Japanese empire indeed found itself increasingly isolated in the Anglo-American order when its expansion into Northeast Asia rapidly intensified. Yet Barbosa's words also pointed to a surprisingly warm relationship between the governments of Japan and Brazil, two increasingly authoritarian regimes in the 1930s. In the wake of the Manchurian Incident, mounting tensions between Japan and the Anglo-American powers pushed Tokyo to explore South America as an alternative supplier of raw materials, leading to unprecedented Japanese interest in the Brazilian market. As the Vargas regime sought to revitalize the national economy following the Great Depression, the sharp growth in Japanese investments and raw material purchases was met with great enthusiasm by Brazil. This intimate trade partnership brought dazzling economic opportunities to Japanese settlers in Brazil.

At the same time, the decade preceding World War II presented serious challenges to the settlers. The Vargas era was marked by the rise of Brazilian ethnic nationalism that celebrated Brazil's long history of racial mixing and its unique racial identity alongside Brazil's cultural and economic independence from Europe and North America. As inclusive as this racial discourse appeared, it did not have a place for the Japanese. Advocates of Japanese immigration such as Barbosa found themselves in the minority in the 1930s. Defining the Japanese as racially unassimilable, anti-Japanese politicians pushed through a quota to restrict immigration from Japan. As a result, the annual number of new Japanese immigrants dropped sharply, from 21,930 in 1934 to 3,306 in 1936, then to 1,414 in 1939.[3] This was only one of a series of setbacks that the settler community suffered as a result of Rio's new policies. Restriction on immigration was soon followed by the forced closure of Japanese schools and a ban on all Japanese-language newspapers by the outbreak of the Pacific War.

Given these contexts, the lives of Japanese settlers in Brazil during the 1930s were marked by three broad changes: the increasing capitalization and economic prosperity of the community, the settlers' search for new identities, and the settlers' new connections with the empire. First, the capitalist turn in the community was twofold. Following the decline in migration, Japanese expansion in Brazil became increasingly capital based. It was marked by the rapid growth of Japanese business interests and investments in agriculture in both the Amazon region and São Paulo. On the other hand, the ratio of owner-farmers in the Japanese Brazilian community grew steadily and nearly doubled through the 1930s. By 1942, when Japan and Brazil terminated their diplomatic relationship, almost 60 percent of Japanese immigrants in Brazil had become landowners.[4] This change took place hand in hand with the shift from coffee to cotton as the primary crop of Japanese farming settlers.

Second, political and economic changes in local and global contexts led the Japanese settlers to search for new identities. The approach of strategic biculturalism that the community elites promoted in the 1920s faltered in the new decade. As ethnic nationalism continued to rise in the Shōwa empire and the Estado Novo, Japanese Brazilian elites grew divided over how to redefine their racial identity in Brazil. This not only resulted in a heated debate on whether the settlers should return to Asia and join the empire's "holy war," but it also led to a bitter confrontation in the settler community that lasted until two decades after World War II.

Third, new developments in the Japanese Brazilian community interacted closely with Japan's ongoing expansion on the other side of the globe, allowing Japanese settlers in Brazil to form new ties with the empire in Asia. Either directly or indirectly, they functioned as the arms of the empire to acquire raw materials from both the Amazon and southeastern Brazil. A small number of settlers also repatriated and participated in the empire's expansion in Southeast Asia and the South Seas. Their relocation and activities were facilitated by Japanese companies in Brazil that were also shifting their operations to the Asia-Pacific region.

This chapter illustrates these three new aspects of Japanese settlers' lives in São Paulo in the 1930s and early 1940s. This was a time marked by a strange mixture of opportunities and failures, rationality and mania, and cosmopolitanism and insularity. The chapter also explores the Japanese Brazilian elites' different approaches to the discourse of identity, analyzing the impacts these approaches had on the Japanese empire as well as their community in Brazil. It begins with a discussion of the rapid development of cotton cultivation among the Japanese settlers in São Paulo and the formation of a new trade partnership between Japan and Brazil in the 1930s. It then examines and compares the two regimes of ethnic nationalism in the Shōwa empire and Estado Novo, illustrating how they worked together in unexpected ways to trigger an identity crisis in the settler community. The chapter ends with a discussion of the different choices made by the settlers in this time of extremes, ranging from returning to Japan to staying in Brazil and assimilating into its society.

FROM COFFEE TO COTTON

Coffee, which dominated the economic lives of Japanese immigrants in São Paulo before the 1930s, was replaced by cotton following the Great Depression. The rapid expansion of cotton cultivation among Japanese settlers in São Paulo secured economic prosperity for the community in the 1930s and during World War II. Further, it created new ties between the settler community and the Japanese empire. These new connections fostered a surprising increase in bilateral trade between Japan and Brazil amid escalating tensions across the Pacific Ocean during the years right before World War II. They also prompted Japanese settlers to renegotiate their identities, though in divergent ways, in terms of how to define their relationship with the two regimes of ethnic nationalism. The arising differences not only led to immediate confrontations but also sowed the seed for chaos in the Japanese settler community both during and after World War II.

Like rice, cotton had been a side crop that the Japanese contract laborers had cultivated to achieve financial independence since the 1910s.[5] Compared to coffee, cotton's advantage was twofold. To start with, it required less capital and expertise upfront and generated returns more quickly. This made cotton an ideal cash crop for plantation laborers who were eager to become independent farmers. Moreover, unlike coffee, cotton was not vulnerable to frost; it was also more suitable to the sandy soil in Alta Paulista and Alta Sorocabana, new areas of settler expansion to the west of São Paulo.[6] Yet up to the 1930s, Japanese immigrants in São Paulo simply adopted the coffee-centered economic mode of local farmers; thus, coffee remained their primary crop.

Two factors spurred the popularity of cotton among the farming settlers in the 1930s. The first was the global Depression and, consequently, the Brazilian government's restriction on coffee production. The trading value of coffee on the international market plummeted during this worldwide crisis. Rising to power amid the Great Depression, Vargas and his followers prioritized mitigating the damage that the Depression had on an economy that disproportionately relied on coffee exportation. To this end, the new regime banned the planting of new coffee trees throughout the country and encouraged economic diversification.[7] This policy, combined with the precipitous drop in coffee prices, pushed coffee farmers to turn to cotton and other cash crops as alternatives.

The impact of these new political and economic changes on the settler community is reflected in Japanese Brazilian literature in the 1930s. *Selling a Coffee Farm* (*Kafēen wo uru*), a short novel by Sugi Takeo that was serialized in *Burajiru jihō* in 1932, told the story of a Japanese farming family in the western part of São Paulo during the chaotic early 1930s. Coming to Brazil with the goal of getting rich, the family acquired a small farm and planted coffee trees. However, instead of achieving financial success, they met one misfortune after another amid the political turmoil and economic depression. On his deathbed, the father attributed the failure of the family farm to its overdependence on coffee. The story ended when the son was forced to sell the coffee farm, seeing the family's years of efforts come to nothing.[8]

The second incentive to switch to cotton came from Japan's government and business leaders. Beginning in the early 1920s, they began to encourage Japanese settlers in Brazil to cultivate cotton by linking the crop with the interest of the empire.[9] The most successful case of Tokyo-guided cotton cultivation was Bastos, the largest among the four settler colonies managed by Burataku, the local agent of Japan's Federation of Overseas Migration Cooperatives. With advanced planning and technical support from Tokyo, Japanese farmers in Bastos responded quickly to the changes of the new era. By 1932, the year that the Japanese empire established Manchukuo in Northeast Asia, cotton had replaced coffee as the primary crop of the colony. Cotton output that year increased nearly sixfold from 1931, and the crop became the colony's biggest source of income.[10]

The success of cotton cultivation in Bastos, in turn, stimulated further attention from Tokyo. Japan began importing raw cotton from Brazil in 1934, shortly after the empire surpassed the United Kingdom to become the world's largest cotton textile exporter as well as the largest raw cotton importer.[11] In response to the growing tensions between the United Kingdom and the Japanese empire after the Manchurian Incident, the Commonwealth countries began boycotting Japanese textiles in 1932. The British Raj, Japan's primary supplier of raw cotton, started to restrict exportation to the empire in 1935.[12] In addition, Japan's relationship with the United States, its top export destination, continued to deteriorate following the Manchurian Incident. These events pushed Japanese policy makers and business elites to explore alternative sources of raw cotton and trading partners in general.[13] The success of cotton cultivation in Bastos came as fortuitous news to those who had always sought ways to make use of the Japanese settlers in Brazil for the empire.

Also in 1935, Tokyo took another step to enhance its economic partnership with Rio by dispatching a special delegation to Brazil led by Hirao Hachisaburō, a business tycoon who also presided over the Federation of Overseas Migration Cooperative Societies. The delegation was received by the Brazilian government with enthusiasm. The amount of Brazilian raw cotton exports to Japan skyrocketed from 2.5 tons (representing 1.8 percent of all Brazilian cotton exports) in 1935 to 43 tons (21.6 percent overall) in 1936.[14] By then, cotton produced by Japanese settlers in São Paulo already made up more than half of the total output in the state. Due to a decrease in cotton exportation from North America at the time, the price of cotton shot up in the international market, leading to a substantial increase in the income of Japanese cotton growers in São Paulo.

In 1936, a year after the delegation's visit, Hirao orchestrated the privatization of the Federation of the Overseas Migration Cooperative Societies' properties in Brazil. He became the founding president of the Nichinan Industrial Company (Nichinan Sangyō Kabushiki Gaisha), a privately funded enterprise that inherited the properties of the federation, including Burataku, which were previously owned by the Japanese government. The Nichinan Industrial Company not only attracted more private investment from Japan to the settler community but also stimulated bilateral trade as a whole.[15] It established the Nanbei Ginkō (South American Bank) in the city of São Paulo to provide financial services to Japanese settlers. It also exported coffee, diamonds, crystal, and other raw materials to Japan through the end of the 1930s.[16]

More Japanese investment and governmental aid poured into the settler community specifically to encourage cotton cultivation. In 1936, the Japanese consul in São Paulo held a two-day workshop to provide the settlers with tips on how to achieve economic success through cotton. Two years later, the consul held another workshop that facilitated the formation of the Cotton Association (Menka Rengōkai), which promoted mutual help among Japanese settlers in the state.[17] Around the same time, the Japanese Brazilian Cotton Company (Nippaku Menka Kabushiki Gaisha) based in Osaka established a factory in São Paulo to process raw cotton before shipping it to Japan.[18] As more assistance from Japan poured into Japanese settler colonies in São Paulo to expand cotton production, the number of Japanese cotton-growing households in the state soared from 14,000 in 1935 to 40,000 in 1942, when Japanese settlers produced as much as 70 percent of the raw cotton output in São Paulo and 30 percent of that in Brazil overall.[19]

The popularization of cotton also served as the final push in the transition of the Japanese settler population's social status from plantation laborers to owner-farmers. Promoting cotton cultivation was a central agenda of the "Gozar a Terra" (Give and Take, also known as GAT) campaign, which included a series of workshops and discussion meetings for the settlers. This social campaign was launched by Burataku in 1934 and grew into a social movement across Japanese villages in São Paulo. Directly responding to the drop in coffee prices caused by the global Depression, the campaign aimed at diversifying the Japanese settler economy and turning away from the slash-and-burn mode of farming that kept them constantly on the move. GAT promoters organized workshops to disseminate tips for cotton cultivation and formed the Cotton Growth Cooperative (Menka Zōshū Kumiai) to encourage cotton production. The ultimate goal of the campaign was to ensure the settlers' commitment to permanent settlement.[20] It disseminated knowledge about how to fertilize the soil for long-term farming, how to choose crops according to soil conditions, and how to develop supplementary farming ventures such as raising pigs, chicken, and silkworms. It also encouraged the settlers to band together for better economic gain and good health.[21] The campaign fell short of its mission of crop diversification: motivated by profit, the settlers quickly embraced cotton as the primary substitute for coffee.[22] However, it did prove effective in terms of fostering permanent settlement by speeding up the transition of Japanese farm laborers to owner-farmers. In the decade between 1932 and 1942, the ratio of owner-farmers among the Japanese farming population more than doubled. By 1942, 59.7 percent of the Japanese farmers in São Paulo had become landowners.[23]

BETWEEN THE TWO REGIMES
OF ETHNIC NATIONALISM

For Koseki Tokuya, architect of the GAT movement, permanent settlement was also a remedy for a pressing crisis the settlers were facing at the time. Koseki had studied agriculture at Hokkaido Imperial University before migrating to São Paulo to become an agricultural engineer and community leader. He observed that most of the Japanese settlers harbored resentment because they wanted to return to Japan but could not afford it. Only the "religion" of permanent settlement (*eijūkyō*), as he called it, could soothe their distress and stabilize the community.[24] The "resentment" described by Koseki was part of a larger identity crisis that plagued the Japanese villages in São Paulo despite their economic prosperity. As ethnic nationalism intensified in both imperial Japan and Brazil, the Japanese settlers in São Paulo found their biculturalism no longer tenable as an identity strategy.

Though emerging in drastically different local contexts, the discourses of ethnic nationalism in Brazil and Japan during this decade bore unexpected similarities. The tradition of racial mixing in Brazil began to be received with increasing positivity after World War I; the publication and immediate popularity of Gilberto

Freyre's *Casa-Grande* marked the decline of the discourse of scientific racism. The latter, which had dominated in Brazil's elite circles since the late nineteenth century, had served to justify the First Republic's decades-long policy of racial whitening, or branqueamento. In its stead, *Casa-Grande* heralded the new discourse of "racial democracy," which gained popularity under the rule of Getúlio Vargas. It celebrated Brazil as a land of racial harmony, where individuals of varying skin tones had equal access to political and social rights, in contrast to the oppression of white supremacy in the United States.[25]

This racial discourse mirrored the theory of racial hybridity that gained popularity in the 1930s in the Japanese empire. Represented by the ideas of Kita Sadakichi and Takamure Itsue, this theory rejected the assumption that the Japanese had a monoracial origin. Instead, it claimed that the Yamato race was a product of long-term interracial marriages among different ethnic groups residing both inside and outside the territory of the Japanese empire.[26] Similar to Freyre's criticism of racial segregation in the United States, advocates of Japanese racial hybridity emphasized the superiority of the Japanese approach over Western practices. Takamure Itsue, for example, argued that history had shown that while the Japanese exemplified how different peoples became one through peaceful means, Westerners could only do so by violent conquest.[27]

In addition to contrasting themselves to racist Euro-Americans, the Japanese and Brazilian discourses of racial mixing were similar in that both were used to advance forced racial assimilation in their settler colonial contexts. Kita's claim about the Japanese's hybrid racial origin conveniently legitimized the ongoing project to assimilate the empire's colonial subjects in Taiwan and the Korean Peninsula. The theory dressed up the violence and coercion associated with this process with the trope of family reunification.[28] It also came with what Takashi Fujitani calls a "polite" form of racism that gained popularity in the Japanese empire around this time. Propelled by the need to procure some degree of consent among the colonial subjects and mobilize them for war, policy makers and cultural elites of the empire were obligated to shun the "vulgar" expressions of racism and openly disavow racial discrimination, even as racism remained omnipresent in the everyday life of the empire.[29]

Similarly, the proclaimed "democratic" tradition of race proved to be useful to the Vargas regime as it sought justifications to enforce the national singularization of language and culture. It also denied the existence of racism in its policies of coerced assimilation and immigration restriction. By this logic, those who became the targets of exclusion could only blame their own failure to assimilate. It was, therefore, not surprising that the Brazilian government promulgated a race-based quota on Japanese immigration just one year after Freyre's book extolled Brazil's tradition of racial mixing. It was also natural that the leaders of anti-Japanese campaigns in Brazil in the 1930s uniformly denied their racist inclinations. Miguel de Oliveira Couto, a university professor and the architect of the proposal to restrict immigration by imposing a quota, made it clear that the Japanese were not inferior.

Instead, he argued that the Japanese should be a target of restriction because they had failed to assimilate into Brazilian society.[30]

The shared nature of exclusivity of these two regimes was also revealed in their redoubled efforts to control the Japanese immigrants in Brazil. Ethnic nationalism in Japan and Brazil simultaneously pushed the Japanese settler elites to drop their strategic biculturalism in favor of more extreme stances. A primary venue through which both regimes exerted their control was education. The Japanese Culture and Education Association (Nihonjin Bunkyō Fukyūkai) was an organization established in 1929 to unify the curricula and administration of Japanese schools in São Paulo. As it was under strong influences from the Japanese consul, it became increasingly nationalistic after the Manchurian Incident.[31] Its leaders acted collectively to boycott a new set of textbooks specifically designed for the settlers' children on the grounds that they lacked patriotism toward Japan. The Japanese government tightened its ideological control over the settlers in 1937, the year when the empire entered a total war with China. Ishi Shigemi, a special officer appointed by Japan's Foreign Ministry to reform the association's leadership, had become its de facto head.[32]

Education was also a core area in which the Vargas regime was projecting power into the settler community. In 1931, Rio promulgated a new law that required all teachers in foreign-language schools in the country to pass an annual standard Portuguese-language test. Ironically, this nationalist decree in Brazil further exposed the Japanese schools in São Paulo to Tokyo's ideological manipulation. In the name of helping Japanese school teachers pass the required Portuguese test, the Japanese Culture and Education Association would organize a special workshop for Japanese school teachers in the state right before the language test each year. Lasting for a period of between two weeks and a month, the workshop not only covered Portuguese-language training but also courses such as Japanese history and language pedagogy. It became a venue for Tokyo to disseminate imperial propaganda to the settlers.[33] This annual workshop continued even after 1938, when the Brazilian government banned foreign-language education for children below the age of fourteen in the countryside. This policy forced all Japanese schools in the state outside the city of São Paulo to shut down.[34]

THE QUESTION OF ASSIMILATION
AND THE IDENTITY CRISIS

Caught between these two fervent ideologies of ethnic nationalism, the biculturalism approach that Japanese settler elites had favored in earlier years quickly crumbled. By the time the Sino-Japanese War broke out in 1937, the community leaders had already become profoundly divided in their responses to the new question of the era: Should they settle permanently or return to Japan (*eijū ka, kikoku ka*)? There were three main approaches, and the question of assimilation, the key to the logics of ethnic nationalism of both imperial Japan and the Estado Novo at the time, was central to each approach. The idea of assimilation was certainly not new to the Japanese settlers, but their internal debate had never been as polarized.

The first approach was to promote permanent settlement in tandem with full assimilation. Its main advocates were those who kept a certain distance from the Japanese empire. An example was Andō Zenpati, who had worked for *Burajiru jihō* as a journalist and then for *Nippaku shinbun* as its editor in chief. Andō had also served as director of the Emeboi Agricultural Practice Farm. He reminded the settlers that the primary reason for their journey to Brazil was to pursue personal success. Despite the empire's lofty designs for them, he pointed out, most of the settlers had simply come here to make money. Accordingly, he urged them to stick to this goal by resolving to settle permanently and transcend the confines of Japanese nationalism. He also suggested that the settlers focus on facilitating their offspring's complete assimilation into Brazilian society.[35]

An even more explicit supporter of this approach was Handa Tomoo, a painter and writer who had also worked for *Burajiru jihō*. In an essay published in 1939, he not only equated permanent settlement with full assimilation but also saw racial mixing as the ultimate path to achieve this goal. "While the blood purity of the Yamato race might be considered critical in Asia," Handa opined, the situation was quite different in Brazil because it was impossible for the Japanese settlers to culturally assimilate while maintaining their blood purity. Following the logic of "racial democracy," Handa believed that the future of the Japanese community in Brazil depended on the settlers' complete mixture with Brazilians, both in mind and in blood.[36]

Wako Shūngorō, journalist and cofounder of the Aliança Colony, was another supporter of full assimilation through racial mixing. Unlike Andō and Handa, Wako was a faithful believer in Japanese racial superiority. He went as far as to claim that assimilation would help purify the Brazilian racial stock: once the superior blood of the Japanese flowed in Brazilian veins, it would "purge its impurities" (*sono nigori wo jōkashite*). To Wako, this would turn Brazil into a model nation that purified humankind (*jinrui jōka*), which was in tune with both the Japanese tradition and Brazil's national spirit.[37]

Supporters of the other two approaches, however, firmly embraced Japan's expansionist ideology. They distanced themselves from Brazilian society and refused to assimilate. The main difference between the second and third approaches was that one called for permanent settlement and the other urged settlers to return to Asia. Despite this ideological divergence, both lines of thinking were deeply influenced by Tokyo. The second approach still promoted permanent settlement, but unlike Andō and Handa, its advocates saw this as the ultimate means for the settlers to fulfill their mission of Japan's imperial expansion in South America. Kishimoto Kōichi was a key supporter of this approach. He founded the Gyōsei School (Gyōsei Gakuen) in 1932 in the city of São Paulo and designed it as a private boarding school for Japanese children who came to urban São Paulo for advanced education.[38] Contrary to Handa and Wako, Kishimoto opposed assimilation and believed that the Japanese would never become good Brazilian citizens through assimilation. Being assimilated into one's environment, as he saw it, only served as evidence of one's weak character.[39] For him, staying in South America was the settlers' duty to the empire. Certain of Japan's expansionist destiny, Kishimoto regarded Japanese migration to South America as an essential part of this historical process. Though he recognized the political and social changes that the settlers were facing in Brazil, he urged them to overcome these difficulties and settle permanently to defend the empire's frontier.[40]

This approach suited the policy makers in Tokyo who had consistently urged immigrants to settle in Brazil permanently. To this end, the Japanese consul in São Paulo, Sakane Junzō, not only sponsored the GAT campaign and provided aid to Japanese farmers in the state but also propagated the idea of permanent settlement via the settler newspapers.[41] In response to the rising call for repatriation in the settler community, the consul issued a special announcement to the settlers in 1939, urging them to stay in Brazil. Their loyalty to the empire, he claimed, was measured by the extent of their resolution to stay. Those who returned to Asia without preparation, Sakane warned, would only suffer failure.[42] The following year, the new Japanese ambassador, Ishii Itarō, issued a similarly strong warning to Japanese settlers in Brazil and commanded them to give up the thought of return.[43]

With similar sentiments, *Burajiru jihō*, Kaikō's mouthpiece, published an anthology of biographies of Japanese settlers in the states of São Paulo, Rio de Janero, Minas Gerais, and Mato Grosso in 1941. Sponsored by the Japanese consul in São Paulo, this book came out to celebrate the 2,600th anniversary of Emperor Jimmu's mythical ascension. It featured the stories of those who were able to become landlords and business owners to showcase the Japanese settlers' accomplishments while putting down roots in South America. In his enthusiastic preface to the anthology, the Japanese deputy consul in São Paulo referred to the settlers as "brethren on the front lines" (*dai'issen no dōhō*). On the one hand, he praised them for their contributions to the empire's "holy war" by donating money and providing moral support. On the other hand, he urged the settlers to fulfill their own duty to the empire by maintaining their foothold in Brazil, as this would be their ultimate way to participate in the empire's grand mission to "put the entire world under one roof" (*hakkō ichiu*). More specifically, he listed a series of virtues that the "brethren on the front lines" should maintain based on Tokyo's expectations. In addition to believing that Japan was the paramount empire of the world, they should practice obedience, perseverance, agility, and modesty to ensure success for their permanent settlement in Brazil.[44]

The third approach was for the settlers to return to the Japanese empire. Kōyama Rokurō, founding editor of *Seishū shinpō*, was an early advocate, and one of the most vociferous, of this strategy. A brief look at how his idea evolved illustrates the development of this discourse. Though he once had been a strong supporter of permanent settlement, Kōyama began calling for repatriation as early as 1935. He divided the Japanese settlers in Brazil into two distinct groups: those who could assimilate and those who could not. While the former should fully assimilate and become 100 percent Brazilians, the latter would be better off if they returned to Asia.[45] His stance became more assertive in 1938, after Rio banned all Japanese schools for children under the age of fourteen in the countryside. In a number of articles that he published between the end of 1938 and the beginning of 1939, Kōyama argued that because of the racial discrimination that the Japanese experienced in Brazil and the country's increasingly exclusionist policies, there was no longer room for them in Brazil. It would be better for all the settlers to return to Asia, where they actually belonged, in "a retreat with glory" (*kōei aru taikyaku*).[46] Moreover, like many of his peers, Kōyama was not immune from racism himself: he believed that the settlers' racial mixing with Brazilians would lead to the racial degradation of the Japanese.[47]

As the Japanese empire continued to expand southward and occupied the island of Hainan in spring 1939, Kōyama saw yet one more reason for the settlers to return. The Japanese Brazilian settlers' decades-long experience navigating the subtropical forests in Brazil, he reasoned, prepared them both physically and mentally for the colonization of Southeast Asia and made them the most suitable group of Japanese to facilitate the empire's expansion in this new frontier. Kōyama went as far as to claim that God brought them to Brazil some three decades earlier to prepare them precisely for this purpose.[48]

Kōyama's *Seishū shinpō* explicitly advocated for the settlers' return, a position that put it at odds with *Burajiru jihō* and *Nippaku shinbun*, the other largest settler newspapers, which generally supported permanent settlement. However, this did not mean that the voice for return was an anomaly among the settlers. In fact, it represented the majority opinion at the end of the 1930s. After completing a 1939 survey among the Japanese population in the northwest of São Paulo, where more than half of the settlers resided, Wako Shūngorō lamented that 85 percent of the respondents indicated that they wished to return to Japan, while only 10 percent would like to stay in Brazil, with the remaining 5 percent undecided.[49]

This overwhelming inclination to return, to some extent, was a result of misleading information propagated by the Japanese government. Although Japanese consular personnel had repeatedly emphasized the importance of permanent settlement, the Japanese consul's increased control over the community's education and its indoctrination of Japanese nationalism contributed to the increasing popularity of repatriation. In addition, Tokyo had recruited several notable leaders in the settler community to advance the empire's expansion in Asia. One of these leaders was Umetani Mitsusada, an executive director of the Federation of Overseas Migration Cooperative Societies who purchased the land for the four major settler colonies managed by Burataku in São Paulo and northern Paraná. As early as 1932,

Umetani was already working for the Kwantung Army in Manchuria by directing its migration department.[50] Nagata Shigeshi, president of the Japanese Striving Society who cofounded the Aliança Colony with Wako Shūngorō, helped Tokyo with migration planning and recruitment for its colonial expansion in Asia.[51] Saibara Seitō, who remigrated to Brazil from Texas and had managed farms in São Paulo and Pará, also moved back to Asia. After conducting a Tokyo-sponsored investigative trip in Manchuria, he turned southward to promote Japanese rice and sugar cultivation in Taiwan. Both by deed and by rhetoric, he became a passionate advocate for Japanese expansion in Southeast Asia and the South Pacific.[52]

Koseki Tokuya, a leader of Burataku and the GAT movement, also returned to Asia. There he was employed by Japan's Ministry of Colonial Affairs to investigate the island of Hainan as a destination for Japanese farmer migration. Summarizing his observations in Asia and his sixteen years of experience in Brazil, he penned a book for the purpose of, in his words, "providing reference for the empire's plan for its southward expansion" and the "construction of the Greater East Asia (*Daitōa kensetsu*)."[53] Based on the three decades of Japanese migration and community building in Brazil that he described as a success earned by the settlers' "sweat and blood," Koseki made a wide range of suggestions for the empire's ongoing colonial migration to Southeast Asia. These included theoretical points such as the general relationship between migrants and land, as well as the significance of settler migration for the empire itself. He also offered concrete advice on how and where to build settler villages, how to turn forests into farmland, how to choose crops based on local conditions, and how to provide the settlers with both mental and physical training.[54]

Though the desire to return was shared by the majority of the settler population, those who actually returned remained few in number, as the majority could not afford the cost of remigration. Those who could afford it and managed to return were farmers who benefited from the cotton boom. The home archipelago was the initial destination of almost all the returnees, but many had difficulty finding their place in Japanese society. As a result, each year saw a substantial portion of the returnees remigrating elsewhere. A small number of them returned to Brazil; others moved to the front lines of the wartime empire such as Southeast Asia and southern China.[55]

While the Japanese government discouraged the settlers in Brazil from repatriating, it did allow those who already returned to remigrate to the empire's frontiers in Asia so that they could contribute to the empire's wartime expansion. To this end, Tokyo worked closely with Kaikō by providing financial and political support, allowing the latter to investigate possible locations in Asia to accommodate the returnees and transport them there.[56] The Federation of Overseas Migration Cooperative Societies too joined Kaikō to relocate the returnees with the state's support.

TABLE 4 Annual number of Japanese returnees from Brazil and subsequent remigrants, 1932–1938

	1932	1933	1934	1935	1936	1937	1938
Returnees	236	655	1,267	826	1,093	1,586	1,113
Remigrants	28	95	192	182	167	184	187
Remigrants' ratio	12%	15%	15%	22%	15%	12%	17%

SOURCE: Based on letter from Takemoto Takeo to Nakano Takeshi (July 26, 1939), in Gaimushō Gaikō Shiryōkan, *Honpō imin toriatsukainin kankei zakken: Kaigai Kōgyō Kabushiki Gaisha*, vol. 10, J.1.2.0, J 3–1.

Transporting the returnees from Japan proper to the empire's actual front lines was part of the overall geographic shift that the Japanese enterprises in Brazil had taken. After Brazil's 1934 Constitution put a quota restriction on Japanese immigrants, the Federation of the Overseas Cooperative Societies began to facilitate relocating Japanese subjects to areas in the Asia-Pacific region such as the Philippines and northern Borneo.[57] The Nichinan Industrial Company, which inherited all the federation's property in Brazil, also moved its businesses to Japan and Southeast Asia.[58] Nantaku too shifted its migration and agricultural businesses from the Amazon to the South Seas after the Brazilian government cut off its diplomatic relationship with Japan in 1942.[59]

. . .

In an article published in *Seishū shinpō* right before the Brazilian government's ban of all foreign-language newspapers took effect, the editor, Kōyama Rokurō, observed that for the settlers, the Japanese-language newspapers were the "only fountain of wisdom and source of comfort" (*yuiichi no chie no izumi to ianmono*). Without them, he lamented, most settlers would become blind, deaf, and dumb. Along with the ban on Japanese schools, this new law would block the community's cultural development, leading the settlers down a dark path of degeneration and immorality. Only the breaking dawn in Asia, Kōyama argued, could bring them out from this darkness.[60] Yet as this chapter has shown, the Vargas regime was not the only reason for the predicament that the Japanese settlers in Brazil found themselves in. The imperial government in Tokyo also tightened its control of the community via settler media and schools, contributing to the intensification of nationalism and polarization among the settler elites.

In this community-wide debate on identity and the future, the young Nisei generation was similarly divided. Some aligned with Kishimoto, resisting assimilation, while others heeded Kōyama's call and were keen to migrate to Asia. A different faction, particularly those who had migrated from rural areas to urban centers for higher education, endorsed Andō's vision of complete assimilation. Illustratively, the governing council of the Japanese Student League in São Paulo (Sanpauro Gakusei Renmei) chose to publish its official journal exclusively in Portuguese.

In the journal's first issue in 1939, council members declared their commitment to the ideals of Brazilian ethnic nationalism and pledged to become fully naturalized Brazilian citizens.[61]

This identity debate continued after the outbreak of the Pacific War, when the Vargas regime joined the war as a member of the Allies and designated Japan an enemy country. Brazil cut off the sea routes with Japan, completely stopped the migration flow, and confiscated Japanese businesses. Brazil also banned all Japanese-language media and jailed those it deemed spies. The valley of darkness foretold by Kōyama had indeed come to pass. What Kōyama hailed as the "dawn of Asia," however, proved to be a false hope. The escalated expansion of the Japanese empire in Asia only worsened the Japanese settlers' political situation in Brazil, placing them under increasing scrutiny from Rio. Tokyo appreciated the settlers' remittances and the cotton they produced but did not want them back physically. If Japan was an orphan empire in the Anglo-American order, as Ishikawa Tatsuzō observed at the beginning of the 1930s, then the Japanese settlers in Brazil had become the actual "orphans of the world" by the end of this decade: they were unable to find a place as the two ethnic nationalist regimes were in conflict.

As Kōyama also predicted, the community fell prey to irrationality due to severe censorship and the lack of reliable media sources. Identity-centered divisions continued to grow, eventually resulting in a violent and bitter community-wide split that would last until a decade after World War II. It was from this chaotic legacy that the Japanese Brazilian community began to reinvent itself in the 1950s. Some of the key participants of the previous identity debate played critical roles in this process, one that was intimately connected with Japan's own national reinvention during the Cold War.

PART IV

WORLD WAR II AND ITS AFTERMATH, 1930s–1970s

7

Conquering the Tropics

Collaborative Settler Colonialism in the Amazon

"Controlling the Amazon is controlling the world," declared Uetsuka Tsukasa in 1931, the same year that the Manchurian Incident broke out. As founder and director of the Amazonia Industrial Research Center, a landmark Japanese enterprise in the region, Uetsuka's view reflected that of many Japanese political leaders and business elites of the day. In their imagination, the white colonizers were incapable of colonizing this rich and vast land because they were physically unprepared for its tropical climate, nor were there enough Indigenous people laboring for them. The Japanese, on the other hand, were uniquely qualified to civilize this tropical land thanks to their special racial characteristics. They would turn the Amazon into an endless source of natural resources that would sustain the Japanese empire's worldwide expansion.[1]

A few years later, the Estado Novo, headed by Getúlio Vargas, rolled out its landmark program to speed up its own colonization of the Amazon with an influx of U.S. investment and technical aid. Dubbed "the March to the West," this government-led program built medical facilities in the region and created a host of state agencies at both the central and local levels to advance land distribution, agricultural development, and the transportation system.[2] The regime also established a series of codes to regulate the utilization of water, minerals, and forests.[3] "The Speech of the Amazon River," which Vargas made during his visit to the region in 1940, illustrated the settler colonial logic behind this program. What his regime would achieve, he claimed, was bringing order and progress to this savage land by conquering "valleys of the great equatorial torrents, transforming its blind force and extraordinary fertility into disciplined energy." For Vargas, this was "the greatest task for civilized man" that the Brazilians, people of an expanding power, were destined to accomplish.[4]

This chapter examines the often-overlooked history of Japanese colonization of the Brazilian Amazon by focusing on its connections with Japanese colonial expansion in the Asia-Pacific region. It also situates Japanese presence in the Amazon in the context of Brazil's own settler colonialism as well as U.S. expansion in the region.[5] Similar to the process of Japanese community making in São Paulo, the development of Japanese settler villages in the Amazon exemplified the nature of collaborative settler colonialism and was a joint product of the migration states of Japan and Brazil. The chapter begins with a brief history of Brazilian colonization of the Amazon before Japanese migration, then examines the early phase of Japanese expansion in the Amazon during the 1920s, which went hand in hand with Japanese colonization of German Micronesia following World War I. While the 1930s following the outbreak of the Manchurian Incident have been commonly understood as a decade of escalated Japanese expansion in Northeast Asia, as this chapter shows, the same decade was marked by the further growth of Japanese colonial presence and investment in the Amazon. This development was jointly stimulated by geopolitical changes in Asia and the Brazilian government's renewed push for its own settler colonialism in the Amazon. The chapter concludes by discussing a resurgence of Japanese migration to the Amazon after World War II, emphasizing the transwar continuity of Japanese and Brazilian settler colonialism in the region.

A SHORT-LIVED RUBBER BOOM

Lying between the Andes and the Atlantic Ocean, the Amazon Basin encompasses 2,700 square miles of tropical forest that spans the territories of Venezuela, Colombia, Bolivia, and Brazil. Most of the basin is located in Brazil, primarily inside the state of Amazonas in the upper basin and Pará in the lower. From the sixteenth century on, leaders of colonial and imperial Brazil launched various campaigns to colonize the land by military and religious means. Other than causing a sharp decline in the Indigenous population, none of these campaigns was successful.[6] Due to the region's unique ecological features and climate, it does not support the cultivation of common cash crops like tobacco, coffee, cocoa, or sugar. As a result, it was relatively insulated from the influences of global capitalism until the rubber boom in the mid-nineteenth century.[7]

The Paraguayan War and the rubber boom in the second half of the nineteenth century motivated the Rio government to commit more resources to the Amazon region, leading to its economic and political integration into the country. The devastating war that the Brazilian empire and its allies fought with Paraguay pushed Brazilian leaders to take serious measures to secure the empire's northwest. Through a series of maneuvers, Brazilian diplomats led by José Maria da Silva Paranhos made the Brazilian empire the ultimate winner of what Susanna Hecht called the "scramble for the Amazon" in the late nineteenth century.[8] The imperial and later republican governments alike sponsored Rondon to survey the Amazon and construct telegraph lines that would connect the Amazon inland with the southeastern metropole.[9]

The rubber boom was another reason for strengthened connections between the Amazon and other parts of the country during the late nineteenth century. Starting in the 1850s, crude rubber came into huge demand in Europe and North America as a basic material for making tires. It was primarily taken from a plant native to the Amazon called the Pará rubber tree (*Hevea brasiliensis*). Between the 1850s and 1910s, Amazon rubber dominated the global market. In the 1890, the region supplied as much as 90 percent of the crude rubber in the world. Rubber quickly became Brazil's second most important cash crop after coffee, accounting for 40 percent of the total value of its exports by 1910.[10] The rubber boom attracted a historical wave of migrants from northeastern Brazil to the region looking for economic opportunities. Manaus and Belém, the capitals of Amazonas and Pará, respectively, saw rapid demographic growth and modernization.[11]

The rubber boom attracted countless settlers from various parts of Brazil to the upper Amazon in pursuit of prosperity and success. However, this movement had catastrophic consequences for the local Indigenous populations. The new settlers overhunted the area's wildlife and spread deadly diseases such as measles, leading to a significant loss of life among the native people. The settlers also waged violent campaigns, known as *correrias*, against Indigenous communities, resulting in the razing of villages, the killing and displacement of inhabitants, and the seizure of their territories.[12]

In 1876, the British smuggled *H. brasiliensis* seeds out of Brazil and transplanted the crop to its Southeast Asian colonies. Due to heavy capital investment, state subsidies, modernized transportation, and cheap labor, rubber produced in British Southeast Asia was more competitive in both price and quality than its Amazonian counterpart, which was produced in a more traditional setting. As a result, the Amazon's global domination of rubber production collapsed. By 1932, the share of its rubber in the global market had shrunk to 1 percent.[13] The end of the rubber boom brought rapid economic decline and a decrease in public and private investment in the Brazilian Amazon. The harm inflicted on the Indigenous cultures and populations was irreversible.

RESOURCES, POPULATION, AND COLLABORATIVE SETTLER COLONIALISM IN THE 1920S

To reverse this course of events, the states of Amazonas and Pará adopted aggressive policies to attract foreign capital and immigrants by granting free land. Both Japan and the United States responded enthusiastically to this development. Ascendant after World War I, both were hungry for additional raw materials and further economic expansion. The Amazon, therefore, became a competing ground for these two Pacific empires. With a booming U.S. automobile industry and its growing demand for tire-making materials, Washington, DC was particularly eager to secure rubber suppliers that were alternatives to Southeast Asia in order to bypass the British monopoly. In the 1920s, it sponsored a number of investigative trips to the Amazon and sent positive reports to American business leaders that portrayed the region as a lucrative opportunity. In 1927, Henry Ford acquired 2.5 million acres along the Tapajós River in Pará. There he built a U.S. settler town named Fordlândia with the goal of cultivating *H. brasiliensis* and experimenting with mass production of rubber.[14]

Japanese investment and settler migration to the Amazon took place at around the same time. The Japanese expansionists' growing interest in the region was stimulated by a national anxiety over the lack of resources (*shigen*) in the archipelago, which became a central concern for Japan's policy makers due to the impact of World War I. As the first total war in human history, the Great War demanded each participating nation to thoroughly mobilize both human and material resources, blurring the line between battlefield and home front. Recognizing the decisive role that resources played in the outcome of the war, the Japanese government established the Bureau of Resources (Shigenkyoku). Reporting directly to the cabinet, the bureau took charge of investigating and collecting information on material resources throughout the archipelago and assisted the cabinet in making policies and plans to utilize them.[15]

Japan's annexation of German Micronesia during World War I turned the South Seas, including the South Pacific and Southeast Asia, into a potential resource supplier for the empire.[16] Taking a well-read page from Western colonial discourse, Japanese expansionists argued that the North was the world of humankind, home to progress, technology, and civilization; in contrast, the South was merely the world of materials, home to abundant natural resources but precious little else.[17] Not only did this North-Human/South-Material discourse (*hokujin nanbutsu ron*) undergird Japanese colonial expansion in the South Seas since the 1920s, it also encouraged Japan's colonial ambitions in the Amazon at around the same time. Japanese expansionists began to look at the rainforest in northern Brazil through the lens of tropical colonialism, as they had done in the South Seas.

The colonial imagination of the Amazon, spurred by the fear of scarce natural resources, developed alongside a growing anxiety regarding overpopulation and food shortage in the archipelago. They became the two main justifications for Japan's capital exportation and emigration to the region. The formation of the Kansai-based Japan-Brazil Association (Nippaku Kyōkai/Associação Nipo-Brasileira) in 1926 symbolized the alliance between Japanese business elites and the advocates for Japanese migration to Brazil, particularly the Amazon. With business elites and politicians as its board members and the governor of Hyōgo Prefecture as the president, the association vowed to tackle the issues of overpopulation and resource shortage that plagued the archipelago by promoting migration

FIGURE 22. This image appeared in the popular journal *Shokumin* (Colonial Review) in Japan in 1930. It contrasted an overpopulated Japan with an empty and resource-filled Amazon. Source: *Shokumin* 9, no. 8 (August 1930): 113.

to Brazil and bilateral trade.[18] It published a journal, *Burajiru: ishokumin to bōeki* (Brazil: Colonial Migration and Trade), to disseminate information about opportunities for migration to and investment in Brazil as well as advice for Japanese investors and migrants. For the same purpose, it also launched a series of lectures and events, including an exhibition on Brazil titled *Burajiru jijō tenrankai* (Exhibition of Brazil's Situation) in the Mitsukoshi Department Store in Kobe.[19] The exhibition, demonstrating a variety of material outputs ranging from diamonds and precious minerals to exotic animals and tropical plants, presented to the Japanese public a Brazil that had boundless empty land and unlimited natural wealth waiting for the Japanese to occupy and make use of.[20]

FIGURE 23. A section of the exhibition "Burajiru Jijō Tenrankai" at the Mitsukoshi Department Store in Kobe in 1927. It aimed to showcase the abundance of Brazil's mineral deposits. Source: "Burajiru Jijō Tenrankai: Kobe Mitsukoshi Gofukuten ni okeru," *Burajiru: ishokumin to bōeki* 1, no. 9 (October 1927): 95.

FIGURE 24. Another section of the exhibition "Burajiru Jijō Tenrankai" at the Mitsukoshi Department Store in Kobe in 1927. This one shows Brazil's primitive nature by displaying its exotic animals and insects. Source: "Burajiru Jijō Tenrankai: Kobe Mitsukoshi Gofukuten ni okeru," *Burajiru: ishokumin to bōeki* 1, no. 9 (October 1927): 95.

Japanese settler colonialism in the Amazon was managed by Japan's migration state using the Kaikō model (see chapter 4). In other words, Tokyo oversaw the migration and community-making processes through companies that provided assistance for both migrant recruitment and settlement. For Japanese business elites in the 1920s, the most attractive region in Brazil was the Amazon because of its abundant natural resources and local governments' policies that encouraged foreign immigration and investment. The formation of the Nanbei Takushoku Kabushiki Gaisha, or Nantaku (South American Colonization Company serves as a good example. After the Japanese ambassador to Brazil, Tazuke Shichita, obtained the promise of a free 500,000-hectare land grant from the governor of Pará, Tokyo sponsored a tour to the state in 1925 to evaluate local conditions for establishing Japanese colonies.[21] The tour was funded by the Kanebo Textile Company, the biggest textile company in Japan, as it was searching for raw cotton suppliers outside of Asia. The delegation was headed by Fukuhara Hachirō, a director of Kanebo, and included several government bureaucrats as well as experts in agriculture and medicine.[22]

Based on his investigation in Pará, Fukuhara concluded that Japanese capital exportation and migration to the region was indeed full of promise. The land of the Amazon was not only ten times cheaper than that of São Paulo but also boasted abundant natural resources. Fukuhara observed that while civilized people in other parts of the world were busy competing for resources to survive, Brazilians, due to the abundance of resources in their land, enjoyed a slow pace of life. For the same reason, the Indigenous peoples in the Amazon, he argued, were especially mild-natured, obedient, and easy for the Japanese to manipulate (*oshiyasui*). Because of the local residents' lack of diligence and the small size of their population, he argued, the Amazon remained largely a virgin land waiting for the Japanese to explore.[23]

Fukuhara urged Japan's business elites and investors to become trailblazers in the empire's expansion in the Amazon. The failure of Japanese migration to the United States, he reasoned, was because the migrants did not have a solid economic foundation in the host society. Land, manpower, and capital were the three indispensable pillars of successful migration. Although the Brazilian land was full of natural wealth and the Japanese settlers were incredibly diligent, they still lacked a solid economic foundation. Accordingly, Fukuhara urged Japan's business leaders to act on behalf of the empire by joining Japanese expansion into the Brazilian Amazon.[24]

Encouraged by Fukuhara's report, Prime Minister Tanaka Gi'ichi hosted a meeting with over sixty Japanese business leaders in March 1928. From this meeting, Nantaku was born. Kanebo took on Nantaku's principal financial and managerial responsibilities by holding 25 percent of Nantaku's stocks. A few other big companies also purchased substantial stocks. Fukuhara himself became the first president of the company. At the end of that year, he arrived in Pará again and established the Japan Plantation Company of Brazil (Companhia Niponica

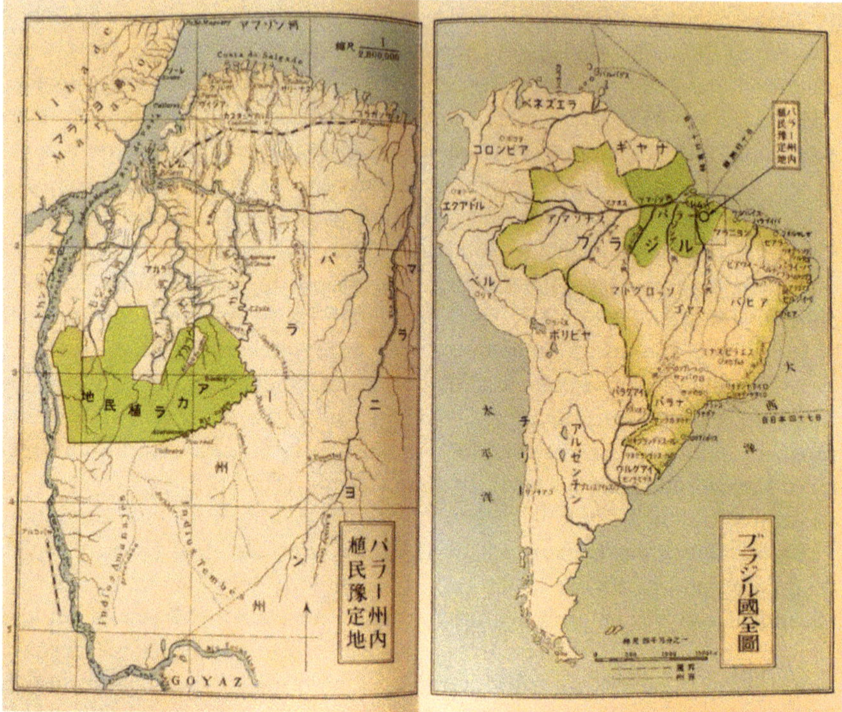

MAP 5. The location of the Japanese Acará Colony managed by Nantaku in Pará. Source: *Burajirukoku Parā shū shokumin nannai* (1930), in Gaimushō Gaikō Shiryōkan, *Honpō imin toriatsukainin kankei zakken: Nanbei Takushoku Kabishiki Gaisha*, vol. 2, J120. J 3–2.

de Plantação do Brasil) as a local agent of Nantaku. He also signed a concession agreement with the state government of Pará, securing the land in Acará, Monte Alegre, and three other areas for Nantaku.

Nantaku established Japanese colonies in both Acará and Monte Alegre, where it built a host of public facilities such as clinics, schools, playgrounds, warehouses, and grocery stores. The company recruited migrants in Japan and settled them in these two colonies as farmers. It provided each migrant family with free housing and inexpensive leases on the land, promising to transfer the land's ownership to the farming families at a low cost later on. In addition to managing migration and community building, the companies established laboratories in the colonies to experiment with new technologies in farming and pest control and to provide professional guidance to the farming settlers. The company's profits mainly came from the sale of crops produced in the colonies, such as cotton and rice, which it encouraged the migrants to cultivate.[25]

Fukuhara's investigation also paved the way for the formation of a few other Japanese settler colonies in Pará and Amazonas in the same decade. Encouraged by the investigation, a group of Japanese Americans founded a company called

South American Business Co. Ltd (Nanbei Kigyō Kabushiki Gaisha) in Delaware. They contracted with Fukuhara to secure a tract of land in Castanhal, where they established a settler farm staffed primarily with Japanese American remigrants. In 1929, the farm merged with the Acará Colony, which was managed by Nantaku.[26] Ōishi Kosaku, a participant in Fukuhara's investigation, obtained a land grant in the state of Amazonas and established a Japanese settler colony near Maués.[27] In a move facilitated by Tazuke Shichita, the Tokyo business owner Yamanishi Gensaburō and the former Japanese diplomat Awazu Kinroku jointly secured a free land grant of 100 hectares in the state of Amazonas. With the financial support of his allies, Awazu established the Amazon Business Co. Ltd, or ABC (Amazon Kōgyō Kabushiki Gaisha), to manage the community and its related businesses.[28]

Yet, at the same time, Japanese settler elites in São Paulo greeted Tokyo's efforts in the Amazon with doubt and resentment. They asserted that the anchor of Japanese expansion in Brazil should be in the Southeast, which enjoyed far better infrastructure and a more pleasant climate. As the Japanese settlers were still on the way to securing their foothold in São Paulo, it was unwise for the empire to waste resources trying to explore the wild Amazon. Miura Saku, editor of one of the three most influential Japanese settler newspapers in Brazil before 1945, was firmly in this camp. After investigating the Amazon region in person, he penned a series of articles and published them in *Asahi shinbun* in Japan. By arguing that expanding into the Amazon was too hasty, Miura tried to sway public opinion in order to stop Tokyo's efforts.[29]

Nevertheless, despite competing for resources and migrants from Japan, the settlers in the Amazon and São Paulo were linked on the leadership level. Tatsuke Shichita, the first Japanese ambassador to Brazil (1923–27), played a central role in obtaining a Japanese land concession in the state of Pará.[30] Tatsuke was also a primary planner of Fukuhara's investigative trip that led to the formation of Nantaku.[31] After his post in Rio de Janeiro ended, Tatsuke became the founding director of the Federation of the Overseas Migration Cooperative Societies, which was in charge of recruiting and transporting Japanese migrants bound for southeastern Brazil.[32] The federation's board of directors included Inoue Masaji, president of Kaikō during the height of its Brazilian migration and settlement programs in southeastern Brazil from 1924 to 1937, as well as Mutō Sanji, head of Kanebo, which financially backed Japanese expansion into the Amazon.[33]

UETSUKA TSUKASA AND A NEW DISCOURSE OF JAPANESE TROPICAL COLONIALISM

As the 1930s progressed, the dramatically changing political landscape in East Asia and South America presented both challenges and opportunities for Japanese collaborative settler colonialism in the Amazon. On the one hand, Japan's intensified expansion in Northeast Asia and China proper dulled its elites' appetite for Brazil. On the other hand, deteriorating relations between Japan and the

Anglo-American powers meant that the empire was subject to an increasing number of trade sanctions. This forced the Japanese elites to consider the Amazon region more seriously as an alternative supplier of raw materials.

Compared to the 1920s, Japanese presence in the Amazon in the 1930s saw both continuities and changes. The number of settlers in the region kept growing, and Japanese investments continued to pour in to sustain and expand the colonial projects first started in the 1920s. However, although the discourse of a resource-hungry Japan stayed constant throughout these decades, the underpinning ideological timbre had changed. Whereas Japanese leaders initially saw their foray into the Amazon as the empire's participation in the Anglo-American-led mission to civilize the region, by the 1930s, they increasingly described their efforts as a challenge to the Anglo-American world order and global white supremacy.

The logical foundation of this new discourse of Japanese expansionism were the self-proclaimed racial characteristics of the Japanese as the ideal colonizers. First, it described the Japanese as uniquely benevolent among the colonizers in the world. Different from the selfish Westerners who only knew how to exploit the colonized, the Japanese wanted to cooperate with local peoples and share the fruits of progress. As explained in chapter 5, this idea mirrored the collective identity of the Japanese settlers in São Paulo that took shape around the same time. It was also echoed by the new discourse of Japanese expansionism in Asia in the 1930s and 1940s that undergirded the rhetoric of the Greater East Asia Co-Prosperity Sphere.

These "special characteristics" of the Japanese included an unmatched capacity to survive in and explore the tropics. Japanese expansionists embraced the existing popular belief among Westerners that white people were unsuccessful in colonizing the tropics because they could not adjust to the climate. *Shizen no kankyō to hakujin jinkō mondai* (Natural Environment and the Problem of the White Population), a book by Kaikō's director, Inoue Masaji, published in 1929, offered a good example of this argument. White colonizers were unsuccessful in the tropics, Inoue argued, for two reasons. First, because of their European racial origin, they were naturally unprepared, both physically and mentally, to live in the tropics. Compared to other races, they were not only more vulnerable to local diseases but also suffered from low fertility and productivity in the hot climate. To make matters worse, such disadvantages forced them to rely on the locals as the primary labor force. Inoue claimed that the Indigenous peoples in the tropics were hopelessly inferior in terms of their intelligence and physical strength, making them an unreliable source of labor for the white colonizers.[34]

In contrast, Inoue claimed, the Japanese had unmatched adaptability to the tropics thanks to their mixed racial origin. As some of their ancestors were from tropical regions in Southeast Asia and the Pacific Islands, the Japanese were naturally immune to tropical diseases and physically prepared to work in hot temperatures. Blessed with their exceptional productivity in the tropics, the Japanese did not need to depend on the Indigenous population as the main source of labor. These two factors, for Inoue, together ensured Japanese success in their colonization of the tropics.[35]

The symbol of Japanese presence in the Amazon in the 1930s was the Amazonia Industrial Research Center, the activities of which fit perfectly in this new colonial discourse. The center's founder and director, Uetsuka Tsukasa, was a cousin of the São Paulo community leader Uetsuka Shūhei.[36] Uetsuka Tsukasa had been a supporter of Japanese expansion to both South America and Asia since his university days, when he led a study group focused on South America. After graduation, he spent eight years working for the Southern Manchuria Railway Company (Mantetsu), investigating the natural deposits and geography of Manchuria, China proper, and the Korean Peninsula for the company and the imperial government. He then returned to Japan and became a member of the Imperial Diet in 1920.

In 1928, Uetsuka Tsukasa took over the rights to the one-million-hectare concession in Amazonas from Yamanishi Gensaburō, who had failed to establish a settler colony there due to the bankruptcy of his own business.[37] Uetsuka sent out two survey teams, both of which were jointly funded by the imperial government and a group of business tycoons. Once the investigation concluded, Uetsuka and his followers purchased land near Parintins City and named it Villa Amazonia. There they established the Amazonia Industrial Research Center, an institution in charge of settler community building, land exploration, and agricultural research and development.[38]

A key feature that separated Uetsuka's Amazon venture from previous programs of Japanese emigration was its emphasis on education. He established the Kokushikan Colonization School (Kokushikan Kōtō Takushoku Gakkō, or Kōtaku) in Tokyo, a private school that trained migrants before their departure. It partnered with the Kokushikan Academy and shared its facilities and campus. Kōtaku required that its students complete a middle school education before enrollment.[39] Its one-year curriculum combined ideology with concrete skills, offering courses such as national morality (*kokumin dōtoku*), history of colonialism and colonial policies, Portuguese, South American geography, agriculture, animal husbandry, and construction.[40] By design, Kōtaku's mission was to cultivate colonial leaders who would bring the unique blessings of the Japanese empire to South America. For this reason, a highlight in the curriculum was the course, "History of Colonialism and Colonial Policies," taught by Uetsuka himself. By studying the failure of Western colonial powers such as the Portuguese, Spanish, British, and French, the course aimed to send a clear message to students: the Japanese should learn from the selfish Westerners' mistakes and conduct their own colonial expansion with benevolence.[41]

Similar to Uetsuka's endeavor in the Amazon, which combined the practice of settler colonialism with education, was that of Sakiyama Hisae. Sakiyama established the Overseas Colonial Migration Academy (Kaigai Shokumin Gakkō) in Tokyo in 1918 in the hope of training vanguards to realize the empire's overseas ambitions. After investigating the Amazon in 1929, he decided to participate in Japanese expansion in the region himself by moving to the Maués Colony and turning it into a migration destination for his followers.[42] Two years later, Kaikō reproduced this model in São Paulo and formed its own colonial school, Emeboi Agricultural Practice Farm (Emeboi Nōji Jisshūjo / Instituto de Prática Agrícola de São Paulo). Its students were unmarried migrants who received full subsidies from the imperial government; the school provided them with two years of training in order to turn them into future leaders of Japanese settler colonies.[43]

While these schools promoted the idea of Japan's "benevolent" colonialism, Japanese elites celebrated the settlers' agricultural achievement in the Amazon as evidence.[44] The Amazonia Industrial Research Center's jute cultivation was particularly illustrative. As the primary material for making coffee bags, long fiber jute was in huge demand in Brazil, yet the crop was only cultivated in India and its production and sale was monopolized by the British. Given India's and the Amazon's shared tropical climate, as well as the crop's economic potential, Uetsuka saw transplanting it to Brazil as a critical mission of the center.[45] Through years of experiment in different locations in the Amazon, the center successfully brought the Amazon-grown long fiber jute to the international market in 1937.[46] Japanese settler elites described this success as a triumph of Japan's "benevolent" colonialism. As they saw it, while the British stole the seeds of rubber trees from the Amazon and caused the collapse of Brazil's rubber industry, the Japanese benefited Brazil by transplanting jute from India, unselfishly sharing the rewards of this venture with the local Brazilian people.[47]

In reality, however, the Amazonia Industrial Research Center and Japanese settlers in the Amazon in general were the immediate beneficiaries of jute production and trade. Jute quickly became a stable source of profit for the center because it maintained a monopoly on jute seeds, and the crop helped the center survive a major setback in the mid-1930s. It also became a major source of income for Japanese settlers in the region in general. Unlike its predecessor, the regime of Getúlio Vargas emphasized central control over state governments by banning them from granting land parcels larger than 10,000 hectares without the federal senate's permission. Though the concession of one million acres was given to Uetsuka before the constitution took effect, he had to apply for an extension because of delays in meeting the conditions of the concession. In 1934, when he applied to extend the concession for the second time, the federal senate vetoed it on the grounds of national security. As a result, Uetsuka was only allowed to keep the research center's existing properties and lost all unclaimed land. With the promising development in jute cultivation, the Japanese government took action to secure the center's existing properties by providing necessary financial assistance to turn the center into a stock-issuing land developing company renamed Amazonia Sangyō Kabushiki Gaisha (Amazonia Industrial Company, or AIC) in 1935. Its four primary shareholders were Tokyo-controlled Japanese companies, Mitsubishi, Sumitomo, Yasuda, and Tōtaku.[48]

Most Japanese enterprises in the Amazon suffered from both the immigration quota imposed by Brazil and a decrease in financial support as the Japanese empire shifted its focus to the Asian continent in the second half of the 1930s. However, the Amazonia Industrial Company continued to grow thanks to its success in jute cultivation. In 1938, it expanded its business to Pará. The state government granted the company 10,000 hectares and allowed it to build two new laboratories to experiment with jute cultivation in Breves and Santarém.[49] In 1940, it took over the Maués Colony, established and previously managed by the Japanese American–funded ABC and turned the primary crop of local Japanese settlers from guarana to jute.[50]

Another crop that the Japanese settlers successfully transplanted to the Amazon from Asia was pepper (*koshō*), which was achieved in the 1930s by Nantaku-affiliated Japanese settlers in Tomé-Açu. Similar to the case of jute, Japanese elites celebrated the success of transplanting pepper as evidence of the benevolent nature of Japanese settler colonialism. In their imagination, both achievements also served as proof of the unmatched capacity of the Japanese race to harness the tropics.[51] Moreover, the transplantation of pepper was a chain in the link between Japanese colonial expansion in the South Seas and the Amazon. The idea of transplanting pepper originated with Takaki Saburō, a Japanese agricultural specialist who was based in Southeast Asia before Nantaku hired him to head the administration of the Acará Colony. His observation of the Chinese settlers' pepper cultivation in Southeast Asia inspired him to experiment with the crop in the Amazon.[52]

TRANSWAR JAPANESE COLLABORATIVE SETTLER COLONIALISM

The new discourse of Japanese tropical colonialism in the Amazon in the 1930s was matched by an unexpectedly similar approach of Brazilian expansionism in the same region. Mirroring Japan's expansion into Manchuria since the beginning of the decade, the Vargas regime strived to increase its geopolitical influence in the Amazon, the Caribbean, and the Pacific. Like Japanese empire builders who embraced Malthusian expansionism and justified their military campaigns in Northeast Asia as protecting the "lifeline" of the empire, Vargas and his supporters saw their efforts as the means to secure the lebensraum of the Estado Novo.[53]

For Brazilian expansionists of the day, the Amazon Basin was critical to securing the nation's northern and western borders and establishing Brazil's geopolitical hegemony in Latin America. They imagined that Brazilian success in "civilizing" this savage land would also demonstrate the Brazilians' racial superiority to their colonial competitors. Like their Japanese counterparts, Brazilian elites embraced the popular claim that the white colonizers were naturally incapable of managing tropical land and asserted that their hybrid racial origins made them uniquely suited for the task. Gilberto Freyre, widely known as the architect of the Brazilian discourse of racial democracy, praised military expansion into the Amazon as proof of the extraordinary capacity of the Brazilian *mestiço* to harness the tropical land.[54]

The Vargas regime also considered the full integration of Indigenous peoples vital to its expansionist policies in the 1930s and 1940s, promoting them as national symbols in its propaganda. The state celebrated their perceived positive attributes, such as valor and generosity, culminating in the establishment of April 19 as the Day of the Indian in 1943, officially recognizing the Indigenous importance to Brazil.[55] Nevertheless, this facade masked the government's true intentions to assimilate Indigenous peoples and harness them for national progress, portraying them as noble yet inherently flawed individuals in need of transformation into productive citizens. This allowed the government to systematically ignore Indigenous voices, downplay atrocities, and appropriate Indigenous land.[56]

Collaborative settler colonialism in the Amazon in the early twentieth century brought catastrophic consequences to the Indigenous peoples. The story of the Karajá, who built their community along the Araguaia River, was especially illustrative. The Karajá have a distinctive language and are famous for their inventive feather ornaments and clay pottery. Their religion involves a mask cult, in which shamans dance in conical straw capes. Wary of outside visitors, the Karajá were described as "dignified and independent." In 1927, the government had created a post in Santa Isabel and sought to establish a museum and a football field and also hold workshops. But when the journalist and traveler Peter Fleming visited Santa Isabel, the main village of the Karajá people, in 1932, the culture and the community of the Karajá were gone. Referring to the government's programs to "civilize" the Karajá, Fleming lamented, "Good work was done while the funds lasted; but when we arrived there were only the labels left to show how zeal had been expended. . . . The outposts of culture had been evacuated. Only the brave green and yellow notices [the national colors of Brazil] remained."[57]

Growing tensions between the United States and Japan during this decade further motivated the Brazilian government to intensify its expansion into the Amazon. Japan's growing influence in Southeast Asia, the primary supplier of raw rubber, pushed U.S. policy makers to explore alternative rubber sources. The Brazilian Amazon emerged as an ideal substitute. In 1937, the same year the Japanese empire embarked on a total war with China, the Brazilian government launched its "March to the West" campaign to escalate its colonization of the Amazon. Vargas's colonial project was marked by its pragmatism. To achieve its goal, the regime strategically utilized both external and internal resources. It took advantage of the growing rivalry between the United States and Germany over access to the Brazilian market and natural resources: Brazil received low-interest loans and a variety of technical aid from the United States in exchange for restricting its exports to Germany.[58] Similarly, though surging ethnic nationalism led to widespread anti-Japanese sentiment and an immigration quota, Vargas nevertheless saw the Japanese settlers as valuable resources. In another pragmatic move, not only did Rio postpone the quota from taking effect on Japanese immigration for a few years, but it also continued to support the economic activities of the Japanese settlers in general and those in the Amazon in particular.

Vargas believed that Japanese settlers and enterprises in the Amazon were well matched with his vision for the region's development. He met twice with Uetsuka Tsukasa, head of a Japanese flagship enterprise in the Amazon, during his 1940 visit to the region. Their first meeting took place in Villa Amazonia where Uetsuka, accompanied by the mayor of Parintins, explained to Vargas the Japanese success in transplanting jute and laid out his plan to increase jute production in the region. They met again a few days later, after Vargas reviewed Uetsuka's written appeal for the Brazilian government to establish regulations on jute rating. The president promised to continue his support for the Japanese settlers' cultivation of jute and their related businesses in Villa Amazonia.

Vargas kept this promise. In early 1941, he granted the Amazonia Industrial Company the exclusive right to jute rating and packaging. By supporting the Japanese settlers, Vargas aimed to promote domestic jute production in the Amazon and decrease the nation's dependence on imports from India.[59] Stimulated by support from both the central and local administrations, Uetsuka made bold plans to expand jute cultivation and increase the company's capacity for packaging and processing raw jute. He also envisioned the formation of an industrial center based in Villa Amazonia, which would manage a variety of other businesses such as sugar and food processing.[60]

The outbreak of World War II, however, doomed Uetsuka's efforts, as well as those of other Japanese settlers in the region. While the Vargas regime did not declare war against Japan until near the end of the war, it was quick to categorize Japan as an enemy country. It banned Japanese immigration completely and confiscated properties owned by Japanese businesses or the Japanese government. A majority of the Japanese employees of the Amazonia Industrial Company were forced to resign and returned to Japan. When Brazilian soldiers raided the company's headquarters in September 1942, they arrested the eight remaining Japanese employees, who were accused of being spies.

Nantaku and other Japanese enterprises in the region met a similar fate. The Brazilian authorities turned Tomé-Açu, Nantaku's headquarters in Pará, into a detention center for enemy aliens. The detainees in Tomé-Açu included both the first generation of Japanese immigrants and the second generation who lived in nearby cities and spoke fluent Portuguese.[61] They were joined by German and Italian detainees who had previously lived in northern Brazil.[62] The forced relocation of these so-called enemy aliens was a part of the Vargas regime's larger wartime campaign to populate the region and redistribute its labor resource. To this end, Rio also relocated nearly fifty-five thousand free migrants from northeastern Brazil to the Amazon as rubber laborers by offering them attractive subsidies.[63]

Although World War II brought catastrophe to the Japanese settlers in the Amazon, it did not end the process of settler colonialism in the region. With a quick surge in the Amazon's working population due to the Brazilian government's wartime relocation campaign, Vargas was able to speed up the process of colonization. He temporarily stepped down from the presidency amid the growing wave of democratization immediately after the war but won the national election in 1951 with a nationalist agenda and returned to the presidential office. His settler colonial project in the Amazon resumed, and the Japanese settlers continued to play a role in his blueprint for the region.

The Empire of Japan collapsed at the end of the war, and the archipelago was occupied by the United States for seven years. However, when the occupation came to an end, old and new Japanese expansionists again began to promote overseas emigration, reviving the connections established during the imperial era. Armed with the Cold War discourse of modernization, they looked to the Amazon once more as a destination for Japanese emigration. This time around, they saw emigration as a means for Japan to reenter the world as a member of the Western Bloc. In 1951, the same year Vargas returned to power, Uetsuka Tsukasa lost his election campaign for the governorship of Kumamoto Prefecture and returned to the Amazon. After meeting with political leaders in Amazonas and Pará, he flew to Rio de Janeiro with his onetime colleague and Amazonian resident, Tsuji Kotarō, to meet Vargas, who was eager to increase raw material extraction in the Amazon. Uetsuka and Tsuji persuaded the president to reopen Brazil to Japanese immigration by promising that it would substantially increase jute production in the region.[64] Tsuji then obtained an official agreement from the Agency for Immigration and Colonization under the Brazilian Ministry of Agriculture, which allowed him to bring eighteen migrant families from Japan in 1953 to join the Japanese settlers already in the Amazon. The Tsuji emigration marked the beginning of Japanese migration to Brazil after World War II.

. . .

In 1939, Takaoka Kumao, the doyen of Japanese colonial policy studies at Hokkaido Imperial University and a longtime supporter of Japanese migration to Brazil, was invited to deliver a speech at the graduation ceremony at Tōhoku Imperial University.[65] In this speech, titled "The Japanese as Tropical Colonizers," Takaoka provided a systematic explanation of why the Japanese were more competent than white people as colonizers in the tropics. In addition to having a more advanced civilization, he reasoned, successful colonizers in the tropics should be able to cooperate and share the fruits of progress with Indigenous peoples; they also needed to maintain high fertility and labor productivity. Whereas white men failed to meet either of these requirements, there was ample evidence that the Japanese could accomplish both. Echoing Tokyo's overall strategy of expanding south into Southeast Asia, Takaoka urged the young empire builders to shift their gaze from the temperate zone to the resource-rich tropics, where Japan's true manifest destiny lay.

Takaoka Kumao's speech also pointed to the decades-long connections between Japan's migration to the Amazon and the empire's expansion into the South Seas. Not only did the former emerge in tandem with the Japanese occupation of Micronesia, the expansionists also held up the Japanese experience in the Amazon as evidence of Japan's success in colonizing the tropics and used it to justify the empire's expansion in Southeast Asia. Nantaku, a flagship Japanese enterprise in the Amazon, moved its migration and agricultural businesses to Southeast Asia after the Brazilian government cut off its diplomatic relationship with Japan in 1942.[66]

In addition to its intellectual and institutional connections with Japanese expansion in Southeast Asia and the South Pacific, Japanese presence in the Amazon evolved along with Brazil's own expansion in the region. The convergence of these two brands of tropical colonialism led to the formation and prosperity of Japanese settler enterprises such as Nantaku and the Amazonia Industrial Company. The Vargas regime's ambition to speed up the colonization of the Amazon and its pragmatic approach enabled Japanese settlers to have even greater success in the 1930s.

Decades later, as both Japan and Brazil strived to reemerge as regional powers by reviving and revising their colonial past during the Cold War, the colonization of the Amazon once again proved to be in their mutual interest. Indeed, the Amazon became the restarting point of postwar Japanese migration to Brazil. The 1953 Tsuji emigration in Pará was joined by another migration project led by Matsubara Yasutarō, a Japanese Brazilian farm owner and a friend of Vargas's, which brought twenty-two families to Mato Grosso, a state that shared the Amazon Basin with Amazonas and Pará. These two projects were followed by many other programs that relocated Japanese farmers, agricultural trainees, and technicians to São Paulo and other Brazilian states in the 1950s and 1960s, the golden period of Japanese Brazilian migration in the postwar era.

8

———

Reinventing Japan
and Japanese Brazilians

The Japanese settler community in Brazil reached its nadir in the years immediately following World War II. When the Shōwa emperor Hirohito's announcement of Japan's unconditional surrender on August 15, 1945, reached Brazil via radio, most Japanese settlers received it with doubt and confusion. Few were willing to believe it. After Rio banned Japanese-language media in 1941, Japanese settlers relied on radio broadcasts from Tokyo as their sole source of news regarding Japan and the ongoing war. The propaganda from Tokyo led its listeners in Brazil to believe that the empire was well on track to victory. Consequently, a long-lasting and bitter split emerged among the settlers with regard to whether to acknowledge Japan's defeat.

The roots of this split had existed among the settlers decades earlier because of the social gap between the elites and the general population. Before the war, community leaders were mainly affiliated with Tokyo-sponsored big enterprises such as Kaikō, Tozan, and Burataku; they were also close to the Japanese embassy and had strong influence on mainstream Japanese newspapers in São Paulo. With their economic privileges and political power, community leaders kept their distance from average settlers and lived in an insulated circle.[1] After the Brazilian government suspended Japan's diplomatic apparatuses, confiscated Tokyo-owned enterprises, and banned Japanese-language media, the existing settler leadership collapsed. Given this power vacuum and the lack of reliable sources of information, some previously marginalized individuals seized the chance to rise as new leaders of the community. They presented themselves as representatives of the downtrodden and vowed to do away with the elitism of the previous leadership.[2]

The question of whether to recognize Japan's defeat continued to fester amid the battle over the new settler leadership. Those who accepted Japan's defeat were

FIGURE 25. Brazilian president Artur da Costa e Silva greeting Japan's Crown Prince Akihito with a welcome toast during his visit to Brasília. Source: *Paulista Gurafu, Kōtaishi gofusai Burajiru no tabi*, July 1967, 2–3.

known as the *makegumi* or the *ninshiki ha* (defeat or recognition faction), while those who refused to accept the defeat were known as the *kachigumi* (victory faction). Among the kachigumi, a militant group known as Shindō Renmei carried out terrorist attacks to retaliate against and threaten fellow settlers who accepted Japan's defeat. The organization soon caught the attention of the Brazilian police, which arrested and jailed all its core leaders in 1947.[3] The extremism of Shindō Renmei stimulated a new anti-Japanese campaign among Brazilian politicians who sought to ban Japanese immigration permanently. Though this campaign failed to write the ban into Brazil's new constitution of 1946, the image of the Japanese settler community suffered tremendously. With few connections with war-torn Japan, the settlers were utterly isolated.

Yet in 1967, when Japan's then crown prince Akihito and his wife arrived in Brasília, Brazil's newly established capital, Brazilian society not only recognized the Japanese as one of the most successful ethnic groups but also celebrated them as vital agents of the two nations' cultural and economic exchange. Brazil's invitation to Akihito to come to Brasília, a milestone achievement of the nation's setter colonialism, symbolized the reintegration of Japanese setters into Brazil's settler colonial history as partners. In São Paulo, the Japanese settlers themselves organized a magnificent welcoming ceremony for the Akihito couple and greeted them in Pacaembu Stadium with a crowd of eighty thousand.[4] The couple also visited Japanese settler businesses and farms in both São Paulo and the Amazon and were showered with appreciation. Akihito's visit, therefore, also

FIGURE 26. Crown Prince Akihito visiting a Japanese coffee farm during his visit to Brazil in 1967 in recognition of Japanese settlers' historical contribution to Brazilian society. Source: *Paulista Gurafu, Kōtaishi gofusai Burajiru no tabi*, July 1967, 1.

FIGURE 27. A crowd of 80,000 Japanese immigrants greeting Crown Prince Akihito and his wife in the Pacaembu Stadium in the city of São Paulo. Source: *Paulista Gurafu, Kōtaishi gofusai Burajiru no tabi*, July 1967, 12–13.

signified the successful reunion of the Japanese settler community after decades of division and turmoil. As the Japanese Brazilian magazine *Jornal Paulista* commented, it was during Akihito's seven-day visit that "the hearts of 600,000 Japanese settlers became one for the first time."[5]

This chapter discusses how Japanese Brazilian elites successfully reunified and rebranded their community in the postwar decades; it also explains how this process of self-reinvention was entwined with and made possible by Japan's own reinvention during the Cold War. The Japanese Brazilian settlers were able to rejuvenate their community through old and new connections with Japanese government and society. By the same process, Japanese Brazilian elites played a critical role in the formation of Japan's national identity after World War II by contributing to the rise of Nihonjinron, a discourse celebrating Japan's cultural uniqueness that continues to influence Japanese society today.

RACE TO CULTURE, EMPIRE TO NATION

Gerald Horne has forcefully argued that World War II was, in fact, a race war.[6] At the same time, it was a war that denied racism. The totality of the war, as Takashi Fujitani observes, forced countries on both sides to alter racial ideologies. In order to mobilize all possible human resources, the states branded themselves as racially inclusive. The traditional and exclusive form of racism, which Fujitani calls "vulgar racism," was no longer publicly acceptable. The new norm that replaced it was a "polite" form of racism that denied the existence of racial discrimination but gave consent to the actual practice of racism in daily life.[7] While the United States and Japan attacked each other as racist, during the total war both embraced this "polite racism." Just as the United States utilized the 442nd Infantry Regiment, which was composed almost entirely of Japanese American Nisei, to showcase its claimed commitment to racial equality, the imperial military of Japan enlisted Koreans and Taiwanese to present the empire's multiethnic profile. The discourse of "racial democracy" that the Vargas regime advocated in the 1930s and 1940s worked in a similar way. By idealizing the interracial harmony in Brazilian society, it justified the authoritarian nature of the government.[8]

In the postwar years, the denial of racial discrimination on the U.S. home front paved the way for the use of "culture" as a strategic term to replace race in public discussions related to racial minorities and foreign countries. Japan's "national culture," a term used in U.S. wartime enemy studies, was popularized among American Japanologists as a result of the rise of the Culture and Personality school in U.S. academia.[9] Best illustrated by Ruth Benedict's 1946 classic, *The Chrysanthemum and the Sword*, this national culture approach treated the Japanese experience as a holistic entity, ignoring its racial and regional diversity.[10] This way of thinking served as an academic guide for policy makers during the U.S. occupation of Japan. It was also embraced with enthusiasm by Japanese intellectuals who, following the lead of Yanagita Kunio, had already begun treating Japanese culture as an integrated entity during the war years.[11]

The concept of national culture also became a political means for postwar Japan to rejoin the world with a new image. In January 1946, Minister of Culture Tanaka Kōtarō called for building postwar Japan as a cultured nation (*bunka kokka*). As he explained it, culture was not merely something to be enjoyed. Instead, it was rooted in justice and associated with universal values such as democracy, pacifism, individualism, and freedom of speech.[12] A few months later, the Ministry of Culture issued the *New Manual for Education*, in which it claimed that the ultimate goal of Japan's national education was to turn Japan into a cultured nation that was committed to democracy and peace. The government distributed 300,000 copies of the manual to schoolteachers throughout the archipelago.[13]

The idea of a cultured nation, with its commitment to pacifism and democracy, served as a cover-up for Japan's colonial past. It created a discursive context in which the traumatic history of expansion, racism, and war atrocities in the imperial era could easily be forgotten in Japan's public discussion. It was therefore no coincidence that the idea of the cultured nation was closely associated with the discourse of the monoethnic nation (*tan'itsu minzuku kokka*), which quickly became popular in postwar Japan. Nambara Shigeru, a leading political thinker who served as president of the University of Tokyo right after the war, was a prominent advocate of both. He celebrated the removal from the archipelago of Japan's former colonial subjects whom he called "racially others from the outside" (*gaichi ishuzoku*). In his mind, their departure and Japan's loss of the former colonies created an opportunity for Japan to return to its supposed former self—that is, a racially pure nation united under the emperor.[14] This invention of Japanese racial purity allowed Nambara, who quickly became one of the most influential opinion leaders of the day, to conveniently remove the history of imperialism and its devastating consequences from public discussion. On the other hand, Nambara's call for creating a new national culture and turning Japan into a cultured nation aimed to enable Japan to rejoin the world as a member of the Western camp in the Cold War. For him, Japan's previous failure was due to its lack of historical experience equivalent to the Renaissance and the Reformation in Europe. The making of Japan's new national culture was to remedy this flaw by allowing the Japanese to catch up with white Europeans and Americans through a similar historical development.[15]

A group of Japanese settler elites in São Paulo, who had accepted Japan's defeat, was closely monitoring these new developments in Japanese and world politics. In 1946, they established an organization called the Saturday Club (Doyō Kai), the founding members of which were associated with the *Horizon* (*Chiheisen*), a Japanese Brazilian literary journal founded by Andō Zenpati. The club's key members included individuals like Yamamoto Kiyoshi, who managed Casa Tozan; attorney and graduate of the University of São Paulo, Suzuki Tei'ichi; writer and artist,

Handa Yukio; and Nisei anthropologist, Saitō Hiroshi. Most of them were well-educated urban elites and had close connections with the settler leadership before the war. The club members embraced the idea of Japanese national culture with enthusiasm and sought to solve the internal and external problems that the settler community was facing by reviving their connections with Japan. Just as postwar Japan required a new national culture, they believed, the Japanese settlers in Brazil needed a cultural movement (*bunka undō*) in order to save themselves.[16]

The Saturday Club's passion for the concept of culture was a result of the comparability of Brazil's and Japan's racial ideologies during the transitional period from World War II to the Cold War. Unlike the discourse of the monoethnic nation that dominated postwar Japan, Brazilian politicians and intellectuals continued to celebrate the idea of racial democracy and praised the nation as a melting pot of all races.[17] Yet, much like how the discourse of a monoethnic Japan in practice tended to emphasize the whiteness of the Japanese and portrayed Japan as a quasi-white nation, Brazil's racial democracy in fact served as a cover for racial whitening, a century-long belief that persisted in the minds of Brazilian elites. They too used "culture" as a code word for race. An example was the 1943 book by Fernando de Azevedo, a professor of sociology and an influential thinker in the Vargas era. Translated into English in 1950 with the title *Brazilian Culture*, the book was widely recognized as a seminal exposition of Brazilian culture. It predicted that as Europe was suffering from the devastating effects of war, Brazil would become the new center of European culture, a torch bearer of Western civilization, thanks to its historically successful process of racial whitening.[18]

More specifically, the concept of culture worked for the Saturday Club members in three ways. First, they believed that if Japanese settlers could lay claim to an advanced culture, it would improve their situation in Brazilian society. The hostilities that the Japanese settlers were facing on a daily basis in Brazil, they concluded, stemmed from cultural differences rather than racism. As Yamamoto Kiyoshi reasoned, "Although we can conquer the primitive forests, if we cannot defeat culture-based discrimination, we will still be subject to exclusion."[19] Building an advanced culture in the community, therefore, was critical to fighting discrimination from the outside. This call for an advanced culture appeared in tandem with the Saturday Club's denial of the existence of racism against the Japanese in Brazil. Similar to the mind-set of the elites in Japan, race remained the foundation of the club members' reasoning. They advocated for building an advanced culture in order to prove the whiteness of the Japanese while discriminating against the nonwhite and Indigenous peoples in Brazil. This was revealed in a discussion meeting of the Saturday Club regarding restarting Japanese migration to Brazil after World War II. At the meeting, aiming to dissuade Japanese from migrating to the Amazon, Andō Zenpati went so far as to claim that the Japanese settlers there would only head down the path of racial degradation due to the local environment and their offspring would become monkeys.[20]

Second, culture was regarded as a medium through which the Japanese Brazilians could contribute to the creation of a new Japanese nation and culture. The settler elites supported Japan's policy makers' and intellectuals' vision of postwar Japan as a cultured nation. To achieve this goal, the settler elites maintained that Japan's national culture should not be isolated. Instead, it must be able to expand overseas and influence others. In their minds, as a young nation rooted in European culture, Brazil was an ideal country where Japan's national culture could exert its influences. Accordingly, Japanese settlers in Brazil would contribute to the formation of Brazil's own culture as agents of Japan, which in turn would attest to the global significance of Japan's new national culture.[21]

The Saturday Club took the lead in this cultural movement. They regularly held meetings to discuss key issues in both postwar Japan and Brazil such as democratism, Japan's rural economy, the situation of the Japanese Brazilian Nisei, and the development of the Japanese language in Brazil. In 1947, the club members started the journal the *Era* to disseminate these discussions. The articles in the *Era* showed how closely the members connected themselves with the discourse of national culture and the invention of a new national identity in Japan. The first article of the inaugural issue was a discussion of the very concept of the nation-state.[22] In another article, Handa Yukio provided an outline on how to establish a new culture in the Japanese Brazilian community.[23] In the third issue, Andō Zenpati published an article explaining the definition of culture and his thoughts on how to construct a cultured nation.[24] In the same and the next issues, Saitō Hiroshi wrote review essays and introduced to his readers the two books crucial to the post–World War II invention of Brazilian and Japanese national cultures, respectively. They were Gilberto Freyre's *Interpretação do Brasil*, which celebrated Brazil's national identity centered on the ideas and practice of racial mixing; and Ruth Benedict's *The Chrysanthemum and the Sword*, which promoted an isolated and ahistorical Japanese national character.[25] Both Freyre and Benedict had studied at Columbia University under the anthropologist Franz Boas, who developed the theory of cultural relativism that was critical to the rise of the Culture and Personality school in U.S. academia.

In addition to spearheading the cultural movement, the Saturday Club members launched two successful social campaigns in the last half of the 1940s. One was to appeal to the Brazilian government for the return of properties confiscated during the war; the other was to raise funds in the settler community to be donated to Japan for war relief. The former aimed at changing the image of Japan in Brazil from an enemy during World War II to an ally in the Cold War. Meanwhile, the goal of the latter was to unify the Japanese settler community itself, which was bitterly split on the recognition of the empire's defeat. Most settlers, whether or not they believed Japan was defeated, were willing to make donations. Thus, this campaign created an occasion for the two opposing camps to join hands and work for a common cause.[26]

Third, the concept of culture gave the Saturday Club members a new language to reinterpret the community's past and present it as a saga of immigration and cultural progress. A central issue of the reunification of the Japanese settler community was how to explain and deal with the kachigumi extremists represented by Shindō Renmei. Though Shindō Renmei's violence claimed the lives of at least twenty-three people, among whom was a Saturday Club member, the majority of the club members remained sympathetic to its cause and to the kachigumi in general. Suzuki Tei'ichi, for example, described Shindō Renmei's activities as part of the Japanese settlers' cultural resistance to the tyranny of Brazilian ethnic nationalism. Saitō Hiroshi went so far as to claim that the rise of Shindō Renmei belonged to the collective efforts of the Japanese settlers to defend their own culture.[27]

Perhaps a more revealing example of how the club members interpreted the story of Shindō Renmei was the 1949 book, *The Forty Years of History of Immigration* (*Imin yonjūnen shi*), written by Kōyama Rokurō with support from the Saturday Club members. The book was a collective effort of the makegumi settler elites to rewrite the history of the Japanese community in Brazil in commemoration of the fortieth anniversary of the sailing of the *Kasato Maru*. It described the history of the Japanese settler community as an epic story revolving around how Japanese migrants contributed to Brazilian society and how they succeeded in preserving their own culture by overcoming various challenges. It mentioned the split of the community only in the appendix and interpreted Shindō Renmei's extremist violence as an unpleasant but forgivable episode in the laudable saga of Japanese immigration.[28]

The sympathy that the Saturday Club members had for this ultranationalist association revealed the shared commitment of the kachigumi and makegumi groups to Japanese ethnic nationalism and their resentment toward the exclusionary policies and anti-Japanese sentiments in Brazil. For the settler elites, the concept of culture served as a convenient way to reunite the community and cover up the division, violence, and close ties with Japanese imperial expansion in the recent past. This mirrored a similar strategy adopted by Japan's political and cultural leaders right after World War II. On the one hand, they embraced the concept of culture to advance the new image of Japan as a democratic, pacifist, and modernizing nation and to cut off its historical connections with the militant and expansionist Japanese empire in the past. On the other hand, they continued to revere the Shōwa Emperor as the central symbol of the national culture and denied his responsibility and role in the war and its atrocities.[29]

It was, therefore, unsurprising that the elites in both Japan and the Japanese Brazilian settler community eventually joined hands to reinterpret the *kachi/make* split by separating it from the overall positive image of Japanese culture. In 1952, the United Nations Educational, Social and Cultural Organization (UNESCO) appointed the Japanese cultural anthropologist Izumi Sei'ichi to investigate the issue of the kachigumi group. After arriving in São Paulo, Izumi met with Saitō

Hiroshi, who introduced him to other Saturday Club members and brought him to club meetings. Izumi hired Saitō as his assistant and translator when he conducted interviews with individual Japanese settlers as he traveled around rural São Paulo. Though terrified by some kachigumi diehards who perceived his arrival as proof of Japan's World War II victory and feeling personally endangered during the investigation, Izumi concluded in his report that the settlers' support for Shindō Renmei was an understandable reaction to their dashed hopes of returning to Japan. He and Saitō tried their best to argue that the extremist behaviors of Shindō Renmei members and their supporters was the sole result of the Japanese settlers' anxiety about the Brazilian government's oppressive wartime policies. In this way, they categorically denied the link between Shindō Renmei and Japanese culture, which they presented as inherently democratic and pacifist.[30]

FRONTIERSMEN AND PEACEMAKERS: DISCOVERING AUTHENTIC JAPANESENESS IN BRAZIL

The concept of culture served as a medium for the Japanese settler elites in Brazil to reconnect with Japan in the late 1940s. In the next two decades, against the backdrop of the Cold War, the Japanese in Brazil participated further in Japan's process of redefining its national identity and culture. In this role they were aided by the restarting of Japanese migration to Brazil in 1952, which led to a rapid increase in economic and cultural exchange between the two nations.

The temporary end of Vargas's presidency right after the war did not stop the close alliance between Brazil and the United States, which was substantially strengthened during World War II. Though having profound differences, Brazil and Japan were similar in terms of their positions as Cold War allies of the United States and recipients of U.S. financial aid. Therefore, both countries embraced the discourse of democracy and capitalist modernization at the same time. During the Cold War, as the settler colonial history of American frontier expansion became a story of the global triumph of democracy, freedom, and development, Japanese and Brazilian elites alike sought to incorporate similar themes into their new national narratives.[31]

One event that exemplified this endeavor on Japan's side occurred in 1948, when a bust of William S. Clark, which was melted down during the war, was recast and unveiled on Hokkaido University's campus. This event was illustrative of how the educated Japanese celebrated the history of Japan's colonization of Hokkaido as a shared experience of frontier expansion of the Japanese and the Americans, with an emphasis on the role played by the American experts in the process.[32] The reinvention of Japanese identity in the logic of settler colonialism took place hand in hand with the reemergence of Japan's migration state. Immediately after the conclusion of the U.S. Occupation, Tokyo started programs to relocate Japanese subjects to Latin American countries by reviving migration networks and organizations that existed before World War II.[33] As the Latin American country that received the largest number of Japanese immigrants before the war, Brazil naturally became the first Latin American destination of Japanese emigration after the war. In 1953, two groups of Japanese migrants reached the Brazilian shores. Known as the Tsuji migrants and the Matsubara migrants, they settled in the Amazon Basin and the state of Mato Grosso, respectively. They were followed by Tokyo-sponsored programs of emigration to southeastern Brazil and other Latin American countries such as Bolivia, Paraguay, Argentina, and the Dominican Republic.

Around the same time, Brazilian intellectuals continued to eulogize the bandeirantes (also known as Paulistas and Mamelucos) as brave frontiersmen who relentlessly expanded the country's borders, describing their tireless spirit as the national character of every Brazilian.[34] A commercial in 1954 praised "those men who came from other lands to mix their sweat and their blood to forge a race of daring people. Paulistas from every state of Brazil and from all the nations of the world here have fused together in the heat of a shared ideal of hard work."[35] The celebration of frontier history in Brazil was coupled with the nation's renewed efforts to attract immigrants after World War II.[36] The renewed state-sponsored immigration in Brazil after the war worked in tandem with the continuation of its internal settler colonialism. A landmark event was the establishment of Brasília as the new national capital in 1960 under the presidency of Juscelino Kubitschek, who embraced the Cold War ideology of modernization to legitimize Brazil's settler colonial past and present. Located in the state of Goiás, six hundred miles from the east coast and designed according to modern and futuristic concepts, Brasília symbolized the government's commitment to colonizing the interior, legitimized by the ideas of progress, national unification, and urbanization.[37]

Brazil's quadricentennial celebration of the founding of São Paulo in 1954 became an occasion where the Japanese and Brazilian narratives of frontier expansion converged. The Saturday Club members seized this opportunity to improve the Japanese settlers' image in Brazilian society at large. They pointed to the parallels between Japanese and Brazilian settler colonial narratives and positioned the Japanese immigrants in Brazil as agents of modernization. By doing so, they were able to present Japanese immigration as an important chapter in the glorious story of São Paulo–driven national progress, describing Japanese immigrants as indispensable contributors to the modernization of Brazil.

As the first step of this campaign, the Saturday Club members reached out to Ishigurō Shirō, Japanese consul general in São Paulo, as early as 1952. They emphasized the importance of Japanese settlers' active involvement in the occasion and sought financial aid from Tokyo. Yamamoto Kiyoshi, director of the Tozan Farm who led the Japanese settlers' committee for the quadricentennial celebration, traveled to Japan to raise awareness—and funds—from both the Japanese government and the general public for the forthcoming ceremony. Through migration networks established before World War II, Yamamoto was able to connect with a host of Japanese political and business leaders. He distributed pamphlets to them that explained the current situation of the Japanese community in Brazil, the significance of participating in the ceremony, and the request for financial aid. Yamamoto's seven-month stay in Japan proved to be successful: he obtained Tokyo's commitment of 190 million yen for building a Japanese pavilion for the ceremony.[38] More importantly, acting as an advocate for the Japanese Brazilian settlers, he was able to convince Japanese leaders that the Japanese settlers in Brazil were both important to and useful for Japan. In 1958, Yamamoto returned to Japan, this time seeking financial and political support to celebrate the fiftieth anniversary of Japanese migration to Brazil. He scored an even bigger victory: in addition to Tokyo's commitment of financial support, Prince Mikasa came to São Paulo to participate in the ceremony as an official representative of the Japanese royal family.[39]

At around the same time, Izumi Sei'ichi and Saitō Hiroshi jointly published a book explaining the past and present of the Japanese settlers in the Amazon region. The book was the result of a two-month field trip that the two had conducted in Tomé Açu (Pará) and Maués (Amazonas) during Izumi Sei'ichi's first visit to Brazil. Titled *The Amazon: Its Climate, Land, and the Japanese*, the book argued that Japanese settlers had proved themselves to be agents of progress in the region. By highlighting the settlers' success in transplanting jute and spice pepper from Asia to the Amazon and turning them into cash crops in Brazil, the book emphasized not only the dedication of the Japanese to the local community but also their superiority vis-à-vis the white settlers in adapting to the tropical climate. It also contained an ethnographic study of local women who married Japanese settlers, presenting them as happy wives. By doing so, the authors portrayed the Japanese settlers in the region as both open and well adapted to interracial marriage. This new narrative aimed to challenge the commonly assumed Japanese preference for endogamy due to their adherence to racial purity and refusal to assimilate.[40]

A few years later, Izumi Sei'ichi, who had already become a central figure in the field of Japanese cultural anthropology in the postwar era, arrived in São Paulo again with a team of researchers. His goal this time was to conduct a comprehensive study of the social conditions of Japanese settlers across Brazil. The final report, published as a book in 1957, made two interlocked claims. First, Izumi believed that the experience of migration provided a critical lens to examine the Japanese national character. Accordingly, he saw Brazil as a useful site to study the nature of Japaneseness. Second, having been well trained in the recent theories of assimilation in the United States, Izumi presented the Japanese settlers as champions of assimilation. He argued that with an advanced culture and a spirit for assimilation, the Japanese had successfully molded themselves into indispensable members of Brazilian society.[41]

As Izumi was heavily involved in Tokyo-sponsored research on colonial subjects during the imperial era, it was not a surprise that he uncritically embraced the concept of assimilation. Assimilation was viewed as the equivalent of the Japanese term *dōka*, an idea that the imperial government adopted to legitimize its cultural suppression of colonial subjects in Taiwan and Korea.[42] Through the experience of Japanese settlers' assimilation into Brazilian society, Izumi claimed, assimilation in human history was a natural and inevitable process. Accordingly, he made the crimes of Japanese colonialism in the recent past both forgivable and forgettable. Moreover, faithfully following the principles of the Culture and Personality school in the United States, Izumi assumed there was a Japanese culture and character that remained unchanged across space and time. As such, he saw the Japanese Brazilian experience as an extension of that of the Japanese. By describing Japanese assimilation into Brazilian society as contributing to modernization and development, Izumi redefined Japan's national character as both cosmopolitan and Western.[43]

To emphasize the shared character of the Japanese in Japan and the Japanese settlers in Brazil, Izumi termed the latter *imin*, the Japanese who migrated, and *Burajiru ni okeru Nihonjin*, the Japanese in Brazil. He also used these terms interchangeably with *koronia*, a term that the Japanese settler elites embraced after World War II as well.[44] The Portuguese word *colônia* had already been commonly used to refer to immigrant communities in Brazil. By naming their community Nikkei koronia (Colônia Japonesa), the Japanese settler elites sought to present themselves as part of the process of Brazilian nation making that combined settler colonialism with immigration. On the other hand, *colônia* could also be translated as "colonist" (*shokumin*) or "colony" (*shokuminchi*), which connected the stories of Japanese settlers in Brazil with the history of Japan's emigration-driven expansion. In this way, the settlers were presented as both fully integrated and contributing members of Brazilian society and subjects of the Japanese nation and empire. In the context of renewed emigration to Brazil, the term "Nikkei koronia" reflected how the settler elites positioned themselves as model Japanese subjects; they described themselves as a bridge between two countries and pioneers in Japan's mission to contribute to the world's modernization and development via peaceful emigration.

Izumi was not alone in his quest to reexamine the idea of Japaneseness in Brazil. Gamō Masao, a student of Izumi and a participant in his research in Brazil, adopted Izumi's approach in his own research. He later served as president of the Japanese Society for Cultural Anthropology, and in 1960 he published a book that considered the Japanese settler villages in Tomé Açu an important site for examining what he called the multisystemic nature (*takeisei*) of the structure of Japanese daily life (*Nihonjin no seikatsu kōzō*). Arguing against the prevailing claim of the closeness and homogeneity of Japanese culture advanced by scholars like Ruth Benedict, Gamō presented Japanese culture as heterogeneous and even self-contradictory. For him, Japan's great success in its ready embrace of Western democracy and modernization was precisely because of the open and multisystemic nature of Japanese culture and social experience.[45] The settler village in Tomé Açu, with what Gamō described as vibrant interactions with local residents and their smooth assimilation to Brazilian society, served as proof of this theory.[46]

The prominent journalist and writer Ōya Sōichi echoed this academic discourse. When he visited Brazil in 1954, he claimed that he saw a Japanese settler village that had preserved the spirit of Meiji- and Taishō-era Japan.[47] His observation was in line with the postwar narrative that extolled Meiji and Taishō as Japan's golden eras of Westernization while designating early Shōwa as a dark but abnormal period of militarism and destruction. For Ōya, the spirit of Meiji and Taishō was the true spirit of Japaneseness, which was marked by Westernization, democracy, and progress. To him, the Japanese settlers in Brazil were free of the taint of early Shōwa; therefore, they were the true representatives of Japaneseness, and their economic and cultural success in Brazil was proof of their cultural purity. "To see the Meiji and Taishō eras," he claimed, "you'd better go to Brazil."[48]

Mishima Yukio, one of the most widely read and controversial Japanese writers, also used the Japanese experience in Brazil as a lens to examine postwar Japanese society and lament the loss of its traditional spirit. Inspired by a trip to Brazil in 1951, he wrote an acclaimed play titled *A Termite Nest* (*Shiroari no su*), the main characters of which were two Japanese couples, one of them owners of a coffee farm in São Paulo and the other their driver and his wife. The owner, a seemingly generous and cultured man, was called a "democratic farm owner" (*minshu teki na enshu*): not only did he treat the farm employees with respect and was he willing to dine at the same table with them, but he also forgave his wife and the driver for their affair. However, he was eventually referred to as "a walking dead" who had lost his human vitality. On the other hand, though the driver's wife resented her husband's prior dalliance, she was eager to marry the owner and dreamed about herself becoming the new termite queen in the house. Termites, which constantly increase their colonies through reproduction and territorial expansion, served as an effective metaphor for Japanese settler colonialism in Brazil. For Mishima, the story of this coffee farm epitomized the society of postwar Japan, which embraced the Western language of democracy only to become culturally corrupted and lose its spiritual self.

In fact, the influence of the Japanese community in Brazil on the process of making and remaking Japaneseness is far from surprising; after all, the Cold War-era school of Japanese studies had originated from U.S. intellectuals' ethnographic research on Japanese Americans during World War II. For the same reason, Japanese Brazilians were not the only Japanese overseas who had shaped the debate surrounding Japaneseness. Japanese Americans too were crucial in the evolution of this knowledge production. However, the Japanese community in the United States served as a source of the past more than the future. Although Japanese migration to the United States resumed in 1952 with the McCarran-Walter Act, the number of migrants was restricted to 185 per year. As a major destination of Japanese immigration both before and after World War II, Brazil was a point of historical convergence where the Japanese community was positioned as a representation of both the past and the future of Japaneseness.

An example of this phenomenon was the nationwide population survey of Japanese settlers led by Suzuki Tei'ichi, a central leader of the Saturday Club. Stimulated by Izumi Sei'ichi's investigation, the settler elites launched the survey as the community's own project to record their history and achievements. Spanning six years, this project collected detailed information on Japanese settlers across Brazil that covered almost every aspect of their lives: age, occupation, location, economic status, marriage, education, family members, religion, language, and political participation. The survey arrived at the conclusion that the settlers achieved remarkable growth in population and brought economic prosperity to their host country. The settler elites employed the discourse of Malthusian expansionism, which Japan's empire builders had used to legitimize its migration-driven expansion before 1945, and blamed overpopulation as the primary reason for Japan's militarism.[49] By showcasing the settlers' great achievements in numbers, the survey presented Japanese migration to Brazil as a solution to the problem of overpopulation in Japan and the Japanese settlers as peacemakers of the world.[50] This claim fit impeccably with postwar Japanese elites' efforts to rebrand Japan as a pacifist country and the Japanese as a peace-loving people. In short, the survey provided much-needed evidence for elites in Japan to legitimize overseas emigration as an altruistic effort contributing to global peace and prosperity.

The survey was also an illustration of how the community building efforts of Japanese settlers in Brazil entwined with the reinvention of postwar Japan. To maximize the scope and depth of the investigation and overcome budgetary limitations, the Saturday Club members traveled to train local volunteers who would conduct the survey at the village level. Common settlers welcomed their efforts enthusiastically. The project itself, in effect, became a community building event that evolved into what Brazilian mainstream media claimed was the biggest population survey ever completed by a nongovernmental group.[51] By widely interacting with common settlers at the individual level, the survey also served as a critical occasion for the Saturday Club members to diffuse their elite-centered settler identity and further unite the community.

Fully aware of the potential value of the survey for Japan, the settler elites successfully lobbied Tokyo for both financial and technical assistance. Suzuki penned an article in the *Asahi shinbun*, arguing that the survey was important for the international image of the Japanese in general.[52] He brought the entire data set to Japan and completed the final analysis with researchers at Tohoku University and the University of Tokyo. The final results of the survey were published by the University of Tokyo Press in English under the title, *The Japanese Immigrant in Brazil* (*Burajiru no Nihon imin*), in 1964.[53]

THE DIVERGENCE BETWEEN JAPANESE AND JAPANESE BRAZILIANS

The year 1964 saw the peak of the collaborative efforts between the elites in Japan and the Japanese Brazilian community in the invention of the new Japanese national identity. In addition to publishing *The Japanese Immigrant in Brazil*, the Japanese Cultural Center opened in São Paulo that year. The building would become the home of a number of social and cultural associations for the Japanese settlers. Its centerpiece, Centro de Estudos Brasilerios (Sanpauro Jinbun Kagaku Kenkyūjo, or Jinmonken), would take shape the next year. Initially staffed and headed by the Saturday Club members, Jinmonken has served as the headquarters for the study of Japanese culture and the Japanese Brazilian community in Brazil ever since. It has functioned as a hub for collaboration between scholars in Japan and Brazil in Japanese studies and is the primary sponsor of most Brazil-based research on the Japanese Brazilian community. The opening of the Cultural Center also saw the unveiling of the bust of Yamamoto Kiyoshi, who had died a year earlier. The bust was placed inside the Cultural Center as a tribute to Yamamoto's leadership and contribution to postwar reconstruction of the settler community.[54]

The death of Yamamoto signified the end of an era in which elites on both sides of the Pacific Ocean collaborated closely to reinvent the national identity of postwar Japan. They had worked together to prove that the Japanese settlers in Brazil embodied and exemplified the ideal version of Japaneseness. In the late 1960s, however, the two sides' paths began to diverge. While Japanese mass media and intellectuals continued to view Japanese settlers in Brazil as representatives of Japaneseness who showcased the superiority of Japanese culture, the number of immigrants who saw themselves primarily as Japanese subjects declined quickly.

The Tokyo Olympics in 1964 heralded Japan's successful return to the global stage, this time as a modernizing, peace-loving, and democratic nation. By then, Japan had secured its position as a pivotal ally of the United States in East Asia. The Japanese economy had also started its decades-long high-speed growth that would turn the country into one of the largest economies in the world. These changes transformed studies of Japaneseness in the archipelago. Such studies in the 1950s primarily interpreted Japan's cultural uniqueness as evidence of Japan's ability to replicate the Euro-American process of modernization in the recent past. In the late 1960s, however, scholars and popular writers in Japan began to emphasize the differences between Japan's culture and that of the West. By doing so, they sought to prove the superiority of the former over the latter. The publication and popularity of Nakane Chie's *Japanese Society* in 1970 ushered in the golden age of Nihonjinron. In the following years, many Nihonjinron books were published that highlighted the family (*ie*) as the structural core of Japan's group-oriented society, in contrast to individual-centered Western societies.[55] It was this cultural difference, Nakane and her followers argued, that accounted for Japan's uniquely successful economic growth.

The conclusion of the Nihonjinron school spearheaded by Nakane Chie differed from that of the Culture and Personality school represented by Izumi Sei'ichi in terms of Japan's cultural location vis-à-vis that of the West. However, the impact of the discourse on national culture promoted by Izumi and his Japanese Brazilian collaborators in earlier decades on the rise of Nihonjinron was evident in the academic career of Nakane herself: she studied with Izumi Sei'ichi at the University of Tokyo and then joined him as a colleague at the same institution. The two had been academic collaborators since the 1950s.[56] They had coedited two volumes titled *Ningen no shakai* (Human Societies) in 1960 and 1961, which examined various societies across the globe by treating each as an isolated cultural system.[57]

Japan's growing economy also generated increasing domestic demand for labor. Emigration, as a result, was no longer a priority for Tokyo. Brazil—and Latin America in general—soon became a target of Japanese investment and economic exportation instead of a migration destination. Nevertheless, cultural elites in Japan continued to refer to Japanese settlers in Brazil and other Latin American countries as exemplifiers of Japanese excellence, though now for a very different reason. While they had previously focused on praising the Japanese ability to assimilate into their host society, now they were no longer interested in assimilation if not outright opposed to it. Instead, they emphasized the supposedly unique capacity of the Japanese to modernize the local society.

The Japanese government endorsed these efforts and sponsored some of these writers' trips to Brazil.[58] One of the Tokyo-backed writers was Tsunoda Fusako, a prolific and award-winning nationalist author who penned several books in the 1960s and 1970s, including two about the Amazon that celebrated the Japanese sacrifice and achievement in civilizing Brazil's primitive land.[59] Around the same period, Tsunoda published two books that described the Japanese settlers in Manchuria as victims of war and colonialism.[60] According to Tsunoda, the experiences of Japanese migrants to the opposite sides of the Pacific ended very differently: those in Brazil successfully carried out their mission, whereas those in Manchuria were met with tragedy due to the collapse of the Japanese empire. However, in Tsunoda's description, both groups of Japanese settlers were innocent and sacrificial agents of modernization.

Some Western scholars supported this new approach. For example, the British scholar Philip Staniford used the case study of Tomé Açu to argue that the unique social and cultural norms of the Japanese allowed them to become successful farmers and modernizers in the Amazon region.[61] Yet others, like the Japanologists John B. Cornell at the University of Texas at Austin and Robert Smith at Cornell University, remained committed to the framework of assimilation. Cornell and Smith came to Brazil in the 1960s and 1970s and conducted a study titled "Texas, Cornell, and São Paulo Research Project." It examined Japanese immigrants' assimilation process in southeastern Brazil.[62] Maeyama Takashi, who emerged during this period as one of the most cited scholars in Japan in the study of the Japanese Brazilian experience, worked closely with Cornell and Smith on this project. Yet Maeyama, like other mainstream scholars in Japan during this period, had his doubts about the assimilation approach. He later criticized Cornell and Smith's research as West-centered in the sense that it saw Western civilization as the standard for human progress and judged non-Western societies based on how well they were able to replicate or adapt to the Western model.[63]

While the assimilation approach lost popularity in Japan during this period, elites in the Japanese Brazilian community continued to hold it as their central value. In addition to economic and political changes in East Asia, this divergence between Japan and the Japanese community in Brazil reflected the generational shift and change in social status of Japanese Brazilians. The Issei, the generation of Japanese settlers in Brazil who had the strongest ties with Japan, were passing into history. Saturday Club members like Saitō Hiroshi and Suzuki Tei'ichi continued to be active in the 1970s, but even they had shifted their focus to ensuring the next generation could become mainstream Brazilians. This generational shift proceeded hand in hand with a "middle-class" transformation of the settler community's economic and social status between the 1930s and 1950s, taking place in the context of the state of São Paulo's rapid industrialization and urbanization.

Taking advantage of the transwar economic boom in São Paulo and the wealth accumulated thanks to the price increase of agricultural goods during World War II, many Japanese farming settlers moved to the cities and started family businesses like fruit shops and cleaning services. These business-owning families were joined by a fast-growing Nisei population that moved to cities like São Paulo to pursue higher education and entered white-collar occupations on graduation.[64] While 92 percent of Japanese settlers in the state of São Paulo resided in the countryside in 1934, nearly half of the settler population had moved to urban areas by 1958.[65] This number climbed to 90 percent in 1988.[66]

The change in socioeconomic status took place in tandem with Japanese settlers' increased domestic political participation in Brazil. Beginning with Tamura Yukishige, who became the first municipal (1948), state (1950), and then federal (1954) lawmaker of Japanese ancestry in Brazil, more and more Nisei became elected policy makers. This number reached 28 in 1968 and grew to 137 in 1972. In 1969, Fabio Yasuda became the first minister of Japanese ancestry in the federal government.[67] For the Nisei and their descendants, Japanese ethnicity continued to be an important identity that marked them as what Gaku Tsuda called a "positive" minority in Brazil.[68] Yet, at the same time, interracial marriage between Japanese Brazilians and other ethnic groups skyrocketed: in 1958, 13 percent of Japanese settlers were in interracial marriages; by 1988, the number had increased

FIGURE 28. A photo of the Japanese crown prince Akihito and the Brazilian president Ernesto Geisel greeting a crowd of 80,000 Japanese immigrants in São Paulo during the ceremony for the seventieth anniversary of Japanese migration to Brazil. Source: *Shūkan Sankei: Tokubetsu Gurafu,* no. 81 (1978): 3.

to 58 percent.[69] Accordingly, while only 6 percent of the Nisei Japanese Brazilians were interracial, among the *sansei* (third generation) and *yonsei* (fourth generation), the interracial rate climbed to 42 percent and 62 percent, respectively.[70]

In 1978, the *Mainichi shinbun* sponsored an international symposium titled, "Nippaku shinjidai to kokusai kōryū" (The New Era of Japan and Brazil and International Exchange). The event brought to light a clear separation between the elites in Japan and the Japanese Brazilian community in terms of their understanding of Japanese Brazilian identity. Though the symposium had aimed to find a common ground, it ultimately revealed an unbridgeable gap. Umesao Tadao, director-general of Japan's National Museum of Ethnology, was the symposium's keynote speaker. He argued that history had proved that racial assimilation was an unsuccessful and outdated approach to nation making and predicted that Brazil would become a new model of the multicultural nation. Each of the ethnic groups in the nation should be able to maintain their own cultural identities. The Japanese in Brazil, he argued, would make a critical contribution in this regard. Suzuki Tei'ichi, then director of Jinmonken in São Paulo, was also invited to speak at the symposium. Contrary to Umesao, Suzuki asserted that the Japanese immigrants in Brazil were destined to become fully assimilated Brazilians. He also happily proclaimed that complete assimilation was only a matter of time thanks to the superb assimilating power of the Japanese race, which, he argued, was attested by both history since ancient times and the present demographic change of the Japanese community in Brazil.[71]

The year 1978 also saw the ceremony for the seventieth anniversary of Japanese Brazilian migration in São Paulo. Known as the last anniversary ceremony hosted by the Issei, the event symbolized the end of Issei leadership in the community. Japan's then crown prince, Akihito, arrived in São Paulo again and attended the ceremony with Brazilian president Ernesto Geisel. The ceremony presented Japanese Brazilians as a unified, prosperous, and patriotic ethnic group in Brazil. As part of the celebration, the Historical Museum of Japanese Immigration in Brazil (Museu Histórico da Imigração Japonesa no Brasil) opened to the public in São Paulo. The primary designer of the museum, Saitō Hiroshi, modeled it after the Historical Museum of Hokkaido (Hokkaido Kaitaku Kinenkan) in Sapporo. Much like how the latter presented the history of Japanese colonization of Hokkaido as a triumph of human civilization, the Historical Museum of Japanese Immigration in Brazil described the history of Japanese collaborative settler colonialism in Brazil as a consistent story of modernization and development.[72] The opening of the museum, however, also marked the end of the Issei-centered narrative, which itself had become the history on display in the museum.

In the same year, the Nisei intellectual Saitō Hiroshi published a book in Japan titled, *The Japanese Who Have Become Foreigners* (*Gaikokujin ni natta Nihonjin*). It synthesized a collection of essays that Saitō had published in Japan and Brazil in past decades and presented assimilation as a natural and inevitable path for the Japanese in Brazil, one that began with the sailing of the *Kasato Maru* and ended with interracial marriages. Saitō described this process as a linear history and divided it into three stages. He defined the Japanese migrants at each of the stages as Nihonjin (Japanese), Nikkeijin (Japanese Brazilians, or Japanese overseas), and Burajirujin (Brazilians). The happy ending of this process, accordingly, was when Japanese migrants became fully assimilated Brazilians.[73]

The migration states of Japan and Brazil, as examined in this study, eventually came to an end. Following rapid economic growth and an increasing demand for labor in Japan, Tokyo ceased sponsoring emigration abroad in the 1970s, and

Japan has become an immigrant-receiving country. Conversely, Brazil was struck by an economic recession and reversed its migration policy, transforming from a recipient to a sender of migrants. These transformations in Japan and Brazil jointly led to the onset of labor migration of Brazilians of Japanese ancestry to Japan.

. . .

This chapter explains how Japanese Brazilian Issei elites reunited their community by reviving their connections with Japan immediately after World War II. Rebuilding their cultural ties with Japan allowed them to rebrand the image of Japanese settlers in Brazil. At the same time, they also participated in the reinvention of Japan's postwar national and cultural identity. The interactions between Japanese elites and intellectuals in the Japanese Brazilian community consolidated and popularized the idea of a unique and progressive Japanese national character among Japanese intellectuals and public media in the 1950s and 1960s. It eventually fostered the rise of Nihonjinron, a popular school of thought that holds sway in Japan even today.

The rise of Japan as an economic powerhouse took place simultaneously with generational and social status changes within the Japanese Brazilian community. These two factors together led to the demise of the once-close ideological alliance between Japanese Brazilian elites and their counterparts in Japan. The former maintained that the only future path for the Japanese community was their full assimilation into Brazilian society. Accordingly, they saw the success of this assimilation as evidence of Japanese racial superiority. The latter, on the other hand, had discarded the concept of assimilation. Instead, they highlighted the uniqueness of the Japanese cultural and social experience and saw it as the primary reason for postwar Japan's unparalleled success in economic development and modernization.

The intellectual divergence between Japanese and Japanese Brazilian elites led to the end of the Japanese Brazilians' participation in the ongoing process of Japanese identity making. However, Saitō's theory of the three-stage development of the Japanese Brazilian community failed to materialize. The full assimilation model proved unpragmatic, as Brazilians of Japanese ancestry continued to benefit from their Japaneseness. On the one hand, they enjoyed the ethnic and social privileges associated with being the "positive minority" in Brazil.[74] On the other hand, given the increasingly wide economic gap between Japan and Brazil, descendants of Japanese immigrants in Brazil began to migrate to Japan as foreign workers. Referred to as the *dekasegi*, they often filled a demand for cheap labor. However, they were paid more than they would have been paid in Brazil and enjoyed a special visa status as Nikkeijin that gave them the legal right to a long-term stay in Japan. In this way, they continued to be part of the process of Japanese identity making. However, whereas their predecessors in the 1950s and 1960s were held up as exemplifiers of the authentic Japan, the dekasegi Nikkeijin would serve as a foil to genuine Japaneseness because of their Latin American cultural and racial background. In this sense, they joined other marginalized ethnic groups in Japan such as the Koreans, Okinawans, and the Ainu as the living legacies of Japan's colonial empire.

Conclusion

In 1961, at the age of twenty-eight, Maeyama Takashi, born in Hokkaido and raised in northeastern Honshu, left Japan for Brazil. During his studies for a bachelor's degree in philosophy, Maeyama had encountered *Tristes tropiques*, a memoir by the French anthropologist Claude Lévi-Strauss that documented his experiences and thoughts while conducting ethnographic studies of Indigenous tribes in Brazil. Deeply inspired, Maeyama decided to go to Brazil to study Indigenous cultures.[1] However, after he began studying at the University of São Paulo, he was invited by Saitō Hiroshi, then professor at the university, to join a collaborative research project led by the American Japanologists John B. Cornell and Robert Smith on the Japanese community in Brazil.[2] After completing his PhD in Latin American Studies at Cornell University and teaching for a couple of years at the University of São Paulo, Maeyama returned to Japan, where he went on to become one of the most influential and innovative scholars in the study of the Japanese Brazilian community.

Trained as a cultural anthropologist, Maeyama's academic career demonstrates the evolution of the ethnic studies framework in the study of the Japanese community in Brazil. Maeyama started studying Japanese immigrants in Brazil by joining Cornell and Smith's project, which was centered on the Japanese immigrants' assimilation into Brazilian society. Maeyama's participation in the project, however, led him to question the usefulness of the concept "assimilation" in terms of fully grasping the experience of Japanese settlers in Brazil.[3] His first monograph, *Hisōzokusha no seishinshi* (A Psychohistory of the People of No Inheritance Rights), examines the history of Japanese immigrants in Brazil by focusing on the social status of the migrants in their homeland and its impact on their new life in Brazil.[4] The impressive success of Japanese immigration to Brazil, he reasoned, was the result of a unique mentality possessed by the first-generation Japanese immigrants. Most of them were second and third sons in the Japanese countryside and by law had no inheritance rights in their own households. Maeyama argued that it was their lack of access to familial wealth that made them especially eager to succeed in the new land as migrants. Thanks to this distinctively Japanese "hisōzokusha" (people of no inheritance rights) mentality, the immigrants were frugal and hardworking, which allowed them to achieve economic success despite facing racial discrimination and marginalization in Brazil.[5]

Maeyama's next monograph, *Imin no Nihon kaiki undō* (The Immigrants' Movement of Returning to Japan), went a step further to explore the changes and divides among Japanese immigrant elites regarding their ethnic identities in Brazil. In particular, Maeyama explained how the Japanese settler elites were caught between Tokyo's nationalist propaganda and the tide of ethnic nationalism in the Estado Novo, a situation that eventually led to a long-lasting divide in the community that continued after World War II.[6] His third major book, *Esunishitei to Burajiru Nikkeijin* (Ethnicity and Japanese Brazilians), explained the ways the Japanese immigrants' identity took shape as a result of their in-betweenness, namely, as imperial subjects of the Japanese empire and as an ethnic minority in Brazil.[7]

Maeyama's scholarship demonstrates both the achievement and limitation of the ethnic studies approach. Unlike the generation of Japanologists before him such as Izumi Sei'ichi, Saitō Hiroshi, as well as Smith and Cornell, Maeyama refused to take the concept of assimilation as a given and situated the identity formation of Japanese settlers in Japan's and Brazil's historical contexts. Different from specialists of modern Brazil whose scholarship on the topic has been exclusively based on Portuguese sources, Maeyama's comprehensive use of primary sources in both Japanese and Portuguese allowed him to analyze the Japanese settlers' minds and activities with increased sophistication. Nevertheless, his scholarship remains confined within the ethnic studies framework, which neglects the settler colonial nature of Japanese immigration. Maeyama's failure to recognize the connections between the predicament of the Indigenous people and the achievements of Japanese immigrants is especially disappointing, as he had ventured into both fields during his dynamic academic career. He initially arrived in Brazil to study Indigenous cultures and only later turned to the study of the Japanese Brazilian community.

Explaining these connections is the starting point of this book, which places Japanese migration and community formation in Brazil in the context of settler colonialism in both Brazil and Japan. I have analyzed Japanese immigration as part of state-driven settler colonialism in Brazil in the late nineteenth and twentieth centuries and termed this process collaborative settler colonialism. Immigrants from Japan, together with those from Europe, served as the Brazilian state's agents in the appropriation of Indigenous land. The Japanese immigrants themselves were also beneficiaries in this process: while most of them arrived in Brazil as plantation laborers, over half had managed to become landowning farmers by the outbreak of the Pacific War, in large part thanks to the land policies of the Brazilian government.[8] Although the Japanese were victims of racial discrimination at all levels of Brazilian society, as this book demonstrates, they were also instrumental for the Brazilian government, at the national and state levels, in carrying out its settler colonial policies.

Acknowledging Japanese immigrants as collaborators of Brazilian settler colonialism also allows us to confront the fact that the Japanese replicated the logic of white racism in Brazil and viewed other residents—especially the Indigenous, caboclos, and other peoples of color—with prejudice. Discussion of racist beliefs and practices by the Japanese immigrants themselves has been generally absent in the ethnic studies scholarship. Such racial discrimination was the product of the convergence of the racial ideologies of both Brazil and the Japanese empire. The immigrant elites used "dojin," the same word that the Japanese used to label Indigenous people in the Japanese empire, to describe the Indigenous people and caboclos in Brazil.[9] In their imagination, these dojin not only had a lower standard of morality, but were incapable of making good use of their own land. This supposed inferiority was derived from the primitivity of the Brazilian land itself, untamed nature waiting for salvation by modern civilization that the Japanese represented. For these reasons, the Japanese settler elites adopted a racist attitude toward the Brazilians in general. They embraced the popular theory of racial assimilation in Brazil that emerged in the early twentieth century and urged Japanese immigrants to uplift the Brazilian racial stock by mixing with the locals through intermarriage.[10] Such racist attitudes continued after World War II and were reinforced by the rapid rise of Japan as an economic powerhouse.[11]

Japanese community and identity making in Brazil was also part of Japan's emigration-driven expansion. Brazil-bound migration shared ideological and material connections with Japan's emigration to its colonial territories in Asia, including Hokkaido, Taiwan, Korea, Manchuria, and the South Seas. By not taking the geographic boundaries of the Japanese empire as inherent limits, I have analyzed the role that Japanese settler elites in Brazil played in the making of Japan's colonial empire and its postwar transition to a nation-state. Moreover, by acknowledging Japanese emigration to Brazil as part of the history of Japanese settler colonialism, I challenge the conventional periodization of the Japanese colonial empire and propose a new chronology of Japanese settler colonialism, one that begins in the early Meiji era and ends in 1978, the seventieth anniversary of Japanese immigration to Brazil. With a broader definition of settler colonialism, this new chronology transcends both the geographic and temporal boundaries of the Japanese empire. It highlights the impact of anti-Asian racism in the United States on Japanese expansion, on the one hand, and sheds light on the transwar continuity of Japanese emigration, on the other.

The history of Japanese migration and community building in Brazil also epitomizes the convergence of Japan's and Brazil's historical paths. Even before the arrival of the Japanese empire's pioneers in Brazil, the historical trajectories of the two countries in the nineteenth century had already shown similarities in empire building. Elites in both Tokyo and Rio de Janeiro, inspired by the ongoing westward expansion of the United States, associated the concept of migration with colonial expansion. The voyage of the *Kasato Maru*, the ship that transported the first official group of Japanese immigrants to Brazil in the early twentieth century, was the culmination of several historical processes occurring simultaneously across the Pacific Ocean. These included the Japanese expansionists' advocacy of overseas emigration, the rise of anti-Japanese sentiment in the United States, and the rapid growth of Brazil's coffee economy, all of which were indispensable factors at the onset of this migration. The development and proliferation of Japanese farming villages in southeastern Brazil through the 1930s unfolded within three distinct yet interconnected settings: Brazil's railway expansion and new land distribution policies in the state of São Paulo; the evolution of Japanese colonialism in Korea and the South Seas; and the establishment of a new world order after World War I. Consequently, the collective identity of the Japanese immigrants in southeastern Brazil was shaped by both Japan's colonial expansion in Asia and the surge of Brazilian ethnic nationalism. Similarly, the Japanese migration to and investment in the Brazilian Amazon during the 1930s paralleled Japanese expansionism in the Asia-Pacific region and Brazil's settler colonialism in its tropical forests. After World War II, the Brazilian Amazon became a focal point for renewed Japanese migration, attributable to the persisting ideology and practice of settler colonialism in both Japan and Brazil throughout the Cold War. The story of Japanese migration to Brazil further reveals the historical convergence of the modernizing powers in East Asia and Latin America in general, which strove to join the race of modern empires for wealth and power in the nineteenth and twentieth centuries.

"Collaborative settler colonialism" describes the multidimensional connections that Japanese immigrants had with settler colonialism in both Japan and Brazil. This concept also invites a reexamination of the settler/native binary in the broader literature of settler colonialism. Patrick Wolfe asserted a strict binary structure within settler societies, claiming that every non-Indigenous individual is a settler. He even argued that slaves, who were forcibly transported to settler nations and colonies, should be considered settlers because the lack of voluntarism does not change their roles as settlers, as defined by the social structure itself.[12] From the perspective of Indigenous peoples, many scholars endorse Wolfe's position. In a recent edited volume exploring settler colonialism in Hawai'i, a cohort of scholars categorized immigrants from Asian countries, such as Japan, China, and the Philippines, as settlers on the islands. They contend that the immigrants' labor and political campaigns reinforced rather than challenged Hawai'i's existing settler colonial structure.[13] In contrast, there are scholars who contend that immigrants, especially those of color, are neither settlers nor Indigenous. Lorenzo

Veracini, for instance, challenges Wolfe by redefining the structure of U.S. settler colonialism as a "trialogue" among settlers, natives, and Black people.[14] Iyko Day supports this triadic framework by illustrating how the settler colonial structure in North America ultimately facilitated anti-Asian racism, which cast Asian laborers as aliens and legitimized their exclusion.[15]

Both the binary framework and the triadic approach examine immigrants in white settler societies primarily at a conceptual level. Scholars from either perspective have seldom investigated the immigrants' own agency. In contrast, I have focused on the ideas, activities, and identities of Japanese immigrants in transnational contexts. Using the term "collaborative settler colonialism," I have explained in detail how Japanese immigrants adopted the settler colonial ideologies of both Japan and Brazil and partnered with settler colonial regimes as agents of expansion. Consequently, this study proposes a new approach to understanding settler colonialism that places the experiences and agency of immigrants at the forefront of the inquiry.

NOTES

INTRODUCTION

1. Art Institute of Chicago, "Window on the West: Chicago and the Art of the New Frontier, 1890–1940," accessed May 1, 2023, https://archive.artic.edu/window/themes.html.

2. Frederick Jackson Turner, *The Frontier in American History* (New York: Henry Holt and Company, 1921), 1–38.

3. *Nihon gaikō bunsho dejitaru ākaibu* 26 (1893), 614–15.

4. Two million was an estimation by the Japanese Ministry of Foreign Affairs in 2019. Ministry of Foreign Affairs of Japan, "Japan-Brazil Relations," accessed May 1, 2023, https://www.mofa.go.jp/region/latin/brazil/data.html.

5. The Brazilian elites' admiration of U.S. settler colonialism was shared by leaders of a number of other Latin American nations.

6. One of the most impressive exhibitions at the fair was titled "Anthropology: Man and His Works." Curated by Harvard professor Frederic Putnam and his chief assistant, Franz Boas, the exhibition featured an anthropological and archaeological display to showcase the advancement of North American scientific institutions in these fields. Sven Schuster, "The World's Fairs as Spaces of Global Knowledge: Latin American Archaeology and Anthropology in the Age of Exhibitions," *Journal of Global History* 13, no. 1 (March 2018): 75.

7. Nitobe Inazō, *The Imperial Agricultural College of Sapporo* (Sapporo: Imperial Agricultural College of Sapporo, 1893), 1–2. Cited in Michele M. Mason and Helen J. S. Lee, eds., *Reading Colonial Japan: Text, Context, and Critique* (Stanford: Stanford University Press, 2012), 39–40.

8. Schuster, "The World's Fairs as Spaces of Global Knowledge," 80.

9. "Settler colonialism" is a term that has been embraced by scholars in recent decades to describe a specific form of colonialism. The primary distinction between settler colonialism and more common forms of colonialism in modern times is threefold. First, unlike the common forms of colonialism that focused on exploiting native labor, settler colonialism

emphasizes the acquisition of Indigenous land. Second, settler colonialism is characterized by migration, community formation, and permanent settlement, often resulting in settlers becoming the majority population in local societies. Third, as settlers usually become the majority population in the colonized society, settler colonialism typically cannot be overthrown like other forms of colonialism.

10. Jeffrey Lesser, *Negotiating National Identity: Immigrants, Minorities, and the Struggle for Ethnicity in Brazil* (Durham, NC: Duke University Press, 1999), 82–135; and *Immigration, Ethnicity, and National Identity, 1808 to the Present* (New York: Cambridge University Press, 2013), 150–76.

11. In earlier studies I introduced the concept of the migration state, which describes the fact that the Japanese government has played the central role in promoting and managing Japan's overseas emigration since the mid-1920s. See Sidney Xu Lu, *The Making of Japanese Settler Colonialism: Malthusianism and Trans-Pacific Migration, 1868–1961* (New York: Cambridge University Press, 2019), 183–205; and "Toward a Prototype of the Total Empire: Japanese Migration to Brazil and Japanese Colonial Expansion in Asia, 1921–1934," in *The Japanese Empire and Latin America*, ed. Pedro Iacobelli Delpiano and Sidney Xu Lu (Honolulu: University of Hawai'i Press, 2023), 63–92.

In this book, I have revised the meaning of this concept to refer to any government that is heavily involved in migration promotion and management for the purpose of settler colonialism.

12. For example, Mark Choate has explained the critical role of the government in promoting Italian emigration and nurturing nationalism among Italians abroad. Mark Choate, *Emigrant Nation: The Making of Italy Abroad* (Cambridge, MA: Harvard University Press, 2008). Aristide Zolberg, on the other hand, demonstrates how immigration policy had served the U.S. government as an essential tool for nation building in different times in history. Aristide Zolberg, *A Nation by Design: Immigration Policy in the Fashioning of America* (Cambridge, MA: Harvard University Press, 2006).

In the case of Japan, Toake Endoh's research has explained the ideology, intention, and institutions of the Japanese government related to its policies on immigration to Latin America both during the era of the empire and after World War II. Toake Endoh, *Exporting Japan: Politics of Emigration toward Latin America* (Urbana: University of Illinois Press, 2009); and "Turning the Water into Fair Pools: Prewar Japan's Paternalistic Outreach in Its South American Emigration Policy," in Delpiano and Lu, *The Japanese Empire and Latin America*, 16–36.

13. Volker Barth and Roland Cvetkovski, eds., *Imperial Co-operation and Transfer, 1870–1930: Empires and Encounters* (London: Bloomsbury Academic, 2015), 7–14.

14. A notable exception: James Belich, *Replenishing the Earth: The Settler Revolution and the Rise of the Anglo-World* (Oxford: Oxford University Press, 2011), offers a comprehensive analysis of the connections between American westward expansion and British settler colonial expansion across the world. It terms both as a part of the "settler revolution" that led to the rise of what he defined as the "Anglo-World." Yet the book remains West-focused.

15. Tessa Morris-Suzuki, *Re-inventing Japan: Nation, Culture, Identity* (New York: Routledge, 1997), 85.

16. In one of his most influential essays, Fukuzawa urged the Japanese to embrace Western civilization and leave Asian civilization behind. Fukuzawa Yukichi, "Datsua ron,"

in *Fukuzawa Yukichi chosakushū*, vol. 8 (Tokyo: Keiō Gijuku Daigaku Shuppankai, 2003), 261–65.

17. Takahashi Yoshio, *Nihon jinshu kairyōron* (Tokyo: Ishikawa Hanjirō, 1884).

18. Fukuzawa Yukichi, "Fuki kōmyo wa oya yuzuri no kuni ni kagirazu," in *Fukuzawa Yukichi zenshū*, vol. 9 (Tokyo: Iwanami Shoten, 1960), 546.

19. *Hokkaido kaitaku zasshi* (*HKZ*), mouthpiece of the Hokkaido Development Agency, the primary government branch in charge of colonizing Hokkaido, published many articles that emphasized the inferiority of the Ainu and the superiority of the Japanese. To name a few examples, "Kaitaku zasshi hakkō no shushi," *HKZ*, no. 1 (January 31, 1880): 2–3. "Hokkaido wa kosan no chi naru setsu," *HKZ*, no. 17 (September 11, 1880): 387. Nōgu kairyō ron," *HKZ*, no. 3 (February 28, 1880): 59.

20. Richard Siddle, *Race, Resistance, and the Ainu of Japan* (New York: Routledge, 1996), 69–70.

21. For example, Naoko Shimazu has demonstrated that stopping racist campaigns against Japanese immigration in the Anglo-American countries was the primary goal behind Japan's diplomatic efforts to include the "racial equality" clause in the Treaty of Versailles. Naoko Shimazu, *Japan, Race, and Equality: The Racial Equality Proposal of 1919* (London: Routledge, 1998), 68–88.

22. Lesser, *Immigration, Ethnicity, and National Identity in Brazil*, 26.

23. Lesser, *Immigration, Ethnicity, and National Identity in Brazil*, 28–52.

24. Lesser, *Immigration, Ethnicity, and National Identity in Brazil*, 60–62.

25. Todd A. Diacon, *Stringing Together a Nation: Cândido Mariano da Silva Rondon and the Construction of a Modern Brazil, 1906–1930* (Durham, NC: Duke University Press, 1991), 30–51.

26. Diacon, *Stringing Together a Nation*, 115–18.

27. Thomas Skidmore, *Black into White: Race and Nationality in Brazilian Thought* (Durham, NC: Duke University Press, 1992), 121–44.

28. An example is the book *Shokuminchi toshite no burajiru* (Brazil as a Colony), published in Japan in 1914, which described Brazil as an empty land blessed with limitless natural resources waiting for the Japanese to colonize it. It described the original owners, the Indigenous people, as uncivilized and incapable of utilizing the land and its resources. Furthermore, the majority of the existing population, claimed the book, were a racial mixture of whites, Blacks, and Indigenous. For this reason, they did not racially discriminate against the Japanese as white Americans did in the United States. Kawada Shirō, *Shokuminchi toshite no burajiru* (Tokyo: Yūhikaku Shobō, 1914), 1–25, 242.

29. Anna Paulina Lee, *Mandarin Brazil: Race, Representation, and Memory* (Stanford: Stanford University Press, 2018), 37–42.

30. Lesser, *Negotiating Ethnic Identity*, 108.

31. Lesser, *Negotiating Ethnic Identity*, 104–5.

32. Miriam L. Kingsberg, "Japan's Inca Boom: Global Archaeology and the Making of a Postwar Nation," *Monumenta Nipponica* 69, no. 2 (2014): 223–24.

33. Kingsberg, "Japan's Inca Boom," 224.

34. This can be attested by the support offered by Vargas and the governments of Pará and Amazonas to Japanese settlers' jute cultivation and commodification, as chapter 7 shows.

35. Takeyuki Tsuda, *Strangers in the Ethnic Homeland: Japanese Brazilian Return Migration in Transnational Perspective* (New York: Columbia University Press, 2003), 65.

36. One of the most successful public history projects along this line is *100 Years of Japanese Emigration to Brazil*, an online exhibition curated and presented by Japan's National Diet Library. Made available in 2008 to celebrate the centenary of the sailing of *Kasato Maru*, this project exemplifies the narrative of ethnic studies as a saga of immigration. The project, available in Japanese, Portuguese, and English, is ongoing. It continues to expand with newly added primary sources and historical details. Two innovative monographs have synthesized the experience of Japanese immigration to Brazil in the past with the experience of Japanese Brazilian labor migration to Japan in the present through the lens of ethnic studies: Tsuda, *Strangers in the Ethnic Homeland*; Meiko Nishida, *Diaspora and Identity: Japanese Brazilians in Brazil and Japan* (Honolulu: University of Hawai'i Press, 2017).

37. Herbert S. Klein and Francisco Vidal Luna, *Feeding the World: Brazil's Transformation into a Modern Agricultural Economy* (New York: Cambridge University Press, 2018), 11.

38. Joe Foweraker, *The Struggle for Land: A Political Economy of the Pioneer Frontier in Brazil from 1930 to the Present Day* (New York: Cambridge University Press, 1981), 210.

39. See Lesser, *Negotiating National Identity*; and *Immigration, Ethnicity, and National Identity in Brazil*.

40. Erika Lee, "The 'Yellow Peril' and Asian Exclusion in the Americas," *Pacific Historical Review* 76, no. 4 (November 2007): 538.

41. Miguel de Oliveira Couto, the brains behind Brazil's quota restriction on immigration in the 1930s, declared that he did not believe the Japanese were inferior. The immigration quota should be imposed on the Japanese, he said, because they failed to assimilate. Maeyama Takashi, *Imin no nihon kaiki undō* (Tokyo: Nihon Hōsō Shuppan Kyōkai, 1982), 93.

42. This can be seen in the rise of the colonial literature movement among Japanese settler writers in the 1920s and 1930s in São Paulo, as documented by Edward Mack and Seth Jacobowitz. Edward Mack, "Paracolonial Literature: Japanese-Language Literature in Brazil," *Ilbon yŏngu*, no. 16 (2011): 116–21; Seth Jacobowitz, "'A Bitter Brew': Coffee and Labor in Japanese Brazilian Immigrant Literature," *Estudos Japanese*, no. 41 (2019): 13–30.

43. For discussion of the discourse on overseas expansion, see Eiichiro Azuma, *In Search of Our Frontier: Japanese America and Settler Colonialism in the Construction of Japan's Borderless Empire* (Oakland: University of California Press, 2019), 32.

44. For example, in Brazilian Portuguese, "Colônia Italiana" could indicate either individual settler villages built by Italian immigrants or the entire Italian community in Brazil. This book uses the term "colony" as it was used historically in Brazil. It refers to Japanese settler communities as "colonies," and "colonies" and "settler communities" are used interchangeably.

45. Daniel Masterson, *The Japanese in Latin America* (Urbana: University of Illinois Press, 2003), 11–84; Ayumi Takenaka, "The Immigrant-Homeland Connection: The Development of the Japanese Community in Peru," in Delpiano and Lu, *The Japanese Empire and Latin America*, 126–44.

46. Michael Goebel, "Settler Colonialism in Postcolonial Latin America," in *The Routledge Handbook of the History of Settler Colonialism*, ed. Edward Cavanagh and Lorenzo Veracini (London: Routledge, 2017), 139–40, 147–48.

47. In the field of Japanese history, the exemplary works in recent years include but are not limited to Brett Walker, *The Conquest of the Ainu Lands: Ecology and Culture in*

Japanese Expansion, 1590–1800 (Berkeley: University of California Press, 2006); Katsuya Hirano, "Thanatopolitics in the Making of Japan's Hokkaido: Settler Colonialism and Primitive Accumulation," *Critical Historical Studies* 2, no. 2 (Fall 2015): 191–218; Jun Uchida, *Brokers of Empire: Japanese Settler Colonialism in Korea, 1876–1945* (Cambridge, MA: Harvard University Asia Center, 2016); Azuma, *In Search of Our Frontier*; Lu, *The Making of Japanese Settler Colonialism*. Likewise, scholars of Latin American studies have made fruitful critiques of and engagement with the Anglo-American-centered literature in settler colonialism. Two notable and collective efforts are the special issues of *American Quarterly* and *Settler Colonial Studies*, respectively: M. Bianet Castellanos, *Settler Colonialism in Latin America, American Quarterly* 69, no. 4 (December 2017); Lucy Taylor and Geraldine Lublin, *Settler Colonial Studies and Latin America, Settler Colonial Studies* 11, no. 3 (2021).

48. Examples of recent scholarship are Lucy Riall, "Hidden Spaces of Empire: Italian Colonists in Nineteenth-Century Peru," *Past & Present* 254, no. 1 (February 2022): 193–233; Goebel, "Settler Colonialism in Postcolonial Latin America."

49. For example, classic works on settler colonialism that have defined the field itself were almost exclusively situated in Anglo-American contexts. In their critique of settler colonialism, they focused exclusively on the experiences of white settler elites who participated in the formation of the colonial states and societies. None treated the immigrants who arrived afterward as colonial settlers or included their experiences in the discussion of settler colonialism. In this way, the experience of colonial settlers and immigrants were separated from each other, with the former shouldering the guilt and responsibility of colonial crimes and tragedies and the latter deemed completely innocent. See, e.g., Patrick Wolfe, "Settler Colonialism and the Elimination of the Native," *Journal of Genocide Research* 8, no. 4 (December 2006): 387–409; Lorenzo Veracini, *Settler Colonialism: A Theoretical Overview* (Houndsmills: Palgrave Macmillan, 2010); Walter Hixon, *American Settler Colonialism: A History* (New York: Palgrave Macmillan, 2013).

50. The Desert Campaign and subsequent Conquest of the Desert in Argentina during the nineteenth century exemplified the colonial settlers' long-lasting and brutal violence against indigenes in Latin America, which killed and displaced thousands. Richard Gott, "Latin America as a White Settler Society," *Bulletin of Latin American Research* 26, no. 2 (April 2007): 285–86; Alistair Hennessy, *The Frontier in Latin American History* (Albuquerque: University of New Mexico Press, 1978), 147.

51. See Goebel, "Settler Colonialism in Postcolonial Latin America," 147. As Goebel shows, the number of immigrants who arrived in the western South Atlantic region from 1870 to 1930 far exceeded the total number of immigrants who arrived during the past three hundred years.

52. From a different perspective, Garasino's research illustrates this historical convergence by how Shinya Yoshio, a Japanese immigrant intellectual in Argentina, adeptly linked Japanese expansionism with ethnic nationalism in Argentina through the logic of white supremacy and historical progress. Facundo Garaino, "Immigrant Propaganda: Translating Japanese Imperial Ideology into Argentine Nationalism," in Delpiano and Lu, *The Japanese Empire and Latin America*, 208–26.

53. Liang Zhan, "Wenming, lixing, yu zhongzhu gailiang: yige datong shijie de gouxiang," in *Shijie zhixue yu wenming dengji: quanqiushi yanjiu de xinlujing*, ed. Liu He (Beijing: Shenghuo Dushu Xinzhi Sanlian Shudian, 2016), 146–54.

54. Goebel, "Settler Colonialism in Postcolonial Latin America," 142–44.

55. George F. W. Young, *Germans in Chile: Immigration and Colonization, 1849–1914* (New York: Center for Migration Studies of New York, 1974), 26–28.

56. Lucy Taylor, "Four Foundations of Settler Colonial Theory: Four Insights from Argentina," *Settler Colonial Studies* 11, no. 3 (2021): 352–53.

57. Todd A. Diacon, *Millenarian Vision, Capitalist Reality: Brazil's Contestado Rebellion, 1912–1916* (Durham, NC: Duke University Press, 1991), 19.

58. Desiree Poets, "Settler Colonialism and/in (Urban) Brazil: Black and Indigenous Resistances to the Logic of Elimination," *Settler Colonial Studies* 11, no. 3 (2021): 271–91.

59. Warren Dean, *Rio Claro: A Brazilian Plantation System, 1820–1920* (Stanford: Stanford University Press, 1976), 11.

60. Diacon, *Millenarian Vision, Capitalist Reality*, 62.

61. Diacon, *Millenarian Vision, Capitalist Reality*, 63.

62. This research heeds the insights of Eiichiro Azuma, who terms Japanese emigration-driven expansion across the Pacific as a form of "borderless" settler colonialism. Azuma, *In Search of Our Frontier*, 2–9. In a broader sense, it echoes recent scholarship in the study of Japanese emigration that has transcended the boundaries of Japan's formal empire by exploring the intersections between Japanese emigration and colonial expansion both in and outside the imperial territories. Examples of this scholarship are Martin Dusinberre, *Mooring the Global Archive: A Japanese Ship and Its Migrant Histories* (Cambridge: Cambridge University Press, 2023); Jun Uchida, *Provincializing Empire: Ōmi Merchants in the Japanese Transpacific Diaspora* (Oakland: University of California Press, 2023); David Ambaras, *Japan's Imperial Underworld: Intimate Encounters at the Borders of Empire* (New York: Cambridge University Press, 2019). From a global and comparative perspective, Shellen Wu introduces the concept "geo-modernity" to examine the relationship between emigration, science, geography, and the rise of modern empires in Japan, China, the United States, and Germany. *Birth of the Geopolitical Age: Global Frontiers and the Making of Modern China* (Stanford: Stanford University Press, 2023)

63. This study joins recent innovative scholarship that has started exploring the historical connections between modern Japan and Japan's migration to Brazil and Latin America more generally. To name just a few: Miriam Kingsberg, "Becoming Brazilian to Be Japanese: Emigrant Assimilation, Cultural Anthropology, and National Identity," *Comparative Studies in Society and History* 56, no. 1 (2014): 67–97; and "Japan's Inca Boom"; Jacobowitz, "'A Bitter Brew'"; Ignacio López-Calvo, *Japanese Brazilian Saudades: Diasporic Identities and Cultural Production* (Boulder, CO: University Press of Colorado, 2019); Edward Mack, *Acquired Alterity: Migration, Identity, and Literature Nationalism* (Oakland: University of California Press, 2022); Delpiano and Lu, *The Japanese Empire and Latin America.*

64. Examples of such scholarship are Yukiko Koshiro, *Trans-Pacific Racism and U.S. Occupation of Japan* (New York: Columbia University Press, 1999), Shimazu, *Japan, Race, and Equality*; Azuma, *In Search of Our Frontier*; Takashi Fujitani, *Race for Empire: Koreans as Japanese and Japanese as Americans during World War II* (Berkeley: University of California Press, 2011).

65. For details of this colony and its aftermath, see Tsunoyama Yukihiro, *Enomoto Takeaki to Mekishiko ijū* (Tokyo: Dōbunkan Shuppan, 1986), 185–219.

66. The most representative works are the classic trilogy of Japanese imperial history published by Princeton University Press: Ramon Myers and Mark Peattie, eds., *The Japanese*

Colonial Empire, 1895–1945 (Princeton, NJ: Princeton University Press, 1987); Peter Duus, Ramon Myers, and Mark Peattie, eds., *The Japanese Informal Empire in China, 1895–1937* (Princeton, NJ: Princeton University Press, 1989); Peter Duus, Ramon Myers, and Mark Peattie, eds., *The Japanese Wartime Empire, 1931–1945* (Princeton, NJ: Princeton University, 1996).

67. Oguma Eiji, *Nihonjin no kyōkai: Okinawa Ainu Taiwan Chōsen shokuminchi shihai kara fukki undō made* (Tokyo: Shinyōsha, 1999); Walker, *The Conquest of the Ainu Lands*; Michael Thornton, "A Capitol Orchard: Botanical Networks and the Creation of a Japanese 'Neo-Europe,'" *American Historical Review* 127, no. 2 (June 2022): 573–99; Sidney Xu Lu, "Eastward Ho! Japanese Settler Colonialism in Hokkaido and the Making of Japanese Migration to the American West," *Journal of Asian Studies* 78, no. 3 (August 2019): 521–47.

68. To name only a few examples of this growing body of scholarship: Oguma Eiji, *Nihonjin no kyōkai*; Miriam Kingsberg Kadia, *Into the Field: Human Scientists of Transwar Japan* (Stanford: Stanford University Press, 2019); Lu, *The Making of Japanese Settler Colonialism*; Leo Ching, *Anti-Japan: The Politics of Sentiment in Postcolonial East Asia* (Durham, NC: Duke University Press, 2019); Prasenjit Duara, ed., *Decolonization: Perspectives from Now and Then* (London: Routledge, 2003)

69. Recent scholarship has begun to challenge such geography-bound narratives of the empire. To name only a few examples, see Azuma, *In Search of Our Frontier*; David Ambaras, *Japan's Imperial Underworlds: Intimate Encounters at the Borders of Empire* (New York: Cambridge University Press, 2018); Seiji Shirane, *Imperial Gateway: Colonial Taiwan and Japan's Expansion in South China and Southeast Asia, 1895–1945* (Ithaca, NY: Cornell University Press, 2022); Uchida, *Provincializing Empire*.

70. Patrick Wolfe, *Settler Colonialism and Transformation of Anthropology* (London: Cassell, 1999), 2.

71. In 1974, various government-related entities responsible for emigration integrated with other government bodies overseeing international matters, including foreign investment, trade, cultural and educational exchanges, and technological collaboration. This led to the creation of the Japan International Cooperation Agency (JICA), a development that signified a shift in the government's approach to overseas migration, indicating that it was no longer a distinct area in government policy but part of the broader realm of international cooperation.

72. Lu, "Eastward Ho!," 521–47.

73. Japanese thinkers, liberal and conservative, pro-Westernization and ultranationalist alike, called for overseas emigration as a means of colonial expansion in the 1880s and 1890s. Itagaki Taisuke, a forefather of Japan's democratic movement, published an essay advocating colonial expansion through overseas emigration. Fukuzawa Yukichi called for the building of "small Japans" around the Pacific Rim. Nationalist thinkers associated with the Politics and Education Association, such as Sugiura Jūkō and Shiga Shigetaka, also penned books advocating Japan's emigration-driven expansion across the Pacific. Itagaki Taisuke, "Shokumin ron," *Jiyūtō hō*, no. 10 (April 28, 1892), in *Itagaki Taisuke zenshū*, ed. Itagaki Morimasa (Tokyo: Hara Shobō, 1980), 77–79; Fukuzawa Yukichi, "Fuki kōmyo wa oya yuzuri no kuni ni kagirazu," in *Fukuzawa Yukichi zenshū*, vol. 9 (Tokyo: Iwanami Shoten, 1960), 546; Sugiura Jūkō, *Hankai yume monogatari: ichimei shinheimin kaitendan* (Tokyo: Sawaya, 1886); Shiga Shigetaka, *Nan'yō jiji* (Tokyo: Maruzen Shōsha Shoten, 1891).

74. Hayashiya Eikichi, "Nihon to Raten Amerika no gaikō kankei," in *Nihon to Raten Amerika no kankei: Nihon no kokuzaika ni okeru Raten Amerika*, ed. Hajime Mizuno (Tokyo: Instituto Iberoamericano, Sofía University, 1990), 1–13.

75. Two major studies of Japan's emigration-driven expansion, written right before the signing of the Gentlemen's Agreement, captured this intellectual transition: Ōkawadaira Takamitsu, *Nihon imin ron* (Tokyo: Jōbudō, 1905); Tōgō Minoru, *Nihon shokumin ron* (Tokyo: Bunbudō, 1906).

76. For details of the company's formation and its initial settler colonial programs, see Ōkōchi Kazuo, *Maboroshi no kokusaku-gaisha Tōyō Takushoku* (Tokyo: Nihon Keizai Shinbunsha, 1982), 21–74.

77. Sandra Wilson, "'The New Paradise': Japanese Emigration to Manchuria in the 1930s and 40s," *International History Review* 17, no. 2 (May 1995): 262–73.

78. Nawa Tōichi, *Nihon bōsekigyō to genmen mondai kenkyū* (Osaka: Daidō Shoin, 1938), 322–23.

79. Henri Delanghe, "Japanese Import of Brazilian Raw Cotton in the Second Half of the 1930s: The Beginning of Significant Japanese-Brazilian Trade and Investment Relations," *História Econômica & História de Empresas* 2, no. 2 (1999): 93–94.

80. Hiromi Mizuno's seminal research demonstrates the ties between Japanese colonial migration to Asia and Japanese migration to Latin America, specifically, the Dominican Republic. Hiromi Mizuno, "After the Empire: Postwar Emigration to the Dominican Republic and Economic Diplomacy," in Delpiano and Lu, *The Japanese Empire and Latin America*, 227–49.

1. THE U.S. FRONTIER AND THE MAKING OF TWO MIGRATION STATES

1. Nakano Kazunori, "Ezo kyōwakoku no tenmatsu," *Josetsu 2: bungaku hihyō*, August 2002, 37.

2. Founders of the First Republic put "Ordem e Progresso" on the national flag, which is still in use today.

3. Brett Walker has offered a well-researched account of this early modern Japanese expansion. See Brett Walker, *The Conquest of Ainu Lands: Ecology and Culture in Japanese Expansion, 1590–1800* (Berkeley: University of California Press, 2006).

4. Anna Paulina Lee, *Mandarin Brazil: Race, Representation, and Memory* (Stanford: Stanford University Press, 2018), 57.

5. Peter Duus has provided a brief but comprehensive overview of the international context for the rise of Japanese imperialism and expansionism. Peter Duus, *The Abacus and the Sword: The Japanese Penetration of Korea, 1895–1910* (Berkeley: University of California Press, 1995), 2–18.

6. Eiichiro Azuma has shown how Meiji expansionists saw Japanese emigration to the United States as a component of Japanese colonial expansion. Eiichiro Azuma, *Between Two Empires: Race, History, and Transnationalism in Japanese America* (London: Oxford University Press, 2005), 17–33.

7. In 1803, Thomas Jefferson reasoned that the rapid growth of white American farming communities made it necessary for them to acquire more land from Native Americans whose primary livelihood was hunting. He envisioned a mass relocation of Native

Americans west of the Mississippi in order to reserve the entire eastern side of the river for the expanding white farming communities. This idea was eventually carried out, during the presidency of Andrew Jackson, and resulted in the relocation of Native American tribes residing in the southeastern states to the west of the Mississippi. Alison Bashford, "Malthus and Colonial History," *Journal of Australian Studies* 36, no. 1 (March 2012): 104; Barbara Arneil, *John Locke and America: The Defense of English Colonialism* (Oxford: Oxford University Press, 1996), 192–93.

8. Yoshida Hideo, *Nihon jinkō ron no shiteki kenkyū* (Tokyo: Kawade Shobō, 1944), 213–14.

9. "Kaitaku no shisatsu," *Hokkaido kaitaku zasshi*, no. 2, February 14, 1880, 1–4.

10. Hayami Akira, "Jinkō tōkei no kindaika katei," in Kokusei Chōsa Izen, *Nihon jinkō tōkei shūsei*, ed. Naimushō Naikaku Tōkeikyoku, vol. 1 (Tokyo: Tōyō Shorin, 1992), 10.

11. Horace M. Capron, *Memoirs of Horace Capron—Volume I: Autobiography.* Special Collections, National Agricultural Library (1884), 79.

12. Horace M. Capron, *Memoirs of Horace Capron—Volume II: Autobiography.* Special Collections, National Agricultural Library (1884), 92–93, 98.

13. "Kaitaku zasshi hakkō no shushi," *Hokkaido kaitaku zasshi*, no. 1, January 31, 1880, 2–3.

14. Hirano, "Thanatopolitics in the Making of Japan's Hokkaido," 198, 204.

15. Taguchi Ukichi, *Nihon keizai ron* (Tokyo: Keizai Zasshisha, 1878), 73.

16. See, e.g., "Asano," *Hokkaido kaitaku zasshi*, no. 2, February 14, 1880, 9; "Jyagatara imo no rieki," *Hokkaido kaitaku zasshi*, no. 3, February 28, 1880, 56; "Budō saibai no rieki," *Hokkaido kaitaku zasshi*, no. 5, March 27, 1880, 97; "Sake no setsu," *Hokkaido kaitaku zasshi*, no. 10, June 5, 1880, 241.

17. "Nihon teikoku no uchi ni Amerika gasshūkoku wo genshutsu suru wa atarasa ni tōki ni arazaru beshi," *Hokkaido kaitaku zasshi*, no. 3, February 28, 1880, 50–51.

18. Before 1807, the territory of colonial Brazil was not open to non-Portuguese settlers. Oliver Marshall, *English, Irish and Irish American Pioneer Settlers in Nineteenth Century Brazil* (Oxford: Center for Brazilian Studies, Oxford University, 2005), 15.

19. Actual land colonization and utilization were not the immediate goals of these bandeirantes and their sponsors. Richard M. Morse, *The Bandeirantes: The Historical Role of the Brazilian Pathfinders* (New York: Knopf, 1965), 21–28.

20. Pedro II also made an official visit to the United States in 1876 and traveled by railroad across the country with profound interest. He was called "Our Yankee Emperor," showing how the U.S. general public was impressed by the Brazilian leader's familiarity with American culture and customs. Joseph Smith, *Brazil and the United States: Convergence and Divergence* (Athens: University of Georgia Press, 2010), 31.

21. José Juan Pérez Meléndez, "Reconsiderando a política de colonização no Brasil imperial: Os anos da Regência e o mundo externo," *Revista Brasileira de História* 34, no. 68 (2014): 37–38.

22. For example, Rio paid close attention to the ongoing process of land exploration in the United States. Pérez Meléndez has documented how the Brazilian leaders borrowed a page from the American experience by encouraging private associations to build river canals. José Juan Pérez Meléndez, "The Business of Peopling: Colonization and Politics in Imperial Brazil, 1822–1860" (PhD diss., University of Chicago, 2016), 181–83.

23. Pérez Meléndez, "The Business of Peopling," 325–26.

24. Toake Endoh, *Exporting Japan: Politics of Emigration to Latin America* (Urbana: University of Illinois Press, 2009), 27.

25. Clodomir Vianna Moog, *Bandeirantes and Pioneers* (New York: G. Braziller, 1964), 12–13.

26. Lesser, *Immigration, Ethnicity and National Identity*, 14.

27. Emilia Viotti da Costa, *The Brazilian Empire: Myths and Histories* (Chapel Hill: University of North Carolina Press, 2000), xxv.

28. Lesser, *Immigration, Ethnicity and National Identity*, 27.

29. Costa, *The Brazilian Empire*, 78–79.

30. Almir Antonio de Souza, "A Lei de Terras no Brasil Império e os índios do Planalto Meridional: A luta política e diplomática do Kaingang Vitorino Condá (1845–1870)," *Revista Brasileira de História* 35, no. 70 (2015): 111.

31. Alexandre Carlos Gugliotta, "Tavares Bastos (1839–1875) e a Sociedade Internacional de Imigração: Um espaço a favor da modernidade," paper presented at the XII Encuentro Regional de História "Usos do Passado," Asociación Nacional de História de Río de Janeiro (2006), 5–6.

32. Marshall, *English, Irish, and Irish American Pioneer Settlers*, 21–22.

33. Gugliotta, "Tavares Bastos (1839–1875) e a Sociedade Internacional de Imigração," 4–5.

34. Marshall, *English, Irish, and Irish American Pioneer Settlers*, 23.

35. It is estimated that about 20,000 Confederate supporters chose to migrate to Brazil between 1865 and 1885. Lesser, *Immigration, Ethnicity and National Identity*, 45.

36. Scully considered Germans another desirable ethnic group for Brazilian immigration but believed that they lacked self-reliance, imagination, and enterprise in comparison with the English and Irish. Marshall, *English, Irish, and Irish American Pioneer Settlers*, 26.

37. Marshall, *English, Irish, and Irish American Pioneer Settlers*, 25.

38. Lesser, *Immigration, Ethnicity and National Identity*, 32.

39. Lesser, *Immigration, Ethnicity and National Identity*, 32.

40. Lesser, *Immigration, Ethnicity and National Identity*, 71.

41. E. Bradford Burns, *A History of Brazil* (New York: Columbia University Press, 1993), 155.

42. Mauricio A. Font, *Coffee and Transformation in São Paulo, Brazil* (Lanham, MD: Lexington Books, 2010), 14.

43. Font, *Coffee and Transformation*, 14.

44. Lesser, *Immigration, Ethnicity and National Identity*, 68.

45. Lesser, *Immigration, Ethnicity and National Identity*, 67–71.

46. Lesser, *Immigration, Ethnicity and National Identity*, 68, 71.

47. Lesser, *Immigration, Ethnicity and National Identity*, 61.

48. Lesser, *Negotiating National Identity*, 96–97.

49. Fukuzawa, "Fuki kōmyo wa oya yuzuri no kuni ni kagirazu."

50. Tachikawa Kenji, "Meiji zenhanki no tobeinetsu (1)," *Tomiyama Daigaku Kyōyōbu kiyō* 23, no. 2 (1990): 17.

51. Ebihara Hachirō, *Kaigai hōji shinbun zasshishi: tsuketari kaigai hōjin gaiji shinbun zasshishi* (Tokyo: Meicho Fukyūkai, 1980), 106.

52. While an influential Japanese intellectual, Tokutomi Sōhō, called for Japanese expansion into the South Pacific, another thinker, Nagasawa Betten, turned to Latin America. Tokutomi Sōhō, "Nihon jinshū no shin kokyō," *Kokumin no tomo* 6, no. 85 (June 13, 1890): 829–38; Nagasawa Setsu (Betten), *Yankii* (Tokyo: Keigyōsha, 1893), 22.

53. Mark Peattie, *Nan'yō: The Rise and Fall of the Japanese in Micronesia, 1885–1945* (Honolulu: University of Hawai'i Press, 1988), 5–6.

54. Peattie, *Nan'yō*, 6.

55. Peattie, *Nan'yō*, 7; Usui Ryūichirō, *Enomoto Takeaki kara sekaishi ga mieru* (Tokyo: PHP Kenkyūjo, 2005), 221–22.

56. "Shokumin Kyōkai hōkoku hatsuda no riyū," *Shokumin Kyōkai hōkokusho*, no. 1, April 1893, 1–2.

57. Jerry Garcia, "Japanese Immigration and Community Development in Mexico, 1897–1940" (PhD diss., Washington State University, 1999), 54–55.

58. Fujita's report was published by the Foreign Ministry. Fujita Toshirō, *Mekishikokoku Taiheiyō engan shoshūn junkai hōkoku* (Tokyo: Gaimu Daijin Kanbō Iminka, 1891).

59. Fujita, *Mekishikokoku Taiheiyō*, 55–56

60. Fujita, *Mekishikokoku Taiheiyō*, 57.

61. Fujita, *Mekishikokoku Taiheiyō*, 67–83.

62. Nemoto's report ushered in the official start of Japanese migration to Peru in 1899. Kōyama Rokurō, *Imin yonjūnen shi* (São Paulo: Kōyama Rokurō, 1949), 6.

63. Kōyama, *Imin yonjūnen shi*, 6.

64. Nobuya Tsuchida, "The Japanese in Brazil, 1908–1941" (PhD diss., University of California, Los Angeles, 1978), 139–42.

65. Kōyama, *Imin yonjūnen shi*, 23.

2. BEFORE THE SAILING OF THE *KASATO MARU*

1. Cited from Paul Kramer, "Empires, Exceptions, and Anglo-Saxons: Race and Rule between the British and United States Empires, 1880–1910," *Journal of American History* 88, no. 4 (2002): 1325.

2. Starr wrote a book recording his journey to bring this group of Ainu people from Hokkaido to St. Louis. Frederick Starr, *The Ainu Group at the Saint Louis Exposition* (Chicago: Open Court, 1904).

3. Miyatake Kimio, "Hakurankai no kioku: 1904 nen sentoruisu Hakurankai to Ainu," *Hokkaido Daigaku Bungaku Kenkyūka kiyō* 118 (February 2006): 62.

4. The state museum became a part of the University of São Paulo in 1963 and is now known as the Museu Paulista. http://www.mp.usp.br/museu-paulista-da-usp.

5. John Hemming, *Amazon Frontier: The Defeat of the Brazilian Indians* (Cambridge, MA: Harvard University Press, 1987), 474.

6. Tsuchida, "The Japanese in Brazil, 1908–1941," 139–42.

7. Kōyama, *Imin yonjūnen shi*, 20–25.

8. Kōyama, *Imin yonjūnen shi*, 8.

9. Lesser, *Immigration, Ethnicity, and National Identity*, 71.

10. Tsuchida, "The Japanese in Brazil, 1908–1941," 18.

11. Kōyama, *Imin yonjūnen shi*, 9.

12. Kōyama, *Imin yonjūnen shi*, 9.

13. *Nihon gaikō bunsho*, vol. 31, no. 2 (Tokyo: Ministry of Foreign Affairs of Japan, 1898), 141–42.

14. *Nihon gaikō bunsho*, vol. 31, no. 2 (1898), 144.

15. *Nihon gaikō bunsho*, vol. 31, no. 2 (1898), 144–50.

16. Kōyama, *Imin yonjūnen shi*, 10.

17. Katō Masuo, "Kankoku iminron," *Taiyō* 7, no. 1, January 5, 1901, 11.

18. Nitobe Inazō, *Nōgyō honron* (Tokyo: Shōka Shobō, 1898), 137–73, 296–333, 433–51.

19. The importance of agriculture for the colonization of Hokkaido was self-evident in almost all of the issues of the *Hokkaido Development Journal* that Tsuda edited.

20. Nitobe, *Nōgyō honron*, 137–73.

21. Hiraoka Hikotarō, *Nihon nōpon ron* (Tokyo: Yasui Ukichi, 1902), 36–53.

22. Hiraoka, *Nihon nōpon ron*, 56–57.

23. For a historical analysis of the relationship between the overpopulation discourse and Japanese emigration, see Lu, *The Making of Japanese Settler Colonialism*.

24. "Japan's Invasion of the White Man's World," *New York Times*, September 22, 1907, 4.

25. Jordan Sand, "Gentlemen's Agreement, 1908: Fragments for a Pacific History," *Representations* 107, no. 1 (Summer 2009): 91.

26. Tōgō, *Nihon shokumin ron*, 2.

27. Tōgō, *Nihon shokumin ron*, 68–69.

28. Ōkawadaira, *Nihon imin ron*, 182–83, 282–83; Tōgō, *Nihon shokumin ron*, 238–41.

29. Ōkawadaira, *Nihon imin ron*, 266–78.

30. Shin Nichibei Shinbunsha, *Beikoku Nikkeijin Hhakunenshi: hatten jinshiroku* (Los Angeles: Shin Nichibei Shinbunsha, 1961), 120–21.

31. Shin Nichibei Shinbunsha, *Beikoku Nikkeijin hyakunenshi*, 121.

32. Kikugawa Sadami, "Tekisasu beisaku no senkusha: Saibara Seitō to Ōnishi Rihei," *Keizai keiei ronsō* 32, no. 4 (March 1998): 45.

33. Shimizu Seisaburō, "Hokubei Tekisasushu iminchi torishirabe hōkoku," in *Gaimushō Tsūshōkyoku, Imin chōsa hōkoku*, vol. 1, 1908 (repr. Tokyo: Yūshōdō Shuppan, 1986), 3.

34. Yoshimura Daijirō, *Hokubei Tekisasushū no beisaku: Nihonjin no shin fugen* (Osaka: Kaigai Kigyō Dōshikai, 1903), 140.

35. Yoshimura Daijirō, *Tekisasushū beisaku no jikken* (Tokyo: Kaigai Kigyō Dōshikai, 1905), 144–45.

36. Yoshimura, *Tekisasushū beisaku no jikken*, 142.

37. For a more comprehensive analysis of the overall failure of Japanese rice farms in Texas, see Lu, *The Making of Japanese Settler Colonialism*, 144–45.

38. Mamiya Kunio, *Saibara Seitō kenkyū* (Kōchi: Kōchi Shimin Toshokan, 1996), 341–44; Ino Masayoshi, *Kyojin Saibara Seitō* (Tosa-shi: Saibara Seitō Sensei Shōtokuhi Kensetsu Kiseikai, 1964), 116, 319.

39. Mamiya, *Saibara Seitō kenkyū*, 320–36.

40. Mamiya, *Saibara Seitō kenkyū*, 365–67.

41. Burns, *A History of Brazil*, 155.

42. Font, *Coffee and Transformation of São Paulo*, 14.

43. Burns, *A History of Brazil*, 264.

44. Thomas E. Skidmore, *Brazil: Five Centuries of Change* (New York: Oxford University Press, 1999), 71.

45. Thomas W. Merrick and Douglas H. Graham, *Population and Economic Development* (Baltimore: Johns Hopkins University Press, 1979), 91, cited in Skidmore, *Brazil: Five Centuries of Change*, 73.

46. Nestor Ascoli, *A immigração japoneza na Baixada do Estado do Rio de Janeiro* (Rio de Janeiro: Edição da "Revista de Lingua Portuguesa," 1924), 22, cited in Lesser, *Immigration, Ethnicity, and National Identity*, 176.

47. Lee, *Mandarin Brazil*, 127–36.

48. Kōyama, *Imin yonjūnen shi*, 31. The full report of Sugimura is also made available by the National Diet Library of Japan. Sugimura Fukashi, "Hakkoku imin jyōkyō," *Burajiru imin no 100 nen*, https://www.ndl.go.jp/brasil/text/t014.html.

49. Kōyama, *Imin yonjūnen shi*, 15–17.

50. Kōyama, *Imin yonjūnen shi*, 17–19.

51. Mizuno Ryū, "Imin jigyō to watashi," *Burajiru imin no 100 nen*, https://www.ndl.go.jp/brasil/text/t016.html.

52. Kōyama, *Imin yonjūnen shi*, 21–22.

53. Tsuchida, "The Japanese in Brazil, 1908–1941," 136–37.

54. Kōyama, *Imin yonjūnen shi*, 23.

55. Tsuchida, "The Japanese in Brazil, 1908–1941," 139–42.

56. Tsuchida, "The Japanese in Brazil, 1908–1941," 133–43.

57. Kōyama, *Imin yonjūnen shi*, 50–56; Tsuchida, "The Japanese in Brazil, 1908–1941," 154–55.

58. Uetsuka is more fully discussed in chapter 3; Kōyama is discussed in detail in chapters 5 and 6.

59. Tsuchida, "The Japanese in Brazil, 1908–1941," 157–63.

60. Tsuchida, "The Japanese in Brazil, 1908–1941," 160–61.

61. Tsuchida, "The Japanese in Brazil, 1908–1941," 155.

3. SEIZING THE LAND: COFFEE, RAILROAD, AND SETTLER COMMUNITY MAKING

1. Yamamoto Shūsaku et al., *Rejisutoro no rokujūnen* (Registro: Rejisutoro Rokujūnen Shi Kenkō Iinkai, 1978), 1. In a previous book, I have explained how Japan's expansionists at the turn of the twentieth century attributed the rural depression to overpopulation in the Japanese countryside and saw the emigration of Japanese farmers overseas as a solution. Lu, *The Making of Japanese Settler Colonialism*, 131–37.

2. Okabayashi Nobuo, "Jinkō mondai to imin ron: Meiji Nihon no fuan to yokubō," *Doshisha hōgaku* 64, no. 8 (March 2013): 153–54. The author, Namatame Kyokutō, started writing the novel when he lived in the United States and observed the racial discrimination against the Japanese immigrants there.

3. Okabayashi, "Jinkō mondai to imin ron," 153–54.

4. *Tokyo Puck*, vol. 3, no. 17, 1907.

5. Satō Yoshimaru, "Dainihon Bunmei Kyōkai shi shiron," *Waseda Daigaku shi kiyō* 21 (March 1989): 180.

6. In addition to the books introducing modern social sciences, the Great Japan Civilization Association translated histories of British colonial expansion, works on national figures of the Great Britain and the United States, and contemporary colonial strategies of Western powers. Satō, "Dainihon Bunmei Kyōkai shi shiron," 198–201.

7. Ōkuma Shigenobu, "Sekai no daikyoku to imin," *Nihon Imin Kyōkai hōkoku* 1, no. 2 (August 1915; repr. Tokyo: Fuji Shuppan, 2006), 6–7.

8. Mamiya Kunio, "Taibei kehatsu undō to Imin Kyōkai no setsuritsu," in *Reimeiki Ajia Taiheiyō chiiki no kokusai kankei: Taiheiyō mondai chōsakai (I.P.R.) no kenkyū*, Waseda Daigaku shakai kagaku kenkyūjo kenkyū shirīzu, no. 33 (1994), 169–77.

9. Dainihon Bunmei Kyōkai, *Nihonjin no kaigai hatten* (Tokyo: Dai Nihon Bunmei Kyōkai, 1916).

10. Sakaguchi Mitsuhiko, "Kaisetsu," in *Nihon Imin Kyōkai hōkoku: kaisetsu, sōmokuji, shihisha sakuin* (Tokyo: Fuji Shuppan, 2006), 10–11.

11. "Nihon minzoku no bōchō," *Taiyō* 16, no. 15, November 1910; "Nanshin ya? Hokushin ya?" *Taiyō* 19, no. 15, November 1913.

12. Takekoshi Yosaburō, "Nanpō no keiei to Nihon no shimei," *Taiyō* 16, no. 15, November 1910, 20–21.

13. Hyung Gu Lynn, "Malthusian Dreams, Colonial Imaginary: The Oriental Development Company and Japanese Emigration to Korea," in *Settler Colonialism in the Twentieth Century: Projects, Practices, and Legacies*, ed. Caroline Elkins and Susan Pedersen (London: Routledge, 2005), 30, 33.

14. Kanbe Masao, *Chōsen nōgyō imin ron* (Tokyo: Yūhikaku Shobō, 1910), 44–45.

15. Akira Iriye, "The Failure of Economic Expansionism: 1918–1931," in *Japan in Crisis: Essays on Taishō Democracy*, ed. Bernard Silberman and H. D. Harootunian (Princeton, NJ: Princeton University Press, 1974), 251, 253; Wilson, "The New Paradise," 252. The small number of Japanese farming settlers in colonial Korea and Manchuria was in sharp contrast to the much larger Japanese urban populations in these two areas around the same time.

16. See Yamamoto Jōtarō, "Manmō no hatten to Mantetsu no jigyō," *Seiyū*, no. 330 (1928): 13–17, cited from Wilson, "New Paradise," 256; Iriye, "The Failure of Economic Expansionism," 254.

17. Takushoku Daigaku, *Takushoku Daigaku hachijūnen shi: Meiji hen* (Tokyo: Takushoku Daigaku Sōritsu Hachijisshūnen Kinen Jigyō Jimukyoku, 1980), 42–43.

18. Takushoku Daigaku, *Takushoku Daigaku hachijūnen shi: Meiji hen*, 49–50.

19. Kimura Kenji, "Nichiro sengo kaigai nōgyō imin no rekishiteki chii," in *Nihon jinushi sei to kindai sonraku*, ed. Abiko Rin (Tokyo: Sōfūsha, 1994), 153.

20. Kimura, "Nichiro sengo kaigai nōgyō imin no rekishiteki chii," 153.

21. Hyung Gu Lynn, "A Comparative Study of Tōyō Kyōkai and Nan'yō Kyōkai," in *The Japanese Empire in East Asia and Its Postwar Legacy*, ed. Harald Fuess (Munich: Iudicium, 1998), 73.

22. At the end of the 1920s, the total number of Japanese settlers in Micronesia was around 20,000. Mark Peattie, "The Nan'yō: Japan in the South Pacific, 1885–1945," in *The Japanese Colonial Empire, 1895–1945*, ed. Ramon Myers and Mark Peattie (Princeton, NJ: Princeton University Press, 1987), 197.

23. Tsuchida, "The Japanese in Brazil, 1908–1941," 167, 197.

24. Burns, *A History of Brazil*, 276–80.

25. Burns, *A History of Brazil*, 305–6.

26. Walter LaFeber, *The Clash: U.S.-Japan Relations throughout History* (New York: Norton, 1997), 62–64. E. Bradford Burns has explained how Brazilian diplomats, led by José Paranhos, sought to foster a Brazil-U.S. alliance at the turn of the twentieth century. E. Bradford Burns, *The Unwritten Alliance: Rio-Branco and Brazilian American Relations* (New York: Columbia University Press, 1966).

27. Thomas E. Skidmore, "Brazil's American Illusion: From Dom Pedro II to the Coup of 1964," *Luso-Brazilian Review* 23, no. 2 (Winter 1986): 73–74.

28. Burns, *A History of Brazil*, 305–6.

29. Emily S. Rosenberg, "Anglo-American Economic Rivalry in Brazil during World War I," *Diplomatic History* 2, no. 2 (Spring 1978): 131–33, 152.

30. Burns, *A History of Brazil*, 307–11.

31. William R. Summerhill, *Order against Progress: Government, Foreign Investment, and Railroads in Brazil, 1854–1913* (Stanford: Stanford University Press, 2003), 36–37, 44.

32. Summerhill, *Order against Progress*, 56–57.

33. Andō Zenpati, "Nihon Imin no Shakai Shiteki Kenkyū," *Kenkyū repōto* 2 (1967): 64.

34. Summerhill, *Order against Progress*, 56.

35. John Hemming, *Die If You Must: Brazilian Indians in the Twentieth Century* (New York: Macmillan, 2003), 24–27.

36. Font, *Coffee and Transformation in São Paulo*, 102.

37. Font, *Coffee and Transformation in São Paulo*, 25.

38. Summerhill, *Order against Progress*, 195.

39. Andō, "Nihon imin no shakai shiteki kenkyū," 72–73.

40. Thomas Holloway, *Immigrants on the Land: Coffee and Society in São Paulo, 1886–1934* (Chapel Hill: University of North Carolina Press, 2012), 147–53.

41. Font, *Coffee and Transformation in São Paulo*, 25.

42. Diacon, *Millenarian Vision, Capitalist Reality*, 17–21.

43. Diacon, *Millenarian Vision, Capitalist Reality*, 145–47.

44. The Iguape colony included two subcolonies, Katsura Colony and Registro Colony, which were established in sequence.

45. Tsuchida, "The Japanese in Brazil, 1908–1941," 187–90. Also see "Iguape Colony," *Burajiru imin no 100 nen*, https://www.ndl.go.jp/brasil/e/s3/s3_2.html.

46. Tsuchida, "The Japanese in Brazil, 1908–1941," 187–90.

47. Tsuchida, "The Japanese in Brazil, 1908–1941," 187–90.

48. Kōyama, *Imin yonjūnen shi*, 136.

49. Kōyama, *Imin yonjūnen shi*, 136; Andō, "Nihon imin no shakai shiteki kenkyū," 66–67.

50. Andō, "Nihon imin no shakai shiteki kenkyū," 66.

51. "From Colonos to Independent Farmers," *Burajiru imin no 100 nen*, https://www.ndl.go.jp/brasil/e/s3/s3_1.html.

52. Kōyama, *Imin yonjūnen shi*, 136.

53. Andō, "Nihon imin no shakai shiteki kenkyū," 66–67.

54. "From Colonos to Independent Farmers."

55. For Hirano Unpei and Uetsuka Shūhei, see Handa Tomoo, *Imin no seikatsu no rekishi* (São Paulo: Centro de Estudos Nipo Brasileiros, 1969), 262–88. For Miyazaki Hachirō, see Nagata Shigeshi, "Birigui shokuminchi no kusawake," *Shokumin* 6, no. 6 (June 1927): 134–37.

56. Hirano Shokuminchi Nihonjinkai, *Hirano 25 shūnen shi* (São Paulo: Hirano Shokuminchi Nihonjinkai, 1941), 33.

57. Handa, *Imin no seikatsu no rekishi*, 262–88.

58. Aoyagi Ikutarō, *Burajiru ni okeru Nihonjin hatten shi*, vol. 1 (Tokyo: Burajiru ni okeru Nihonjin Hatten Shi Kankō Iinkai, 1941), 358–59.

59. Handa, *Imin no seikatsu no rekishi*, 270–75.

60. The formation of the Registro Colony, for example, was delayed by the land disputes. Yamamoto et al., *Rejisutoro no rokujūnen*, 2–3.

61. Hokkaido Nanbei Ijūshi Henshūshi Iinkai, *Hokkaido Nanbei ijū shi* (Sapporo: Hokuhōken Sentā, 2009), 143.

62. Kawada Shirō, *Shokuminchi toshite no Burajiru* (Tokyo: Yūhikaku Shobō, 1914), 220; Zaihaku Hokkaidō Kyōkai, *Zaihaku Hokkaidōjin shi: Hokkaidō hyakunen kinen* (São Paulo: Zaihaku Hokkaidō Kyōkai, 1968), 171.

63. Kawada, *Shokuminchi toshite no Burajiru*, 222–23.

4. "MAKING THE WORLD OUR HOME": THE HEYDAY OF COLLABORATIVE SETTLER COLONIALISM

1. Inoue Masaji, "Sekai wo ie toshite," *Shokumin* 9, no. 3 (March 1930): 22–23.

2. For public media's opinion, see *Osaka mainichi*, August 2, 1918. For the ideas of the strategists in the imperial military, see the comment of Matsui Iwane, "Hokuman taisaku shiken," mimeograph, June 1, 1923. Cited in Iriye, "The Failure of Economic Expansionism, 1918–1931," 240, 245.

3. *Tokyo asahi*, June 1, 1922. Cited inIriye, "The Failure of Economic Expansionism, 1918–1931," 245.

4. Iriye, "The Failure of Economic Expansionism, 1918–1931," 246–47.

5. Nishita Toshihiro, "Shidehara Kijūrō no kokusai ninshiki: daiichiji sekai taisen go no tenkanki wo chūshin toshite," *Kokusai seiji*, no. 139 (November 2004): 96–99.

6. Frederick Dickinson, *World War I and the Triumph of the New Japan* (Cambridge: Cambridge University Press, 2015), 70.

7. Iriye, "The Failure of Economic Expansionism, 1918–1931," 256.

8. Through the concept of social management, Sheldon Garon has illustrated how Japanese government bureaucrats collaborated and negotiated with leaders of different social interest groups during the interwar years to strengthen state control over society. Sheldon Garon, *Molding the Japanese Minds: The State in Everyday Life* (Princeton, NJ: Princeton University, 1998), 6–7.

9. Examining a selection of Kaikō's advertising materials, Andre Deckrow explains how Kaikō managers tried to mobilize Japan's rural poor by presenting Brazil-bound migration as a solution to their poverty and promising the emigrants landownership in Brazil in the future. Andre Kobayashi Deckrow, "Guiding Settlers: The Overseas Development Company and the Recruitment of Rural Brazil, 1918–1936," in Delpiano and Lu, *The Japanese Empire and Latin America*, 145–67.

10. The migration guides and pamphlets published by Kaikō usually encouraged its recruited migrants to become independent owner-farmers after their labor contracts ended. See, e.g., Kaigai Kōgyō Kabushiki Gaisha, *Nanbei Burajirukoku to Nihon ishokumin* (Tokyo: Kaigai Kōgyō Kabushiki Gaisha, 1922), 1–3.

11. Louise Young, *Beyond Metropolis: Second Cities and Urban Life in Interwar Japan* (Berkeley: University of California Press, 2013), 2.

12. Michael Lewis, *Rioters and Citizens: Mass Protest in Imperial Japan* (Berkeley: University of California Press, 1990), 248–49.

13. Sakaguchi Mitsuhiko, "Dare ga imin wo okuridashita no ka: kan Taihenyō ni okeru Nihonjin no kokusai idō gaikan," *Ritsumeikan gengo bunka kenkyū* 21, no. 4 (March 2010): 55.

14. Iikubo Hideki, "1920 nendai ni okeru naimushō shakaikyoku no kaigai imin shōreisaku," *Rekishi to keizai* 46, no. 1 (2003): 42.

15. Iikubo Hideki, "Kaigai Kōgyō Kabushiki Gaisha to Kaigai Ijū Kumiai Rengōkai: 1920–40 nendai ni okeru kaigai ishokumin toriatsukari kikan no hensen," *Yokohama Shiritsu Daigaku ronsō shakai kagaku keiretsu* 61, no. 1 (2010): 66.

16. These four migration companies were Tōyō Imin, Nanbei Imin, Nittō Shokumin Kabushiki Kōshi Gaisha, and Nihon Shokumin Kabushiki Gaisha. Iikubo, "Kaigai Kōgyō Kabushiki Gaisha to Kaigai Ijū Kumiai Rengōkai," 66.

17. Kaigai Kōgyō Kabushiki Gaisha, *Kaigai Kōgyō Kabushiki Gaisha gensei yōran,* 10–40.

18. The numbers of Japanese migrants to Brazil in these three years were 776 in 1921, 1,087 in 1922, and 757 in 1923, according to the records of the Japanese government. Burajiru Nikkeijin Jittai Chōsa Iinkai, *Burajiru no Nihon imin: kijutsu-hen* (Tokyo: University of Tokyo Press, 1964), 225.

19. Iikubo, "1920 nendai ni okeru naimushō shakaikyoku no kaigai imin shōreisaku," 43.

20. Tsuchida, "The Japanese in Brazil, 1908–1941," 132.

21. Iikubo, "1920 nendai ni okeru naimushō shakaikyoku no kaigai imin shōreisaku," 45.

22. The U.S. doors to Japanese immigration were not officially reopened until 1952.

23. Iikubo, "1920 nendai ni okeru naimushō shakaikyoku no kaigai imin shōreisaku," 47.

24. The founding years of these magazines are *Shokumin* in 1922, *Kaigai* in 1927, and *Burajiru: ishokumin to bōeki* in 1927.

25. Nagata Shigeshi, *Burajiru ni okeru Nihonjin hattenshi,* vol. 2 (Tokyo: Burajiru ni Okeru Nihonjin Hattenshi Kenkōkai, 1953), 32–34.

26. The official magazine of the association, *Umi no soto,* started to circulate in 1922.

27. Nagata Shigeshi, *Shinano kaigai ijūshi* (Nagano: Shinano Kaigai Kyōryokukai, 1952), 91–92.

28. Nagata, *Shinano kaigai ijūshi,* 134.

29. To buy land of 25 chobu in Aliança required 1,500 yen, while to enroll in the contract-farmer program of Aliança required 700 to 800 yen. Nagata, *Shinano kaigai ijūshi,* 134.

30. Nagata, *Burajiru ni okeru Nihonjin hattenshi,* 56; Tsuchida, "The Japanese in Brazil, 1908–1941," 250–51.

31. Tsuchida, "The Japanese in Brazil, 1908–1941," 269; Nagata, *Burajiru ni okeru Nihonjin hattenshi,* 73.

32. Suzuki Iwazō, "Menka seisankoku toshite no Burajiru," *Burajiru: ishokumin to bōeki* 1, no. 1 (January 1927): 21–22.

33. Shibusawa Ei'ichi Kinen Zaidan Kenkyūbu, *Jitsugyōka to Burajiru ijū* (Tokyo: Fuji Shuppan, 2008), 5–6.

34. Unlike others, Nanbei Kigyō Kumiai was funded by a group of Japanese Americans. It established a colony in Castanhal, which was mainly occupied by Japanese American re-migrants. It was merged with the Acará Colony managed by Nantaku in 1929. Azuma, *In Search of Our Frontier,* 148–49.

35. The example of Nantaku is analyzed in chapter 7.

36. Imin Shūyōjo, *Imin Shūyōjo e nyūjo ni tsuite* (Kobe: Imin Shūyōjo, 1928). It was later renamed Kobe Imin Kyōyōjo.

37. "Kugatsu nijūnichi yori hanabanashiku kaijōshita kankanshiki kinen kaikō hakurankai," *Osaka asahi shinbun,* September 28, 1930.

38. *Kaikō hakuran kaishi: kankanshiki kinen* (Kobe: Kobe Hakurankai Kyōkai, 1931), 104.

39. Fukuda Sanji, "Senkō wo assuru ei e aru daikankanshiki ni narabini kaikō hakurankai ni okeru kaigai hattenkan," *Burajiru: ishokumin to bōeki* 4, no. 11 (November 1930): 72–73.

40. *Kaikō hakuran kaishi: kankanshiki kinen* (Kobe: Kobe Hakurankai Kyōkai, 1931), i–ii.

41. For the concrete amounts of money that the Ministry of Colonial Affairs provided to the migration companies to support Brazilian migration, see Iikubo, "Burajiru imin kara Manshu imin e no kessetsuten," 109.

42. For an extended explanation of the minister of colonial cffairs on the responsibilities of the ministry, see Gaimushō Gaikō Shiryōkan, *Honpō imin toriatsukainin kankei zakken: Nanbei Takushoku Kabushiki Gaisha*, vol. 3, J120, J3–2.

43. Led by Naitō Hideo, head of the Colonial Department at Jōchi (Sophia) University, the Colonial Migration Association was the publisher of the magazine *Shokumin*.

44. "Chūzai gaikoku shisetsu wo mukaete: sōgonnaru rekishiteki kōkei no tenkai," *Shokumin* 9, no. 3 (March 1930): 6–11.

45. Nagata Shigeshi, "Manshū no shinano mura (1)," *Rikkō sekai*, no. 347 (November 1933): 21.

46. Nippon rikkō kai sōritsu hyaku shūnen kinen jigyō jikkō iinkai kinenshi hensan senmon iinkai, *Nippon rikkō kai hyakunen no kōseki: reiniku kyūsai, kaigai hatten undō, kokusai kōken* (Tokyo: Nippon Rikkō Kai, 1997), 213.

47. Nagano ken kaitaku jikōkai manshū kaitakushi kankōkai, *Naganoken manshū kaitakushi: sōhen* (Nagano-shi: Nagano Ken Kaitaku Jikōkai Manshū Kaitakushi Kankō Kai, 1984), 89, 150–66.

48. The number of Manchurian migrants from Nagano was more than twice that of their counterparts from Yamagata, which was ranked second. Louise Young, *Japan's Total Empire: Manchuria and the Culture of Wartime Imperialism* (Berkeley: University of California Press, 1998), 329–30.

49. Burajiru Nikkeijin Jittai Chōsa Iinkai, *Burajiru no nihon imin, kijutsu-hen*, 225.

50. Shibusawa Ei'ichi Kinen Zaidan Kenkyūbu, *Jitsugyōka to Burajiru ijū*, 133–34.

51. Tsuchida, "The Japanese in Brazil, 1908–1941," 310. Peru was another Latin American country that supplied cotton, with significant investment from the Japanese textile industry and where Japanese immigrants were essential as cotton producers. Ayumi Takenaka, "The Japanese Immigrant-Homeland Connection: The Development of Japanese Community in Peru," in Delpiano and Lu, *The Japanese Empire and Latin America*, 133–35; Franco Lobo Collantes, "En defensa del mercado interno: Importación japonesa y empresarios textiles en el Perú, 1929–1939," *Apuntes* 86 (primer semestre 2020), 100–110.

52. Gaimushō Gaikō Shiryōkan, *Honpō imin yoriatsukainin kankei zakken:* "Amazonia" Sangyō Kabushiki Gaisha, J120. J3–6.

53. Tagawa Mariko, "'Imin' shichō no kiseki" (PhD diss., Yūshōdō Shuppan, 2005), 129–30.

54. "Establishment of the quota system and movements for Japanese immigrants' exclusion," *Burajiru imin no 100 nen*, https://www.ndl.go.jp/brasil/e/s5/s5_1.html.

55. Burajiru Nihon Imin Hyakushūnen Kinen Kyōkai, *Burajiru Nihon imin hyakunenshi*, vol. 3 (Tokyo: Fūkyōsha, 2010), 113.

56. For a full list of these businesses, see "Zai hakkoku hōjin shōsha seisan kankei," in Gaimushū Gaikō shiryōkan, *Honpō Imin toriatsukainin kankei zakken*, J120. J3.

57. Gaimushō Gaikō Shiryōkan, *Honpō imin toriatsukainin kankei zakken: Kaigai Kōgyō Kabushiki Gaisha*, vol. 10, J120. J3–1.

58. Gaimushō Gaikō Shiryōkan, *Honpō imin toriatsukainin kankei zakken: Kaigai Kōgyō Kabushiki Gaisha*, vol. 11, J120. J3–1. Kaigai Ijū Kumiai Rengōkai, Kaigai Ijū Kumiai Rengōkai jigyō gaiyō, 8–11, in Gaimushō Gaikō Shiryōkan, *Honpō imin toriatsukainin kankei zakken: Kaigai Kōgyō Kabushiki Gaisha*, vol. 30, J120. J 3–5.

59. Nippon Rikkō Kai Sōritsu Hyaku Shūnen Kinen Jigyō Jikkō Iinkai Kinenshi Hensan Senmon Iinkai, *Nippon Rikkō Kai hyakunen no kōseki*, 260–73.

5. LAND, MEDIA, AND THE FORMATION
OF SETTLER COLONIAL IDENTITY

1. Smith, *Brazil and the United States*, 82–94.

2. Morris-Suzuki, *Re-inventing Japan: Time, Space, Nation*, 92; Christopher W. A. Szpilman and Sven Saaler, "Pan-Asianism as an Ideal of Asian Identity and Solidarity, 1850–Present," *Asia-Pacific Journal* 9, issue 17, no. 1 (April 2011): 13–14.

3. What made this transoceanic network of information possible was the vibrant circulation of books, journals, and newspapers published in Japan among the Japanese settler communities in Brazil. For details regarding the circulation of Japanese print media in Brazil, see Hibi Yoshitaka, "Chasing the Transnational Flow of Books and Magazines: Materials, Knowledge, and Network," in Delpiano and Lu, *The Japanese Empire and Latin America*, 191–207.

4. Mori Sei'ichi, Yamamoto Kōsuke, and Suzuki Nao, "Burajiru Nihon imin no isseiki," *Jinmonken*, no. 7 (2009): 66.

5. Mori Sei'ichi, Yamamoto Kōsuke, and Suzuki Nao, "Burajiru Nihon imin no isseiki," 66.

6. The portion of Japanese immigrants in the overall yearly number of immigrants in Brazil grew at an astonishing rate, from 1.1 percent in 1923 to 53.2 percent in 1933. Mori Sei'ichi, Yamamoto Kōsuke, and Suzuki Nao, "Burajiru Nihon imin no isseiki," 64.

7. See chapter 3 for a more comprehensive discussion of the loteamento model.

8. Maeyama Takashi, "Kaisetsu: imin bungaku kara mainoritei bungaku e," in *Koronia shōsetsu senshū*, ed. Koronia Bugakukai, vol. 1 (São Paulo: Koronia Bungakukai, 1975), 304.

9. Wako Jungorō, *Bauru kannai no hōjin* (São Paulo: Fazenda Tietêk, 1938), 18.

10. Iida Kōjirō, *Imin no kaiketsu Hoshina Ken'ichirō no shōgai: Hawai, Tekisasu, Burajiru* (Tokyo: Fuji Shuppan, 2017), 143

11. Nagata, *Burajiru ni okeru Nihonjin hattenshi*, vol. 2, 259, 262, 264.

12. Iida, *Imin no kaiketsu Hoshina Ken'ichirō no shōgai*, 130–34.

13. Nagata, *Burajiru ni okeru Nihonjin hattenshi*, vol. 2, 259–63.

14. Edward Mack, "Diasporic Markets: Japanese Print and Migration in São Paulo, 1908–1935," *Script & Print: Bulletin of the Bibliographical Society of Australia and New Zealand* 29 (2005): 164.

15. Mack, "Diasporic Markets," 172.

16. *Ariansā Jihō* was a newspaper founded and circulated only in the Aliança Colony. *Hokusei Minpō* was primarily for settlers in the Birigui Colony. Hanzawa Noriko, "Burajiru Noroesute chihō ni okeru nihongo shinbun no hatashita yakuwari," *Ritsumeikan gengo bunka kenkyū* 26, no. 4 (March 2015): 99 n. 10.

17. Burajiru Nihon Imin Hyakushūnen Kinen Kyōkai, *Burajiru nihon imin hyakunenshi*, vol. 3, 103.

18. Burajiru Nihon Imin Hyakushūnen Kinen Kyōkai, *Burajiru nihon imin hyakunenshi*, vol. 4 (Tokyo: Fūkyōsha, 2013), 485–86.

19. Nagata, *Burajiru ni okeru nihonjin hattenshi*, vol. 2, 261.

20. Nagata, *Burajiru ni okeru nihonjin hattenshi*, vol. 2, 264.

21. Two representative works published in these two decades, respectively, were Kawada Shirō, *Shokuminchi toshite no Burajiru* (Tokyo: Yūhikaku Shobō, 1914); and Inoue Masaji, *Kaigai yuhi wakaki Nihon no shinro* (Tokyo: Minyūsha, 1929). Both named Brazil as a desirable destination for Japanese emigration.

22. This practice was attested by the accounts of the Japanese settlers in Brazil themselves. See, e.g., Nagashima Kanae, "Jūkanan no shokuminchi seikatsu," *Burajiru: ishokumin to bōeki*, no. 9, October 1927, 72.

23. Hanzawa Noriko, "Senzenki Burajiru sanpauroshū Noroesute chihō to nihongo shinbun: Kōyama Rokurō to *Seishū shinpō*" (PhD diss., Kyoto Joshi Daigaku, 2017), 86–87.

24. "Nōgyōka no torubeki michi (1)," *Burajiru jihō*, no. 483, January 14, 1927, 1.

25. "Ketten wo shiru tokoronin seikō ga aru," *Burajiru jihō*, no. 589, January 31, 1929, 1.

26. For example, see "Nōsakubutsu no sentaku: kangyōbu ni ichigon," *Nippaku shinbun*, no. 730, May 28, 1931, 3.

27. There are two main reasons for this mind-set. First, they believed that it would be in the best interest of the empire if the Japanese emigrants settled down abroad. Second, they accepted the argument of many white exclusionists in the United States, who blamed the Japanese immigrants for their refusal to contribute to the host society because they intended to return to Japan after accumulating enough wealth. Lu, *The Making of Japanese Settler Colonialism*, 132–33, 175.

28. Negawa Sachio, *Burajiru nikkei imin no kyōikushi* (Tokyo: Misuzu Shobō, 2016), 84.

29. Handa Tomoo, *Imin no seikatsu no rekishi: Burajiru nikkeijin no ayunda michi* (Tokyo: Ie no Hikari Kyōkai, 1970), 307.

30. Burajiru Jihōsha, *Burajiru nenkan* (São Paulo: Burajiru Jihōsha, 1933), 108.

31. The total number of Japanese schools created in São Paulo reached 122 by June 1931. The number climbed to 486 by March 1939. Burajiru Nihon Imin Hyakushūnen Kinen Kyōkai, *Burajiru nihon imin hyakunenshi*, vol. 3, 289.

32. Burajiru Nihon Imin Hyakushūnen Kinen Kyōkai, *Burajiru nihon imin hyakunenshi*, vol. 3, 275–76.

33. Matsunaga Toshio, "Watashi no jidō kyōiku mondaikan," *Burajiru jihō*, no. 495, April 8, 1927, 3.

34. "Gutaika shita kyōiku mondai," *Burajiru jihō*, no. 491, March 11, 1927, 1.

35. The Parents' Association was established based on a preexisting organization, the Japanese Education Association in Brazil (Zaihaku Nihonjin Kyōikukai), established under the initiative of the previous consul-general, Akamatsu Hiroyuki, in 1927. Though also formed to unify the operation of Japanese-language schools in the state, it failed to achieve the original goal and was replaced by the Parents' Association. Nagata, *Burajiru ni okeru nihonjin hattenshi*, vol. 2, 199.

36. Negawao, *Burajiru nikkei imin no kyōikushi*, 101.

37. "Manshū mondai to hakkoku imin," *Nippaku shinbun*, no. 775, April 7, 1932, 1.

38. Mori Sei'ichi, Yamamoto Kōsuke, and Suzuki Nao, "Burajiru Nihon imin no isseiki," 73–74.

39. Tsuchida, "The Japanese in Brazil, 1908–1941," 210.

40. Tsuchida, "The Japanese in Brazil, 1908–1941," 213–14.

41. Tsuchida, "The Japanese in Brazil, 1908–1941," 217.

42. "Nihonjin nomi no shokuminchi fuka," *Burajiru jihō*, no. 461, August 13, 1926, 1; "Kaigai ijū kumiai ni chūmon no koto (1)," *Burajiru jihō*, no. 539, February 10, 1928, 1.

43. The best exemplifier of the principle of coexistence and co-prosperity was Aliança, a Japanese settler colony in São Paulo established in 1923. See chapter 4; also see Lu, *The Making of Japanese Settler Colonialism*, 211–22.

44. Maeyama, "Kaisetsu: imin bungaku kara mainoritei bungaku e," 299.

45. *Burajiru jihō*, no. 778, April 14, 1932, cited in Mack, "Paracolonial Literature," 115–16.

46. Koronia Bungakukai, *Koronia shōsetsu senshū*, vol. 1 (São Paulo: Koronia Bungakukai, 1975), 12–20.

47. Kōyama, *Zaihaku ishokumin 25 shūnenkan*, preface, 1.

48. See Burajiru Jihōsha, *Burajiru nenkan* (São Paulo: Burajiru Jihōsha, 1933).

49. A 1929 editorial in *Nippaku shinbun*, for example, claimed that although the Japanese were the strongest in the world in terms of their national character, if left without intervention they would still lose their Japanese identity because of the tremendous power of nature in Brazil. To prevent the Nisei from degeneration, it urged parents themselves to keep the consciousness and pride of being Japanese. "Kokumin teki jikaku," *Nippaku shinbun*, no. 636, August 8, 1929, 1.

50. "Meiyo na shokumin ka?" *Seishū shinpō*, no. 269, February 25, 1927, 1.

51. Maeyama, *Imin no Nihon kaiki undō*, 101–3.

52. Maeyama, *Imin no Nihon kaiki undō*, 103–4.

53. Burajiru Nihon Imin Hyakushūnen Kinen Kyōkai, *Burajiru nihon imin hyakunenshi*, vol. 3, 29.

54. Burajiru Nihon Imin Hyakushūnen Kinen Kyōkai, *Burajiru nihon imin hyakunenshi*, vol. 3, 396.

55. Burajiru Nihon Imin Hyakushūnen Kinen Kyōkai, *Burajiru nihon imin hyakunenshi*, vol. 3, 398.

56. Jeffrey D. Needell, "Identity, Race, Gender, and Modernity in the Origins of Gilberto Freyre's Oeuvre," *American Historical Review* 100, no. 1 (February 1995): 58.

57. Needell, "Identity, Race, Gender, and Modernity in the Origins of Gilberto Freyre's Oeuvre," 68.

58. George Reid Andrews, "Brazilian Racial Democracy, 1900–90: An American Counterpoint," *Journal of Contemporary History* 31, no. 3 (July 1996): 483–85.

59. Hemming, *Die If You Must*, 41–42.

6. "ORPHAN OF THE WORLD": THE MYTH AND REALITY OF RACIAL INCLUSION

1. Ishikawa Tatsuzō, *Saikin Nanbei ōraiki* (1931; repr. Tokyo: Chūō Kōron, 1981), 8.

2. Ishikawa, *Saikin Nanbei ōraiki*, 129–34.

3. Tsuchida, "The Japanese in Brazil, 1908–1941," 239.

4. Burajiru Nihon Imin 8onenshi Hensan Iinkai, *Burajiru Nihon imin 8onenshi* (São Paulo: Toppan Fueisu Insatsu Shuppan Gaisha, 1996), 107.

5. Imasawa Fujisaburō, "Shōwa 4nen Abarē fukin menka jikkyō," *Burajiru: ishokumin to bōeki* 3, no. 12, December 1929, 37–38.

6. Tsuchida, "The Japanese in Brazil, 1908–1941," 258.

7. Northern Paraná was excluded from this ban. Tsuchida, "The Japanese in Brazil, 1908–1941," 266.

8. Jacobowitz, "A Bitter Brew," 24–26. In his pathbreaking study of Japanese immigrant literature in Brazil, Edward Mack demonstrates that Sugi Takeo (the pen name of Takei Makoto) was not only an astute observer of the settler community but also a core participant in the construction of Japanese settler identity itself through literature. Mack, *Acquired Alterity*, 128, 199–200.

9. For example, Caza Tozan's early efforts in cotton cultivation in the 1920s were inspired by the Japanese government–sponsored investigation. See details in chapter 4.

10. Tsuchida, "The Japanese in Brazil, 1908–1941," 257.

11. "British-Japanese Struggle for Asia Textile Markets," *Far Eastern Survey* 5, no. 13 (1936): 134.

12. Nawa, *Nihon bōsekigyō to genmen mondai kenkyū*, 322–23.

13. Henri Delanghe, "Japanese Import of Brazilian Raw Cotton in the Second Half of the 1930s: The Beginning of Significant Japanese-Brazilian Trade and Investment Relations," *História Econômica & História de Empresas* 2, no. 2 (1999): 93–94.

14. Delanghe, "Japanese Import of Brazilian Raw Cotton in the Second Half of the 1930s," 85.

15. Shibusawa Ei'ichi Kinen Zaidan Kenkyūbu, *Jitsugyōka to Burajiru ijū*, 135–38.

16. "Kaisha Enkaku oyobi Jigyō Jōkyō," in Gaimusho Gaikō Shiryōkan, *Honpō ijūsha toriatsukai dantai kankei zakken: Nichinan Sangyō Kabushiki Gaisha kankei*, vol. 3, J.1.1.0.3–1.

17. Kōyama, *Imin yonjūnen shi*, 242.

18. Gaimushō Gaikō Shiryōkan, *Honpō imin toriatsukainin kankei zakken*, J 1.2.0, J.3.

19. Shibusawa Ei'ichi Kinen Zaidan Kenkyūbu, *Jitsugyōka to Burajiru ijū*, 134.

20. Burataku Gatto Undō Sanbōbu, *Gatto undō no shiori*, vol. 1 (São Paulo: Burataku Gatto Undō Sanbōbu, 1934), 2–3.

21. Burataku Gatto Undō Sanbōbu, *Gatto undō no shiori*, vol. 1, 3–60.

22. Mizuno Masano, *Basutosu nijūgonenshi* (Tokyo: Mizuno Masano, 1955), 63–64.

23. Burajiru Nihon Imin Hyakunenshi Hensan Kankō Iinkai, *Burajiru Nihon imin hyakunenshi*, vol. 1 (Tokyo: Fūkyōsha, 2008), 133–34.

24. Kōyama, *Imin yonjūnen shi*, 312.

25. Andrews, "Brazilian Racial Democracy, 1900–90," 483–85.

26. Morris-Suzuki, *Re-inventing Japan*, 91.

27. Morris-Suzuki, *Re-inventing Japan*, 93.

28. Morris-Suzuki, *Re-inventing Japan*, 92.

29. Fujitani, *Race for Empire*, 7.

30. Maeyama, *Imin no Nihon kaiki undō*, 93.

31. The association was initially named the Japanese School Parents' Association in São Paulo and changed to Japanese Education Association in 1936, before changing to Japanese Culture and Education Association in 1938. Fukushima Hiroyuki, "Burajiru nihonjin imin no kyōiku to nihon kokka: Nihonjin no dōka mondai ni kansuru yobiteki kōsatsu," *Fukuoka Daigaku jinbun ronsō* 52, no. 1 (June 2020): 13.

32. Fukushima, "Burajiru nihonjin imin no kyōiku to nihon kokka," 28.

33. Kōyama, *Imin yonjūnen shi*, 308–9.

34. Kōyama, *Imin yonjūnen shi*, 308–9.

35. Kōyama, *Imin yonjūnen shi*, 314.

36. Kōyama, *Imin yonjūnen shi*, 314–15.

37. Wako, *Baurū kannai no hōjin*, 11.

38. Negawa Sachio, "Senzen senchūki Burajiru ni okeru nikkei imin shitei kyōiku no shiteki kenkyū," (PhD diss., Graduate University for Advanced Studies, Sokendai, 2013), 187.

39. Kishimoto Kōichi, *Nanbei no senya ni koritsu shite* (1947; repr. Tokyo: Tōfūsha, 2002), 284–85.

40. Kishimoto, *Nanbei no senya ni koritsu shite*, 190.

41. Japanese diplomats in Brazil had painstakingly urged Japanese settlers to stay, settle down, and keep being hopeful when facing the rising tide of anti-Japanese sentiments in the country. For example, see the article penned by the Japanese consul in São Paulo in 1934: Uchiyama Iwatarō, "Hainichi no jikyoku ni shinmenshite zairyū dōhō ni tsugu," *Seishū shinpō*, no. 860, May 22, 1934, 1.

42. Maeyama, *Imin no nihon kaiki undō*, 133–34.

43. Maeyama, *Imin no nihon kaiki undō*, 134.

44. Narusei Ren, "Kigen nisen rokuhaykunen wo hōshukushite," in *Burajiru ni okeru dai'issen ni katsuyaku suru hitobito*, ed. Ono Shinzen (São Paulo: Burajiru Jihōsha, 1941), preface, 1–3.

45. Maeyama, *Imin no nihon kaiki undō*, 113.

46. Maeyama, *Imin no nihon kaiki undō*, 122–23.

47. Kiyotani Masuji, "Shinbun wa imin ni totte no nendeattaka (2)," *Jinmonken*, no. 3 (1999): 34–35.

48. Kiyotani, "Shinbun wa imin ni totte no nendeattaka (2)," 35–36.

49. Wako, *Baurū kannai no hōjin*, 1.

50. Nagata, "Manshū no shinano mura (1)," 21.

51. Nippon Rikkō Kai Sōritsu Hyaku Shūnen Kinen Jigyō Jikkō Iinkai Kinenshi Hensan Senmon Iinkai, *Nippon Rikkō Kai hyakunen no kōseki*, 213.

52. Mamiya, *Saibara Seitō kenkyū*, 367–68.

53. Koseki Tokuya, "Jijo," in *Nanpō Kaitakusha no shihyō: Nanbei imin no taiken wo mototoshite* (Tokyo: Bunkentō Shoten, 1942), 1.

54. Koseki, "Jijo," 1–4.

55. Takemoto Takeo to Nakano Takeshi, July 26, 1939, in Gaimushō Gaikō Shiryōkan, *Honpō imin toriatsukainin kankei zakken: Kaigai Kōgyō Kabushiki Gaisha*. Vol. 10, J.1.2.0, J 3–1.

56. Takemoto Takeo to Nakano Takeshi, August 12, 1939, and August 31, 1939, in Gaimushō Gaikō Shiryōkan, *Honpō imin toriatsukainin kankei zakken: Kaigai Kōgyō Kabushiki Gaisha*, vol. 10, J.1.2.0, J 3–1.

57. Kaigai Ijū Gaimushō Rengōkai jigyō gaiyō (1943), in Gaimushō Gaikō Shiryōkan, *Honpon imin toriatsukainin kankei zakken: Kaigai Ijū Kumiai*, vol. 30, J.1.2.0, J 3–5.

58. Nichinan Sangyō Kabushiki Gaisha, *Dai nana nendo gyōmu hōkokusho* (1944), in Gaimushō Gaikō Shiryōkan, *Honpō ijūsha toriatsukai dantai kankei zakken: Nichinan Sangyō Kabushiki Gaisha kankei*, vol. 3, J.1.1.0.3–1.

59. Kanegafuchi Takushoku Kabushiki Gaisha no jigyō keika to kaisha kongo no shochi ni tsuite, in Gaimushō Gaikō Shiryōkan, *Honpō imin toriatsukainin kankei zakken, Nanbei Takushoku Kabushiki Gaisha*, vol. 1, J.1.2.0, J 4–1.

60. Kōsonki (Kōyama Rokurō), "Yagate Hōji Shinbun no Hakkin nit suki," *Seishū shinpō*, no. 2205, April 5, 1941, 4.

61. Maeyama, *Imin no Nihon kaiki undō*, 42.

7. CONQUERING THE TROPICS: COLLABORATIVE SETTLER COLONIALISM IN THE AMAZON

1. Uetsuka Tsukasa, "Dai Amazon no Nihon shin shokuminchi," *Kingu* 7, no. 6 (1931): 72–85.

2. Seth Garfield, *In Search of the Amazon: Brazil, the United States, and the Nature of a Region* (Durham, NC: Duke University Press, 2013), 22–23.

3. Garfield, *In Search of the Amazon*, 37.

4. Garfield, *In Search of the Amazon*, 21.

5. This chapter joins Facundo Garasino's recent article that examines the Amazonia Industrial Institute and Company as a joint product of Japan's migration-driven expansionism and Brazil's developmental nationalism. Facundo Garasino, "Japan's Last Colonial Frontier: Settler Migration, Development, and Expansionism in the Brazilian Amazon," in *Transpacific Visions: Connected Histories of the Pacific across North and South*, ed. Yasuko Hassall Kobayashi and Shinnosuke Takahashi (Lanham, MD: Lexington Books, 2021), 111–28.

6. Garfield, *In Search of the Amazon*, 14–15.

7. Garfield, *In Search of the Amazon*, 15.

8. Susanna B. Hecht, *The Scramble for the Amazon and the "Lost Paradise" of Euclides da Cunha* (Chicago: University of Chicago Press, 2013), 84–102.

9. Todd A. Diacon, *Stringing Together a Nation: Cândido Mariano da Silva Rondon and the Construction of a Modern Brazil, 1906–1930* (Durham, NC: Duke University Press, 2004), 15–17.

10. Garfield, *In Search of the Amazon*, 17.

11. Garfield, *In Search of the Amazon*, 17.

12. The anthropologist Darcy Riberio observed that during the rubber boom the Indigenous peoples were subjected to such oppressive exploitation that no community could endure. Hemming, *Die If You Must*, 53–54.

13. Garfield, *In Search of the Amazon*, 18.

14. Ford traded part of his existing land for the land upriver at Belterra in 1934. Garfield, *In Search of the Amazon*, 63.

15. Satō Jin, *"Motazaru kuni" no shigen ron: jizoku kanō na kokudo o meguru mō hitotsu no chi* (Tokyo: Tokyo Daigaku Shuppankai, 2011), 69–70.

16. Satō, *"Motazaru Kuni" no shigen ron*, 76.

17. Yano Tooru, *Nihon no nanshin to Tōnan Ajia* (Tokyo: Nihon Keizai Shinbunsha, 1976), 16.

18. Yamagata Jirō, "Sōkan no ji," *Burajiru: ishokumin to bōeki* 1, no. 1, January 1927, 4–5.

19. The exhibit was also cosponsored by the Hyōgo prefectural government, the Department of Commerce and Industry of the Kobe Municipal Government, the Kobe Chamber of Commerce and Industry, and Osaka Mainichi News Agency. The composition of the cosponsors demonstrated the Kobe-based business elites' profound interest in the opportunities in Brazil. See "Burajiru jijō tenrankai: Kobe Mitsukoshi gofukuten ni okeru," *Burajiru: ishokumin to bōeki* 1, no. 9 (October 1927): 93.

20. "Burajiru jijō tenrankai: Kobe Mitsukoshi gofukuten ni okeru," 93–96.

21. "Amazon kaitaku," *Burajiru imin no 100 nen*, https://www.ndl.go.jp/brasil/s4/s4_2 .html

22. Ikushima Shigekazu, *Amazon ijū sanjūnenshi* (São Paulo: Sanpauro Shinbunsha, 1959), 21.

23. Fukuhara Hachirō, "Zenjin mitō no Burajiru genya wo tōsa shite," *Burajiru: ishokumin to bōeki* 1, no. 4 (May 1927): 26–29.

24. Fukuhara Sei (Hachirō), "Wa ga kuni no ishokumin hatten ni Burajiru no kōya ni hiyaku wo nasu: tōshi jigyō no shōkai," *Burajiru: ishokumin to bōeki* 2, no. 11, November 1928, 58–59.

25. *Burajirukoku Parā shū shokumin nannai* (1930), in Gaimushō Gaikō Shiryōkan, *Honpō imin toriatsukainin kankei zakken: Nanbei Takushoku Kabishiki Gaisha*, vol. 2, J120, J3–2.

26. Azuma, *In Search of Our Frontier*, 148–49.

27. Ikushima, *Amazon ijū sanjūnenshi*, 108–9.

28. Uetsuka Yoshio and Nakano Yorio, *Uetsuka Tsukasa no Amazon kaitaku jigyō* (Chufu: Ten'en, 2013), 36–38.

29. Saitō Hiroshi, "Amazonia no Nikkeijin," *Kenkyū repōto* 8 (1980): 1.

30. Ikushima, *Amazon ijū sanjūnenshi*, 22.

31. Ikushima, *Amazon ijū sanjūnenshi*, 24–25.

32. "Kaigai Ijū Kumiai Sōkai: yūshi jikō kettei," *Osaka mainichi shinbun*, August 7, 1927, 4.

33. "Kaigai Ijū Kumiai Sōkai: yūshi jikō kettei," 4.

34. Inoue Masaji, *Shizen no kankyō to hakujin jinkō mondai* (Tokyo: Kaigai Kōgyō Kabushiki Gaisha, 1929), 15–23. The claim of Japanese racial superiority over white people as colonizers in the tropics enjoyed popularity in the Japanese empire through the 1940s and undergirded its expansion to Southeast Asia and the South Seas until the end of World War II. The same discourse, for example, was used to justify Japanese expansion to New Guinea in 1941. Nanpō Sangyō Chōsakai, *Nanshin sōsho*, vol. 1: *Nyūginia* (Tokyo: Nanshinsha, 1941), 70–74.

35. Inoue, *Shizen no kankyō to hakujin jinkō mondai*, 42–47.

36. See chapter 3 for details about Uetsuka Shūhei.

37. Uetsuka and Nakano, *Uetsuka Tsukasa no Amazon kaitaku jigyō*, 36–38.

38. Gaimushō Tsūshōkoku, *Hakkoku Amazonnasu shū Nihon shokuminchi chiki kakutei narabi shokumin keikaku ni kansuru chō hōkokusho* (Tokyo: Gaimushō Tsūshōkoku, 1931), 405–6.

39. The Kokushikan Academy was established by Shibata Tokujirō in the Azubu district of Tokyo in 1917. It became the Kokushikan University in 1958.

40. After the Manchurian Incident, the president of the Kokushikan Academy, Shibata Tokujirō, wanted the Kōtaku graduates to go to South America instead of Manchuria. Insisting on its focus on the Amazon, Uetsuka pulled Kōtaku out of the Kokushikan campus and moved it to Kanagawa Prefecture. There he managed to establish a new campus with the financial support of the Colonial Ministry and renamed the school Nihon Kōtō Takushoku Gakkō (Japanese Advanced Colonial School).

41. Uetsuka and Nakano, *Uetsuka Tsukasa no Amazon kaitaku jigyō*, 70–71, 107.

42. Uetsuka and Nakano, *Uetsuka Tsukasa no Amazon kaitaku jigyō*, 34–35.

43. Burataku Gatto Undō Sanbōbu, *Gatto undō no shiori*, vol. 1, 652.

44. Ikushima, *Amazon ijū sanjūnenshi*, 131–34.

45. The idea of jute cultivation was originally proposed by Tsuji Kotarō, Uetsuka's follower and alumnus of Kobe Academy of Commerce, after completing an investigation in the Amazon. Ikushima, *Amazon ijū sanjūnenshi*, 102.

46. Ikushima, *Amazon ijū sanjūnenshi*, 103–4.

47. Kōyama, *Imin yonjūnen shi*, 193.

48. Ikushima, *Amazon ijū sanjūnenshi*, 100–101. The financial involvement of Tōtaku, in particular, demonstrated the connections between Japanese colonial business in Asia and the empire's capitalist expansion in the Amazon.

49. Ikushima, *Amazon ijū sanjūnenshi*, 72; Uetsuka and Nakano, *Uetsuka Tsukasa no Amazon kaitaku jigyō*, 235–37.

50. Uetsuka and Nakano, *Uetsuka Tsukasa no Amazon kaitaku jigyō*, 245–47.

51. Saitō, "Amazonia no Nikkeijin," 8–11.

52. Ikushima, *Amazon ijū sanjūnenshi*, 55.

53. Garfield, *In Search of the Amazon*, 31.

54. Garfield, *In Search of the Amazon*, 14, 33–34.

55. Garfield, "The Roots of a Plant," 751–53.

56. Garfield, "The Roots of a Plant," 752–53, 760–61.

57. Hemming, *Die If You Must*, 93.

58. Garfield, *In Search of the Amazon*, 25.

59. Uetsuka and Nakano, *Uetsuka Tsukasa no Amazon kaitaku jigyō*, 243.

60. Uetsuka and Nakano, *Uetsuka Tsukasa no Amazon kaitaku jigyō*, 266.

61. Philip Staniford, *Pioneers in the Tropics: The Political Organization of Japanese in an Immigrant Community in Brazil* (London: Athlone Press, 1973), 18.

62. Staniford, *Pioneers in the Tropics*, 17.

63. Garfield, *In Search of the Amazon*, 127.

64. Ikushima, *Amazon ijū sanjūnenshi*, 168.

65. Takaoka had advocated Japanese migration to Brazil as early as 1925 in response to Japanese exclusion in the United States. Takaoka Kumao, "Burajiru imin ron," *Chūō kōron*, vol. 40, no. 1, January 1925, 53–68.

66. *Kanegafuchi Takushoku Kabushiki Gaisha no jigyō keika to kaisha kongo no shochi ni tsuite*, in Gaimushō Gaikō Shiryōkan, *Honpō imin toriatsukainin kankei zakken: Nanbei Takushoku Kabushiki Gaisha*, vol. 1, J.1.2.0, J 4–1.

8. REINVENTING JAPAN AND JAPANESE BRAZILIANS

1. Suzuki Masatake, *Suzuki Tei'ichi: Burajiru Nikkei shakai ni ikita kisai no shōgai* (São Paulo: San Pauro Jinbun Kagaku Kenkyūjo, 2007), 262–63.

2. Suzuki, *Suzuki Tei'ichi*, 263–64.

3. Fernando Morais, trans. with a critical introduction by Seth Jacobowitz, *Dirty Hearts: The History of Shindō Renmei* (Basingstoke: Palgrave Macmillan, 2021), 4.

4. *Paulista Gurafu, Kōtaishi gofusai Burajiru no tabi*, July 1967, 3.

5. *Paulista Gurafu, Kōtaishi gofusai Burajiru no tabi*, July 1967, 3.

6. Gerald Horne, *Race War! White Supremacy and the Japanese Attack on the British Empire* (New York: New York University Press, 2003), xv.

7. Fujitani, *Race for Empire*, 7. Nazi Germany was a noteworthy exception.

8. Jessica Lynn Graham, *Shifting the Meaning of Democracy: Race, Politics, and Culture in the United States and Brazil* (Berkeley: University of California Press, 2019), 262.

9. The Culture and Personality school originated in the theory of cultural relativism developed by the U.S. anthropologist Franz Boas at Columbia University and was popularized by Boas's students Ruth Benedict and Margret Mead. Scholars of this school treated cultures as isolated subjects and believed that each culture functioned according to its internal logic. Accordingly, they explained each culture based on its claimed "psychological characterization" and "personality type." Sonia Ryang, *Japan and National Anthropology: A Critique* (New York: Routledge, 2004), 16.

10. Ryang, *Japan and National Anthropology*, 37–38.

11. Morris-Suzuki, *Re-inventing Japan*, 70.

12. Sakai Tetsuya, "Sengo shisō to kokusai seijiron no kōsaku: kōwa ronsōki wo chūshin ni," *Kokusai seiji*, no. 117 (March 1998): 121.

13. Nakamura Mihō, "Sengo Nihon no bunka kokka gainen no tokuchō: rekishiteki tenkai o fumaete," *Bunka seisaku kenkyū*, no. 7 (2013): 143.

14. Nambara Shigeru, *Bunka to kokka* (Tokyo: Tokyo Daigaku Shuppankai, 1957), 40–41.

15. Nambara, *Bunka to kokka*, 14.

16. X.Y.Z., "Doyōkai to jidai," *Jidai*, no. 11, 1950, 42–44.

17. Barbara Weinstein, *The Color of Modernity: São Paulo and the Making of Race and Nation in Brazil* (Durham, NC: Duke University Press, 2015), 260–61.

18. Thomas E. Skidmore, *Black into White: Race and Nationality in Brazilian Thought* (Durham, NC: Duke University Press, 1992), 208.

19. Suzuki, *Suzuki Tei'ichi*, 358

20. The discussion script was published in the club's mouthpiece, the *Era* (*Jidai*), and reprinted in *Chūō kōron* in Japan. "Zaihaku hōjin shakai to imin mondai: Burajiru genchi zadankai," *Chūō kōron*, no. 784, June 1951, 88.

21. Yamamoto Kiyoshi Hyōdan Henshū Iinkai, *Yamamoto Kiyoshi hyōdan* (São Paulo: San Pauro Jinbun Kagaku Kenkyūjo, 1981), 183.

22. Emi Kiyotaka, "Kokumin kokka ron," *Jidai*, no. 1, 1947, 1–3.

23. Handa Tomoo, "Shinbunka kensetsu no shihyō," *Jidai*, no. 1, 1947, 15–18.

24. Andō Zenpati, "Bunka no honshitsu to tokushūsei: bunka kokka kensetsu no kokoroe," *Jidai*, no. 3, 1947, 23–26.

25. Saitō Hiroshi, "Shinkan shōkai: Gilberto Freyre, Interpretação do Brasil, 1947," *Jidai*, no. 3, 1947, 22; Saitō Hiroshi, "Shinkan shōkai: Ruth Benedict, *The Chrysanthemum and the Sword: Patterns of Japanese Culture*, Boston, 1946," *Jidai*, no. 4, 1947, 18–19.

26. Suzuki, *Suzuki Tei'ichi*, 318–55.

27. Suzuki, *Suzuki Tei'ichi*, 259–60.

28. Kōyama, *Imin yonjūnen shi*, 430–35.

29. Nambara Shigeru, for example, claimed that the emperor himself symbolized Japan's national morality and spirit and held no responsibility for the war and Japanese imperialism. Nambara, *Bunka to kokka*, 198–99.

30. Kingsberg, "Becoming Brazilians to Be Japanese," 81–82.

31. An example of this trend in US historiography was the concept of the Great Frontier created by Walter Webb, then president of the American Historical Association. See Walter Prescott Webb, *The Great Frontier* (Boston: Houghton Mifflin, 1952).

32. *Frontier News* (March 2011), 3.

33. For more details on the reemergence of Japan's migration state in the 1950s, see Lu, *The Making of Japanese Settler Colonialism*, 247–50.

34. Weinstein, *The Color of Modernity*, 44.

35. Weinstein, *The Color of Modernity*, 261.

36. For more information on the history of immigration in Brazil after World War II, see Lesser, *Immigration, Ethnicity, and National Identity in Brazil*, 179–81.

37. Burns, *A History of Brazil*, 403–5. The fundamental urban layout of Brasília is characterized by the intersection of two primary roads. These roads extend toward Brazil's northern and western frontiers. One road connects Brasília with Porto Velho, which is close to the Bolivian border, and the other leads to Belém, an important port located at the mouth of the Amazon River. Paulo Travaros, "Modern Frontiers: Beyond Brasília, the Amazon." In *Latin American Modern Architectures: Ambiguous Territories*, ed. Patricio del Real and Helen Gyger (Routledge, 2013), 191.

38. Paurisuta Shinbunsha, ed., *Koronia sengō jūnenshi* (São Paulo: Paurisuta Shinbunsha, 1956), 43–46.

39. Suzuki, *Suzuki Tei'ichi*, 359–60.

40. Izumi Sei'ichi and Saitō Hiroshi, eds., *Amazon: So no fūdo to Nihonjin* (Tokyo: Kokon Shoin, 1954), 235–41.

41. Izumi Sei'ichi, ed., *Imin: Burajiru imin no jittai chōsai* (Tokyo: Kokon Shoin, 1956), 127.

42. Leo T. S. Ching has provided a historical analysis of *dōka* as a colonial policy in Taiwan and Korea and discussed its relationship with *kōminka* (the empire's policy of imperialization). Leo T. S. Ching, *Becoming Japanese: Colonial Taiwan and the Politics of Identity Formation* (Berkeley: University of California Press, 2001), 89–132.

43. Kingsberg, "Becoming Brazilians to Be Japanese," 84–85.

44. For example, while Izumi used the term "imin" in the book title itself, he called the Japanese community in Brazil "Burajiru no Nikkei Koronia" in the title of the introduction to the book. Izumi, *Imin: Burajiru imin no jittai chōsa*, 10.

45. Gamō Masao, *Nihonjin no seikatsu kōzō jusetsu* (Tokyo: Seishin Shobō, 1960), 1–2.

46. Gamō, *Nihonjin no seikatsu kōzō jusetsu*, 113–78.

47. Nakamura Shigeo, "Ōya sōichi no 'meigen' wo megutte," *Discover Nikkei*, March 29, 2007, http://www.discovernikkei.org/en/journal/2007/3/29/brazil-nippon-dayori/.

48. Fukasawa Masayuki, "Meiji seishin to koronia nana fushigi," *Burajiru tokuhō*, March 2012, https://nipo-brasil.org/archives/2332/

49. For more information on the term "Malthusian expansionism," refer to Lu, *The Making of Japanese Settler Colonialism*, 3–33.

50. "Yattazō Suzuki San," *Shūkan nikkei*, September 1, 1963, 42–43.

51. Suzuki, *Suzuki Tei'ichi*, 384–85.

52. Suzuki Tei'ichi, "Burajiru imin no jigazō: ashide kaida gojūmannin no kiroku," *Asahi shinbun*, February 13, 1964, 11.

53. Burajiru Nikkeijin Jittai Chōsa Iinkai, *Burajiru no nihon imin, kijutsu-hen* (Tokyo: University of Tokyo Press, 1964).

54. *Colônia*, no. 44, November 1964, 35.

55. Ryang, *Japan and National Anthropology*, 139–48.

56. Izumi and Nakane had coedited two volumes titled *Gendai bunka jinruigaku: daisanmaki ningen no shakai*, vols. 3 and 4. These books examined different societies across the

world by treating each of them as isolated cultural systems according to the approach of the Culture and Personality school.

57. Izumi Sei'chi and Nakane Chie, eds., *Ningen no shakai*, vol. 1 (Tokyo: Nakayama Shoten, 1960); Izumi Sei'chi and Nakane Chie, eds., *Ningen no shakai*, vol. 2 (Tokyo: Nakayama Shoten, 1961).

58. Burajiru Imin 70 Nenshi Hensan Iinkai, *Burajiru imin 70 nenshi* (São Paulo: Sociedade Brasileira de Cultura Japonesa, 1980), 143.

59. Tsunoda Fusako, *Amazon no uta: Nihonjin no kiroku* (Tokyo: Mainichi Shinbunsha, 1966), *Yakusoku no daichi* (Tokyo: Shinchōsha, 1977), and *Burajiru no Nikkeijin: Shintenchi ni ikiru chi to ase no kiroku* (Tokyo: Shinchōsha, 1967). The first two were specifically about Japanese settlers in the Amazon; the third discussed the history of Japanese settlers in Brazil in general.

60. Tsunoda Fusako, *Yukitsubaki no shōgai: Manshū busō imin no tsuma* (Tokyo: Ie no Hikari Kyōkai, 1970); and *Hiroku bohyōnaki hachiman no shisha: Man-mō kaitakudan no kaimesu* (Tokyo: Banchō Shobō, 1972).

61. Staniford, *Pioneers in the Tropics*.

62. Among the results of this research project were Robert J. Smith, John B. Cornell, Hiroshi Saitō, and Maeyama Takashi, *The Japanese and Their Descendants in Brazil: An Annotated Bibliography* (São Paulo: Centro de Estudos Nipo-Brasileiros, 1967); John B. Cornell, Sugiyama Iutaka, and Robert J. Smith, "Nisei Biculturalism in Southern Brazil" (University of Texas at Austin, 1968), mimeograph.

63. Maeyama, *Imin no Nihon kaiki undō*, 26.

64. Mori, Yamamoto, and Suzuki, "Burajiru Nihonjin imin no isseiki," 86–87.

65. Mori, Yamamoto, and Suzuki, "Burajiru Nihonjin imin no isseiki," 86.

66. Mori, Yamamoto, and Suzuki, "Burajiru Nihonjin imin no isseiki," 100.

67. Burajiru Imin 80 Nenshi Hensan Iinkai, *Burajiru imin 80 nenshi* (São Paulo: Sociedade Brasileira de Cultura Japonesa, 1961), 264–65.

68. Tsuda, *Strangers in the Ethnic Homeland*, 73.

69. Mori, Yamamoto, and Suzuki,. "Burajiru Nihonjin imin no isseiki," 100.

70. Mori, Yamamoto, and Suzuki, "Burajiru Nihonjin imin no isseiki," 100.

71. Suzuki, *Suzuki Tei'ichi*, 462–65.

72. Historical Museum of Hokkaido, *Museum Survey and Guide* (Sapporo: Historical Museum of Hokkaido, 2014), 1; Saitō Hiroshi, *Burajiru to Nihonjin* (Tokyo: Simul Press, 1984), 115–19.

73. Saitō Hiroshi, *Gaikokujin ni natta Nihonjin: Burajiru imin no ikikata to kawarikata* (Tokyo: Saimura Shuppankai, 1978), 1–3.

74. Tsuda, *Strangers in the Ethnic Homeland*, 74–77.

CONCLUSION

1. Maeyama Takashi, *Esunishitei to Burajiru Nikkeijin: Bunka Jinruigaku teki Kenkyū* (Tokyo: Ocha no Mizu Shobō, 1996), ii.

2. Maeyama, *Esunishitei to Burajiru Nikkeijin*, iii.

3. Maeyama, *Imin no Nihon kaiki undō*, 26.

4. Maeyama Takashi, *Hisōzokusha no seishinshi: aru Nikkei Burajirujin no henreki* (Tokyo: Ocha no Mizu Shobō, 1981).

5. Maeyama, *Hisōzokusha no seishinshi*, 4–11.

6. Maeyama, *Imin no Nihon kaiki undō* (Tokyo: Ocha no Mizu, 1982).

7. Maeyama, *Esunishitei to Burajiru Nikkeijin*.

8. Burajiru Nihon Imin 80 nenshi Hensan Iinkai, *Burajiru Nihon imin 80 nenshi*, 107.

9. For a few examples in which the Indigenous people and caboclos were referred to as dojin, see "Noroesute ittai hattenshi no ichipeiji," *Burajiru jihō*, no. 753, January 21, 1932, 3; Kōsonki, "Hainichi jiu to tenchōsetsu," *Seishū shinpō*, no. 1080, April 29, 1936, 7; Shimanuki Takeo, "Burajiru shokumin no hajimari (6)," *Nippaku shinbun*, no. 819, February 16, 1933, 4.

10. Wako Shungorō, *Bauru kannai no hōjin* (Bauru: Wako Shungorō, 1939), reprinted in *Nikkei imin shiryōshū dainiki, nanbeihen*. Vol. 25 (Tokyo: Nihon Tosho Sentā, 1999), 11.

11. Robert Smith recorded a conversation that he had with an Issei immigrant in the 1970s in Brazil who called local Brazilians "dojin." When Smith questioned the appropriateness of using this term, the Issei man insisted on it. A Japanese immigrant who relocated from Manchuria to Brazil after World War II and became a farm owner, he claimed that there was little difference between his Brazilian farmworkers and the Chinese coolies in Manchuria. Robert Smith, "The Ethnic Japanese in Brazil," *Journal of Japanese Studies* 5, no. 1 (Winter 1979): 65.

12. Patrick Wolfe, "Recuperating Binarism," *Settler Colonial Studies* 3, no. 3–4 (2013): 263.

13. Candace Fujikane and Jonathan Y. Okamura, eds., *Asian Settler Colonialism: From Local Governance to the Habits of Everyday Life in Hawai'i* (Honolulu: University of Hawai'i Press, 2008)

14. Lorenzo Veracini, "Is Settler Colonial Studies Even Useful?," *Postcolonial Studies* 24, no. 2 (2021): 274. Veracini makes this point when commenting on Tiffany King's brilliant study that explores the intersections between blackness and indigeneity in the settler colonial contexts of the Anglo world. See Tiffany Lethabo King, *The Black Shoals: Offshore Formations of Black and Native Studies* (Durham, NC: Duke University Press, 2019).

15. Iyko Day, *Alien Capital: Asian Racialization and the Logic of Settler Colonial Capitalism* (Durham, NC: Duke University Press, 2016).

BIBLIOGRAPHY

ARCHIVES AND COLLECTIONS

Diplomatic Archives of the Ministry of Foreign Affairs of Japan
Hoji Shinbun Digital Collection, the Hoover Institution Library and Archives, Stanford University
Japanese Overseas Migration Museum
Japanese Striving Society
John B. Cornell Papers, Hoover Institution Library and Archives, Stanford University
Kajiyama Collection, University of Hawai'i at Mānoa Libraries
Museu Histórico da Imigração Japonesa no Brasil, São Paulo
National Archives of Japan
Robert Smith Papers, Cornell University

PRIMARY SOURCES

Andō Zenpati. "Bunka no honshitsu to tokushūsei: bunka kokka kensetsu no kokoroe." *Jidai*, no. 3, 1947.

———. "Nihon imin no shakai shiteki kenkyū." *Kenkyū repōto* 2 (1967): 3–110.

Aoyagi Ikutarō. *Burajiru ni okeru Nihonjin hatten shi*. Vol. 1. Tokyo: Burajiru ni okeru Nihonjin Hatten Shi Kankō Iinkai, 1941.

"Asano." *Hokkaido kaitaku zasshi*, no. 2, February 14, 1880.

"British-Japanese Struggle for Asia Textile Markets." *Far Eastern Survey* 5, no. 13 (1936): 134–35.

"Budō saibai no rieki." *Hokkaido kaitaku zasshi*, no. 5, March 27, 1880, 97.

Burajiru Imin 70 Nenshi Hensan Iinkai. *Burajiru imin 70 nenshi*. São Paulo: Sociedade Brasileira de Cultura Japonesa, 1980.

Burajiru Imin 80 Nenshi Hensan Iinkai. *Burajiru imin 80 nenshi*. São Paulo: Sociedade Brasileira de Cultura Japonesa, 1961.

Burajiru: ishokumin to bōeki, no. 6, July 1927.

———, vol. 1, no. 6, October 1927.

Burajiru jihō, no. 778, April 14, 1932.

Burajiru Jihōsha. *Burajiru nenkan*. São Paulo: Burajiru Jihōsha, 1933.

"Burajiru jijō tenrankai: Kobe Mitsukoshi gofukuten ni okeru." *Burajiru: ishokumin to bōeki* 1, no. 9, October 1927, 93–96.

Burajirukoku Parā shū shokumin nannai (1930). In Gaimushō Gaikō Shiryōkan, *Honpō imin toriatsukainin kankei zakken: Nanbei Takushoku Kabishiki Gaisha*, vol. 2, J120, J3-2.

Burajiru Nikkeijin Jittai Chōsa Iinkai. *Burajiru no nihon imin, kijutsu-hen*. Tokyo: University of Tokyo Press, 1964.

Burajiru Nihon Imin 80 Nenshi Hensan Iinkai. *Burajiru Nihon imin 80 nenshi*. São Paulo: Toppan Fueisu Insatsu Shuppan Gaisha, 1996.

Burajiru Nihon Imin Hyakunenshi Hensan Kankō Iinkai. *Burajiru Nihon imin hyakunenshi*. Vol. 1. Tokyo: Fūkyōsha, 2008.

Burajiru Nihon Imin Hyakushūnen Kinen Kyōkai. *Burajiru Nihon imin hyakunenshi*. Vol. 3. Tokyo: Fūkyōsha, 2010.

———. Burajiru Nihon Imin Hyakushūnen Kinen Kyōkai. *Burajiru Nihon imin hyakunenshi*. Vol. 4. Tokyo: Fūkyōsha, 2013.

Burataku Gatto Undō Sanbōbu. *Gatto undō no shiori*. Vol. 1. São Paulo: Burataku Gatto Undō Sanbōbu, 1934.

Capron, Horace M. *Memoirs of Horace Capron—Volume I: Autobiography*. Special Collections, National Agricultural Library, 1884.

———. *Memoirs of Horace Capron—Volume II: Autobiography*. Special Collections, National Agricultural Library, 1884.

"Chūzai gaikoku shisetsu wo mukaete: sōgonnaru rekishiteki kōkei no tenkai." *Shokumin* 9, no. 3, March 1930.

Colônia, no. 44, November 1964.

Dainihon Bunmei Kyōkai. *Nihonjin no kaigai hatten*. Tokyo: Dai Nihon Bunmei Kyōkai, 1916.

Emi Kiyotaka. "Kokumin kokka ron." *Jidai*, no. 1, 1947.

Frontier News, March 2011.

Fukuda Sanji. "Senkō wo assuru ei e aru daikankanshiki ni narabini kaikō hakurankai ni okeru kaigai hattenkan." *Burajiru: ishokumin to bōeki* 4, no. 11, November 1930.

Fukuhara Hachirō. "Zenjin mitō no Burajiru genya wo tōsa shite." *Burajiru: ishokumin to bōeki* 1, no. 4, May 1927.

Fukuhara Sei (Hachirō). "Wa ga kuni no ishokumin hatten ni Burajiru no kōya ni hiyaku wo nasu: tōshi jigyō no shōkai." *Burajiru: ishokumin to bōeki* 2, no. 11, November 1928.

Fukuzawa Yukichi. "Datsua Ron." In *Fukuzawa Yukichi chosakushū*, vol. 8, 261–65. Tokyo: Keio Gijuku Daigaku Shuppankai, 2003.

"Fuki Kōmyo wa Oya Yuzuri no Kuni ni Kagirazu." In *Fukuzawa Yukichi zenshū*, vol. 9, 546. Tokyo: Iwanami Shoten, 1960.

Fujita Toshirō. *Mekishikokoku Taiheiyo engan shoshūn jūnkai hōkoku*. Tokyo: Gaimu Daijin Kanbō Iminka, 1891.

Fujita Toshirō. Box. 1. Access No. 2017c47–14. 36, Hoover Institution Archives.

Gaimushō Gaikō Shiryōkan. *Honpō imin toritasukainin kankei zakken*, J 1.2.0. J.3.

———. *Honpō imin toriatsukainin kankei zakken: "Amazonia" Sangyō Kabushiki Gaisha.* J120, J3–6.

———. *Honpō imin toriatsukainin kankei zakken: Kaigai Kōgyō Kabushiki Gaisha.* Vol. 10, J120. J3–1.

———. *Honpō imin toriatsukainin kankei zakken: Kaigai Kōgyō Kabushiki Gaisha.* Vol. 11, J120. J3–1.

———. *Honpō imin toriatsukainin kankei zakken: Nanbei Takushoku Kabushiki Gaisha.* Vol. 3. J120. J3–2.

Gaimushō Ryōji Ijūbu. *Waga kokumin no kaigai hatten: ijū hyakunen no ayumi, shiryōhen.* Tokyo: Gaimushō Ryōji Ijūbu, 1971.

Gaimushō Tsūshōkoku. *Hakkoku Amazonnasu shū Nihon shokuminchi chiki kakutei narabi shokumin keikaku ni kansuru chō hōkokusho.* Tokyo: Gaimushō Tsūshōkoku, 1931.

"Gutaika shita kyōiku mondai." *Burajiru Jihō,* no. 491, March 11, 1927.

Handa Tomoo. *Imin no seikatsu no rekishi.* São Paulo: Centro de Estudos Nipo Brasileiros, 1969.

———. *Imin no seikatsu no rekishi: Burajiru Nikkeijin no ayunda michi.* Tokyo: Ie no Hikari Kyōkai, 1970.

———. "Shinbunka kensetsu no shihyō." *Jidai,* no. 1, 1947.

Hirano Shokuminchi Nihonjinkai. *Hirano 25 shūnen shi.* São Paulo: Hirano Shokuminchi Nihonjinkai, 1941.

Hiraoka Hikotarō. *Nihon nōpon ron.* Tokyo: Yasui Ukichi, 1902.

Historical Museum of Hokkaido. *Museum Survey and Guide.* Sapporo: Historical Museum of Hokkaido, 2014.

Hokkaido wa Kosan no Chi Naru Setsu." *Hokkaido kaitaku zasshi,* no. 17 (September 11, 1880): 387.

Ikushima Shigekazu. *Amazon ijū sanjūnenshi.* São Paulo: Sanpauro Shinbunsha, 1959.

Imasawa Fujisaburō. "Shōwa 4nen Abarē fukin menka jikkyō." *Burajiru: ishokumin to bōeki* 3, no. 12, December 1929.

Imin Shūyōjo. *Imin Shūyōjo e nyūjo ni tsuite.* Kobe: Imin Shūyōjo, 1928.

Ino Masayoshi. *Kyojin Saibara Seitō.* Tosa-shi: Saibara Seitō Sensei Shōtokuhi Kensetsu Kiseikai, 1964.

Inoue Masaji. *Kaigai yuhi wakaki Nihon no shinro.* Tokyo: Minyūsha, 1929.

———. "Sekai wo ie toshite." *Shokumin* 9, no. 3, March 1930.

———. *Shizen no kankyō to hakujin jinkō mondai.* Tokyo: Kaigai Kōgyō Kabushiki Gaisha, 1929.

Ishikawa Datsuzō. *Saikin Nanbei ōraiki.* 1931. Reprint, Tokyo: Chūō Kōron, 1981.

Itagaki Taisuke. "Shokumin ron." *Jiyūtō hō,* no. 10 (April 28, 1892). In *Itagaki Taisuke zenshū,* edited by Itagaki Morimasa, 77–79. Tokyo: Hara Shobō, 1980.

Izumi Sei'ichi, ed. *Imin: Burajiru imin no jittai chōsai.* Tokyo: Kokon Shoin, 1956.

Izumi Sei'ichi, and Nakane Chie, eds. *Ningen no shakai.* Vol. 1. Tokyo: Nakayama Shoten, 1960.

———. *Ningen no shakai.* Vol. 2. Tokyo: Nakayama Shoten, 1961.

Izumi Sei'ichi, and Saitō Hiroshi, eds. *Amazon: so no fūdo to Nihonjin.* Tokyo: Kokon Shoin, 1954.

"Japan's Invasion of the White Man's World." *New York Times,* September 22, 1907.

"Jyagatara imo no rieki." *Hokkaido kaitaku zasshi*, no. 3, February 28, 1880.

"Kaigai Ijū Kumiai ni chūmon no koto (1)." *Burajiru jihō*, no. 539, February 10, 1928.

Kaigai Ijū Kumiai Rengōkai. "Kaigai Ijū Kumiai Rengōkai jigyō gaiyō." In Gaimushō Gaikō Shiryōkan, *Honpō imin toriatsukainin kankei zakken: Kaigai Kōgyō Kabushiki Gaisha*, vol. 30, J120. J 3–5.

Kaigai Ijū Kumiai Rengōkai jigyō gaiyō (1943). In Gaimushō Gaikō Shiryōkan, *Honpō imin toriatsukainin kankei zakken: Kaigai Ijū Kumiai*, vol. 30, J.1.2.0. J 3–5.

"Kaigai Ijū Kumiai Sōkai: yūshi jikō kettei." *Osaka mainichi shinbun*, August 7, 1927, 4.

Kaigai Kōgyō Kabushiki Gaisha. *Kaigai Kōgyō Kabushiki Gaisha gensei yōran*. Tokyo: Kaigai Kōgyō Kabushiki Gaisha, 1932.

———. *Nanbei Burajirukoku to Nihon ishokumin*. Tokyo: Kaigai Kōgyō Kabushiki Gaisha, 1922.

Kaikō hakuran kaishi: kankanshiki kinen. Kobe: Kobe Hakurankai Kyōkai, 1931.

"Kaisha enkaku oyobi jigyō jōkyō." In Gaimushō Gaikō Shiryōkan, *Honpō ijūsha toriatsukai dantai kankei zakken: Nichinan Sangyō Kabushiki Gaisha kankei*, vol. 3, J.1.1.0.3–1.

"Kaitaku no shisatsu." *Hokkaido Kaitaku Zasshi*, no. 2, February 14, 1880.

"Kaitaku Zasshi Hakkō no Shushi." *Hokkaido Kaitaku Zasshi*, no. 1 (January 31, 1880): 2–3.

Kanbe Masao. *Chōsen nōgyō imin ron*. Tokyo: Yūhikaku Shobō, 1910.

Kanegafuchi Takushoku Kabushiki Gaisha no jigyō keika to kaisha kongo no shochi ni tsuite. In Gaimushō Gaikō Shiryōkan, *Honpō imin toriatsukainin kankei zakken: Nanbei Takushoku Kabushiki Gaisha*, vol. 1, J.1.2.0. J 4–1.

Katō Masuo. "Kankoku iminron." *Taiyō* 7, no. 1, January 5, 1901.

Kawada Shirō. *Shokuminchi toshite no Burajiru*. Tokyo: Yūhikaku Shobō, 1914.

"Ketten wo shiru tokoronin seikō ga aru." *Burajiru jihō*, no. 589, January 31, 1929.

Kobe hakurankai shuppin mokuroku. Kobe: Kobe Hakurankai Kyōkai, 1931.

Kobe ijū kyōyōjo gaiyō. Kobe: Kobe Ijū Kyōyōjo, 1934.

"Kokumin teki jikaku." *Nippaku shinbun*, no. 636, August 8, 1929.

Koseki Tokuya. *Nanpō Kaitakusha no shihyō: Nanbei imin no taiken wo mototoshite*. Tokyo: Bunkentō Shoten, 1942.

Kōsonki (Kōyama Rokurō). "Hainichi jiu to tenchōsetsu." *Seishū shinpō*, no. 1080, April 29, 1936.

———. "Yagate hōji shinbun no hakkin ni tsuki." *Seishū shinpō*, no. 2205, April 5, 1941.

Kōyama Rokurō. *Imin yonjūnen shi*. São Paulo: Kōyama Rokurō, 1949.

———. *Zaihaku ishokumin 25 shūnenkan*. São Paulo: Kōyama Rokurō, 1934.

Koronia Bugakukai. *Koronia shōsetsu senshū*. Vol. 1. São Paulo: Koronia Bungakukai, 1975.

"Kugatsu nijūnichi yori hanabanashiku kaijōshita kankanshiki kinen kaikō hakurankai." *Osaka Asahi shinbun*, September 28, 1930.

"Manshū Mondai to Hakkoku Imin." *Nippaku shinbun*, no. 775, April 7, 1932.

Matsui Iwane. "Hokuman taisaku shiken." Mimeograph. June 1, 1923.

Matsunaga Toshio. "Watashi no jidō kyōiku mondaikan." *Burajiru jihō*, no. 495, April 8, 1927.

"Meiyo na Shokumin ka?" *Seishū shinpō*, no. 269, February 25, 1927.

Mizuno Masano. *Basutosu nijūgonenshi*. Tokyo: Mizuno Masano, 1955.

Nagasawa Setsu (Betten). *Yankii*. Tokyo: Keigyōsha, 1893.

Nagashima Kanae. "Jūkanan no shokuminchi seikatsu." *Burajiru: ishokumin to bōeki*, no. 9, October 1927.

Nagata Shigeshi. "Birigui shokuminchi no kusawake." *Shokumin* 6, no. 6, June 1927.

———. *Burajiru ni okeru Nihonjin hattenshi*. Vol. 2. Tokyo: Burajiru ni okeru Nihonjin hattenshi kenkōkai, 1953

———. "Manshū no shinano mura (1)." *Rikkō sekai*, no. 347, November 1933.

———. *Shinano kaigai ijūshi*. Nagano: Shinano Kaigai Kyōryokukai, 1952.

Nambara Shigeru. *Bunka to kokka*. Tokyo: Tokyo Daigaku Shuppankai, 1957.

Nanpō Sangyō Chōsakai. *Nanshin sōsho*. Vol. 1: *Nyūginia*. Tokyo: Nanshinsha, 1941.

"Nanshin ya? Hokushin ya?" *Taiyō* 19, no. 15, November 1913.

Narusei Ren. "Kigen nisen rokuhaykunen wo hōshukushite." In *Burajiru ni okeru dai'issen ni katsuyaku suru hitobito*, edited by Ono Shinzen. São Paulo: Burajiru Jihōsha, 1941.

Nawa Tōichi. *Nihon bōsekigyō to genmen mondai kenkyū*. Osaka: Daidō Shoin, 1938.

Nichinan Sangyō Kabushiki Gaisha, Dai nana nendo gyōmu hōkokusho (1944). In Gaimusho Gaikō Shiryōkan, *Honpō ijūsha toriatsukai dantai kankei zakken: Nichinan Sangyō Kabushiki Gaisha Kankei*, vol. 3, J.1.1.0.3–1.

Nihon gaikō bunsho dejitaru ākaibu, vol. 26, 1893.

Nihon gaikō bunsho, vol. 31, no. 2. Tokyo: Ministry of Foreign Affairs of Japan, 1898.

"Nihonjin nomi no shokuminchi fuka." *Burajiru jihō*, no. 461, August 13, 1926.

"Nihon minzoku no bōchō." *Taiyō* 16, no. 15, November 1910.

"Nihon teikoku no uchi ni Amerika gasshūkoku wo genshutsu suru wa atarasa ni tōki ni arazaru beshi." *Hokkaido kaitaku zasshi*, no. 3, February 28, 1880.

Nitobe Inazō. *The Imperial Agricultural College of Sapporo*. Sapporo: The Imperial Agricultural College of Sapporo, 1893.

———. *Nōgyō honron*. Tokyo: Shōka Shobō, 1898.

"Nōgu Kairyō Ron," *Hokkaido kaitaku zasshi*, no. 3 (February 28, 1880): 59.

"Nōgyōka no torubeki michi (1)." *Burajiru jihō*, no. 483, January 14, 1927.

"Noroesute ittai hattenshi no ichipeiji." *Burajiru jihō*, no. 753, January 21, 1932.

"Nōsakubutsu no Sentaku: Kangyōbu ni ichigon." *Nippaku shinbun*, no. 730, May 28, 1931.

Ōkawadaira Takamitsu. *Nihon imin ron*. Tokyo: Jōbudō, 1905.

Osaka Mainichi, August 2, 1918.

Kōtaishi gofusai burajiru no tabi, Paulista Gurafu (July 1967).

Paurisuta Shinbunsha, ed. *Koronia sengō jūnenshi*. São Paulo: Paurisuta Shinbunsha, 1956.

Revista Ilustrada, no. 63, April 1877.

———, no. 301, 1882.

———, no. 564, 1889.

Saitō Hiroshi. "Amazonia no Nikkeijin." *Kenkyū repōto* 8 (1980): 1–15.

———. *Burajiru to Nihonjin*. Tokyo: Simul Press, 1984.

———. *Gaikokujin ni natta Nihonjin: Burajiru imin no ikikata to kawarikata*. Tokyo: Saimura Shuppankai, 1978.

———. "Shinkan shōkai: Gilberto Freyre, Interpretação do Brasil, 1947." *Jidai*, no. 3, 1947.

———. "Shinkan shōkai: Ruth Benedict, The Chrysanthemum and the Sword: Patterns of Japanese Culture, Boston, 1946." *Jidai*, no. 4, 1947.

"Sake no setsu." *Hokkaido kaitaku zasshi*, no. 10, June 5, 1880.

Shimanuki Takeo. "Burajiru shokumin no hajimari (6)." *Nippaku Shinbun*, no. 819, February 16, 1933.

Shokumin 9, no. 8, August 1930.

"Shokumin Kyōkai Hōkoku hatsuda no riyū." *Shokumin kyōkai hōkokusho*, no. 1, April 1893.

Shūkan Nanbei 1, no. 29, 1918.

Shūkan Sankei: Tokubetsu Gurafu, no. 81, 1978.

Sugiura Jūkō. *Hankai yume monogatari: ichimei shinheimin kmaitendan.* Tokyo: Sawaya, 1886.

Suzuki Iwazō. "Menka seisankoku toshite no Burajiru." *Burajiru: ishokumin to bōeki* 1, no. 1, January 1927.

Suzuki Tei'ichi. "Burajiru imin no jigazō: ashide kaida gojūmannin no kiroku." *Asahi shinbun*, February 13, 1964.

Taguchi Ukichi. *Nihon keizai ron.* Tokyo: Keizai Zasshisha, 1878.

Takahashi Yoshio. *Nihon jinshu kairyōron.* Tokyo: Ishikawa Hanjirō, 1884.

Takaoka Kumao. "Burajiru imin ron." *Chūō kōron* 40, no. 1, January 1925.

Takekoshi Yosaburō. "Nanpō no keiei to Nihon no shimei." *Taiyō* 16, no. 15, November 1910, 20–21.

Takemoto Takeo. Takemoto Takeo to Nakano Takeshi, August 12, 1939. In Gaimushō Gaikō Shiryōkan, *Honpō imin toriatsukainin kankei zakken: Kaigai Kōgyō Kabushiki Gaisha*, vol. 10, J.1.2.0. J 3–1.

———. Takemoto Takeo to Nakano Takeshi, August 31, 1939. In Gaimushō Gaikō Shiryōkan, *Honpō imin toriatsukainin kankei zakken: Kaigai Kōgyō Kabushiki Gaisha*, vol. 10, J.1.2.0. J 3–1.

———. Takemoto Takeo to Nakano Takeshi, July 26, 1939. In Gaimushō Gaikō Shiryōkan, *Honpō imin toriatsukainin kankei zakken: Kaigai Kōgyō Kabushiki Gaisha*, vol. 10, J.1.2.0. J 3–1.

Tōgō Minoru. *Nihon shokumin ron.* Tokyo: Bunbudō, 1906.

Tokutomi Sōhō. "Nihon jinshū no shin kokyō." *Kokumin no tomo* 6, no. 85, June 13, 1890.

Tokyo asahi, June 1, 1922.

Tokyo Puck, vol. 3, no. 17, 1907.

Tsunoda Fusako. *Amazon no uta: Nihonjin no kiroku.* Tokyo: Mainichi Shinbunsha, 1966.

———. *Burajiru no Nikkeijin: Shintenchi ni ikiru chi to ase no kiroku.* Tokyo: Shinchōsha, 1967.

———. *Hiroku bohyōnaki hachiman no shisha: Man-mō kaitakudan no kaimesu.* Tokyo: Banchō Shobō, 1972.

———. *Yakusoku no daichi.* Tokyo: Shinchōsha, 1977.

———. *Yukitsubaki no shōgai: Manshū busō imin no tsuma.* Tokyo: Ie no Hikari Kyōkai, 1970.

Turner, Frederick Jackson. *The Frontier in American History.* New York: Henry Holt and Company, 1921.

Uchiyama Iwatarō. "Hainichi no jikyoku ni shinmenshite zairyū dōhō ni tsugu." *Seishū shinpō*, no. 860, May 22, 1934.

Uetsuka Tsukasa. "Dai Amazon no Nihon shin shokuminchi." *Kingu* 7, no. 6, 1931.

X.Y.Z. "Doyōkai to jidai." *Jidai*, no. 11, 1950.

Yamagata Jirō. "Sōkan no ji." *Burajiru: ishokumin to bōeki* 1, no. 1, January 1927.

Yamamoto Jōtarō. "Manmō no hatten to Mantetsu no jigyō." *Seiyū*, no. 330, 1928.

"Yattazō Suzuki San." *Shūkan Nikkei*, September 1, 1963.

Yoshida Hideo. *Nihon jinkō ron no shiteki kenkyū.* Tokyo: Kawade Shobō, 1944.

Yoshimura Daijirō. *Hokubei Tekisasushū no beisaku: Nihonjin no shin fugen.* Osaka: Kaigai Kigyō Dōshikai, 1903.

———. *Tekisasushū beisaku no jikken.* Tokyo: Kaigai Kigyō Dōshikai, 1905.

"Zai hakkoku hōjin shōsha seisan kankei." In Gaimushū Gaikō Shiryōkan, *Honpō imin tori-atsukainin kankei zakken,* J120. J3.

"Zaihaku hōjin shakai to imin mondai: Burajiru genchi zadankai." *Chūō kōron,* no. 784, June 1951.

SECONDARY SOURCES

"Amazon kaitaku." *Burajiru imin no 100 nen.* https://www.ndl.go.jp/brasil/s4/s4_2.html.

Ambaras, David. *Japan's Imperial Underworlds: Intimate Encounters at the Borders of Empire.* New York: Cambridge University Press, 2018.

Andrews, George Reid. "Brazilian Racial Democracy, 1900–90: An American Counterpoint." *Journal of Contemporary History* 31, no. 3 (July 1996): 483–507.

Arneil, Barbara. *John Locke and America: The Defense of English Colonialism.* Oxford University Press, 1996.

Art Institute of Chicago. "Window on the West: Chicago and the Art of the New Frontier, 1890–1940." Accessed May 1, 2023. https://archive.artic.edu/window/themes.html.

Ascoli, Nestor. *A Immigração Japoneza na Baixada do Estado do Rio de Janeiro.* Rio de Janeiro: Edição da "Revista de lingua portuguesa," 1924.

Azuma, Eiichiro. *Between Two Empires: Race, History, and Transnationalism in Japanese America.* London: Oxford University Press, 2005.

———. *In Search of Our Frontier: Japanese America and Settler Colonialism in the Construction of Japan's Borderless Empire.* Oakland: University of California Press, 2019.

Barth, Volker, and Roland Cvetkovski, eds. *Imperial Co-operation and Transfer, 1870–1930: Empires and Encounters.* London: Bloomsbury Academic, 2015.

Bashford, Alison. "Malthus and Colonial History." *Journal of Australian Studies* 36, no. 1 (March 2012): 99–110.

Belich, James. *Replenishing the Earth: The Settler Revolution and the Rise of the Anglo-World.* Oxford: University of Oxford Press, 2011.

Burns, E. Bradford. *A History of Brazil.* New York: Columbia University Press, 1993.

———. *The Unwritten Alliance: Rio-Branco and Brazilian American Relations.* New York: Columbia University Press, 1966.

Castellanos, M. Bianet, ed. "Settler Colonialism in Latin America." *American Quarterly* 69, no. 4 (December 2017).

Ching, Leo T. S. *Anti-Japan: The Politics of Sentiment in Postcolonial East Asia.* Durham, NC: Duke University Press, 2019.

———. *Becoming Japanese: Colonial Taiwan and the Politics of Identity Formation.* Berkeley: University of California Press, 2001.

Choat, Mark. *Emigrant Nation: The Making of Italy Abroad.* Cambridge, MA: Harvard University Press, 2008.

Cornell, John B., Sugiyama Iutaka, and Robert J. Smith. "Nisei Biculturalism in Southern Brazil." University of Texas at Austin, 1968. Mimeograph.

Costa, Emilia Viotti da. *The Brazilian Empire: Myths and Histories.* Chapel Hill: University of North Carolina Press, 2000.

Day, Iyko. *Alien Capital: Asian Racialization and the Logic of Settler Colonial Capitalism.* Durham, NC: Duke University Press, 2016.

de Souza, Almir Antonio. "A Lei de Terras no Brasil Império e os índios do Planalto Meridi-onal: A luta política e diplomática do Kaingang Vitorino Condá (1845–1870)." *Revista Brasileira de História* 35, no. 70 (2015): 109–30.

Dean, Warren. *Rio Claro: A Brazilian Plantation System, 1820–1920.* Stanford: Stanford University Press, 1976.

Delanghe, Henri. "Japanese Import of Brazilian Raw Cotton in the Second Half of the 1930s: The Beginning of Significant Japanese-Brazilian Trade and Investment Relations." *História Econômica & História de Empresas* 2, no. 2 (1999): 93–94.

Delpiano, Pedro Iacobelli, and Sidney Xu Lu, eds. *The Japanese Empire and Latin America.* Honolulu: University of Hawai'i Press, 2023.

Diacon, Todd A. *Millenarian Vision, Capitalist Reality: Brazil's Contestado Rebellion, 1912–1916.* Durham, NC: Duke University Press, 1991.

———. *Stringing Together a Nation: Cândido Mariano da Silva Rondon and the Construction of a Modern Brazil, 1906–1930.* Durham, NC: Duke University Press, 2004.

Dickinson, Frederick. *World War I and the Triumph of the New Japan.* Cambridge: Cambridge University Press, 2015.

Duara, Prasenjit, ed. *Decolonization: Perspectives from Now and Then.* London: Routledge, 2003.

Dusinberre, Martin. *Mooring the Global Archive: A Japanese Ship and Its Migrant Histories.* Cambridge: Cambridge University Press, 2023.

Duus, Peter. *The Abacus and the Sword: The Japanese Penetration of Korea, 1895–1910.* Berkeley: University of California Press, 1995.

Duus, Peter, Ramon Myers, and Mark Peattie, eds. *The Japanese Informal Empire in China, 1895–1937.* Princeton, NJ: Princeton University Press, 1989.

———. *The Japanese Wartime Empire, 1931–1945.* Princeton, NJ: Princeton University, 1996.

Ebihara, Hachirō. *Kaigai hōji shinbun zasshishi: tsuketari kaigai hōjin gaiji shinbun zasshishi.* Tokyo: Meicho Fukyūkai, 1980.

Endoh, Toake. *Exporting Japan: Politics of Emigration toward Latin America.* Urbana: University of Illinois Press, 2009.

"Establishment of the Quota System and Movements for Japanese Immigrants' Exclusion." *Burajiru imin no 100 nen.* https://www.ndl.go.jp/brasil/e/s5/s5_1.html.

Foweraker, Joe. *The Struggle for Land: A Political Economy of the Pioneer Frontier in Brazil from 1930 to the Present Day.* New York: Cambridge University Press, 1981.

Font, Mauricio A. *Coffee and Transformation in São Paulo, Brazil.* Lanham, MD: Lexington Books, 2010.

"From Colonos to Independent Farmers." *Burajiru imin no 100 nen.* https://www.ndl.go.jp/brasil/e/s3/s3_1.html.

Fujikane, Candace, and Jonathan Y. Okamura, eds. *Asian Settler Colonialism: From Local Governance to the Habits of Everyday Life in Hawai'i.* Honolulu: University of Hawai'i Press, 2008.

Fujitani, Takashi. *Race for Empire: Koreans as Japanese and Japanese as Americans during World War II.* Berkeley: University of California Press, 2011.

Fukasawa Masayuki. "Meiji seishin to koronia nana fushigi." *Burajiru tokuhō,* March 2012. https://nipo-brasil.org/archives/2332/.

Fukushima Hiroyuki. "Burajiru nihonjin imin no kyōiku to nihon kokka: Nihonjin no dōka mondai ni kansuru yobiteki kōsatsu." *Fukuoka Daigaku jinbun ronsō* 52, no. 1 (June 2020): 1–43.

Gamō Masao. *Nihonjin no seikatsu kōzō jusetsu.* Tokyo: Seishin Shobō, 1960.

Garasino, Facundo. "Immigrant Propaganda: Translating Japanese Imperial Ideology into Argentine Nationalism." In *The Japanese Empire and Latin America,* edited by Pedro Iacobelli Delpiano and Sidney Xu Lu, 208–26. Honolulu: University of Hawai'i Press, 2023.

———. "Japan's Last Colonial Frontier: Settler Migration, Development, and Expansionism in the Brazilian Amazon." In *Transpacific Visions: Connected Histories of the Pacific across North and South,* edited by Yasuko Hassall Kobayashi and Shinnosuke Takahashi, 111–36. Lanham, MD: Lexington Books, 2021.

Garcia, Jerry. "Japanese Immigration and Community Development in Mexico, 1897–1940." PhD diss., Washington State University, 1999.

Garfield, Seth. *In Search of the Amazon: Brazil, the United States, and the Nature of a Region.* Durham, NC: Duke University Press, 2013.

Garon, Sheldon. *Molding the Japanese Minds: The State in Everyday Life.* Princeton, NJ: Princeton University, 1998.

Goebel, Michael. "Settler Colonialism in Postcolonial Latin America." In *The Routledge Handbook of the History of Settler Colonialism,* edited by Edward Cavanagh and Lorenzo Veracini, 139–51. London: Routledge, 2017.

Gott, Richard. "Latin America as a White Settler Society." *Bulletin of Latin American Research* 26, no. 2 (April 2007): 269–89.

Graham, Jessica Lynn. *Shifting the Meaning of Democracy: Race, Politics and Culture in the United States and Brazil.* Berkeley: University of California Press, 2019.

Gugliotta, Alexandre Carlos. "Tavares Bastos (1839–1875) e a Sociedade Internacional de Imigração um espaço a favor da modernidade." Paper presented at the XII Encuentro Regional de História "Usos do Passado," Asociación Nacional de História de Río de Janeiro, 2006.

Hanzawa, Noriko. "Burajiru Noroesute chihō ni okeru Nihongo shinbun no hatashita yakuwari." *Ritsumeikan gengo bunka kenkyū* 26, no. 4 (March 2015): 87–101.

———. "Senzenki Burajiru Sanpauroshū noroesute chihō to nihongo shinbun: Kōyama Rokurō to *Seishū shinpō.*" PhD diss., Kyoto Joshi Daigaku, 2017.

Hayami, Akira. "Jinkō Tōkei no Kindaika Katei." In Kokusei Chōsa Izen, *Nihon jinkō tōkei shūsei,* vol. 1, edited by Naimushō Naikaku Tōkeikyoku, 3–11. Reprint. Tokyo: Tōyō Shorin, 1992

Hayashiya Eikichi. "Nihon to Raten Amerika no gaikō kankei." In *Nihon to Raten Amerika no kankei: Nihon no kokuzaika ni okeru Raten Amerika,* edited by Hajime Mizuno, 1–13. Tokyo: Instituto Iberoamericano, Sofía University, 1990.

Hecht, Susanna B. *The Scramble for the Amazon and the "Lost Paradise" of Euclides da Cunha.* Chicago: University of Chicago Press, 2013.

Hemming, John. *Amazon Frontier: The Defeat of the Brazilian Indians.* Cambridge, MA: Harvard University Press, 1987.

———. *Die If You Must: Brazilian Indians in the Twentieth Century.* New York: Macmillan, 2003.

Hennessy, Alistair. *The Frontier in Latin American History.* Albuquerque: University of New Mexico Press, 1978.

Hirano, Katsuya. "Thanatopolitics in the Making of Japan's Hokkaido: Settler Colonialism and Primitive Accumulation." *Critical Historical Studies* 2, no. 2 (Fall 2015): 191–218.

Hixon, Walter. *American Settler Colonialism: A History.* New York: Palgrave Macmillan, 2013.

Hokkaido Nanbei Ijūshi Henshūshi Iinkai. *Hokkaido Nanbei ijū shi*. Sapporo: Hokuhōken Sentā, 2009.

Holloway, Thomas. *Immigrants on the Land: Coffee and Society in São Paulo, 1886–1934*. Chapel Hill: University of North Carolina Press, 2012.

Horne, Gerald. *Race War! White Supremacy and the Japanese Attack on the British Empire*. New York: New York University Press, 2003.

"Iguape Colony." *Burajiru imin no 100 nen*. https://www.ndl.go.jp/brasil/e/s3/s3_2.html.

Iida Kōjirō. *Imin no kaiketsu Hoshina Ken'ichirō no shōgai: Hawai, Tekisasu, Burajiru*. Tokyo: Fuji Shuppan, 2017.

Iikubo Hideki. "1920 nendai ni okeru naimushō shakaikyoku no kaigai imin shōreisaku." *Rekishi to keizai* 46, no. 1 (2003): 38–54.

———. "Burajiru imin kara Manshū imin e no kessetsuten." In *Ajia to keiei: shijō, gijutsu, soshiki*, vol. 2, edited by Ihara Motoi, Kikkawa Takeo, and Kubo Fumikatsu, 103–29. Tokyo: Tokyo Daigaku Shakai Kagaku Kenkyūjo, 2002.

———. "Kaigai Kōgyō Kabushiki Gaisha to Kaigai Ijū Kumiai Rengōkai: 1920–40 nendai ni okeru kaigai ishokumin toriatsukari kikan no hensen." *Yokohama Shiritsu Daigaku ronsō shakai kagaku keiretsu* 61, no. 1 (2010): 61–93.

Iriye, Akira. "The Failure of Economic Expansionism: 1918–1931." In *Japan in Crisis: Essays on Taishō Democracy*, edited by Bernard Silberman and H. D. Harootunian, 237–69. Princeton, NJ: Princeton University Press, 1974.

Jacobowitz, Seth. "'A Bitter Brew': Coffee and Labor in Japanese Brazilian Immigrant Literature." *Estudos Japanese*, no. 41 (2019): 13–30.

Kikugawa, Sadami. "Tekisasu beisaku no senkusha: Saibara Seitō to Ōnishi Rihei." *Keizai keiei ronsō* 32, no. 4 (March 1998): 39–58.

Kimura Kenji. "Nichiro sengo kaigai nōgyō imin no rekishiteki chii." In *Nihon jinushi sei to kindai sonraku*, edited by Abiko Rin, 149–68. Tokyo: Sōfūsha, 1994.

King, Tiffany Lethabo. *The Black Shoals: Offshore Formations of Black and Native Studies*. Durham, NC: Duke University Press, 2019.

Kingsberg, Miriam. "Becoming Brazilian to Be Japanese: Emigrant Assimilation, Cultural Anthropology, and National Identity." *Comparative Studies in Society and History* 56, no. 1 (2014): 67–97.

———. "Japan's Inca Boom: Global Archaeology and the Making of a Postwar Nation." *Monumenta Nipponica* 69, no. 2 (2014): 221–54.

———. *Into the Field: Human Scientists of Transwar Japan*. Stanford: Stanford University Press, 2019.

Kishimoto Kōichi. *Nanbei no senya ni koritsu shite*. 1947. Reprint. Tokyo: Tōfūsha, 2002.

Kiyotani Masuji. "Shinbun wa imin ni totte no nendeattaka (2)." *Jinmonken*, no. 3 (1999): 2–63.

Klein, Herbert S., and Francisco Vidal Luna. *Feeding the World: Brazil's Transformation into a Modern Agricultural Economy*. New York: Cambridge University Press, 2018.

Koshiro, Yukiko. *Trans-Pacific Racism and U.S. Occupation of Japan*. New York: Columbia University Press, 1999.

LaFeber, Walter. *The Clash: U.S.-Japan Relations throughout History*. New York: Norton, 1997.

Lee, Ana Paulina. *Mandarin Brazil: Race, Representation, and Memory*. Stanford: Stanford University Press, 2018.

Lee, Erika. "The 'Yellow Peril' and Asian Exclusion in the Americas." *Pacific Historical Review* 76, no. 4 (November 2007): 537–62.

Lesser, Jeffery. *Immigration, Ethnicity, and National Identity in Brazil, 1808 to the Present.* New York: Cambridge University Press, 2013.

———. *Negotiating National Identity: Immigrants, Minorities, and the Struggle for Ethnicity in Brazil.* Durham, NC: Duke University Press, 1999.

Lewis, Michael. *Rioters and Citizens: Mass Protest in Imperial Japan.* Berkeley: University of California Press, 1990.

Liang Zhan. "Wenming, lixing, yu zhongzhu gailiang: yige datong shijie de gouxiang." In *Shijie zhixu yu wenming dengji: quanqiushi yanjiu de xinlujing,* edited by Liu He, 101–63. Beijing: Shenghuo Dushu Xinzhi Sanlian Shudian, 2016.

Lobo Collantes, Franco. "En defensa del mercado interno: Importación japonesa y empresarios textiles en el Perú, 1929–1939." *Apuntes* 86 (primer semestre 2020): 91–115.

López-Calvo, Ignacio. *Japanese Brazilian Saudades: Diasporic Identities and Cultural Production.* Boulder, CO: University Press of Colorado, 2019.

Lu, Sidney Xu. "Eastward Ho! Japanese Settler Colonialism in Hokkaido and the Making of Japanese Migration to the American West." *Journal of Asian Studies* 78, no. 3 (August 2019): 521–47.

———. *The Making of Japanese Settler Colonialism: Malthusianism and Trans-Pacific Migration, 1868–1961.* New York: Cambridge University Press, 2019.

———. "Toward a Prototype of the Total Empire: Japanese Migration to Brazil and Japanese Colonial Expansion in Asia, 1921–1934." In *The Japanese Empire and Latin America,* edited by Pedro Iacobelli Delpiano and Sidney Xu Lu, 63–92. Honolulu: University of Hawai'i Press, 2023.

Lynn, Hyung Gu. "A Comparative Study of Tōyō Kyōkai and Nan'yō Kyōkai." In *The Japanese Empire in East Asia and Its Postwar Legacy,* edited by Harald Fuess, 65–95. Munich: Iudicium, 1998.

———. "Malthusian Dreams, Colonial Imaginary: The Oriental Development Company and Japanese Emigration to Korea." In *Settler Colonialism in the Twentieth Century: Projects, Practices, and Legacies,* edited by Caroline Elkins and Susan Pedersen, 25–40. London: Routledge, 2005.

Mack, Edward. *Acquired Alterity: Migration, Identity, and Literature Nationalism.* Oakland: University of California Press, 2022.

———. "Diasporic Markets: Japanese Print and Migration in São Paulo, 1908–1935." *Script & Print: Bulletin of the Bibliographical Society of Australia and New Zealand* 29 (2005): 163–77.

———. "Paracolonial Literature: Japanese-Language Literature in Brazil." *Ilbon yŏn'gu,* no. 16 (2011): 116–21.

Maeyama Takashi. *Esunishitei to Burajiru Nikkeijin: bunka jinruigaku teki kenkyū.* Tokyo: Ocha no Mizu Shobō, 1996.

———. *Hisōzokusha no seishinshi: aru Nikkei Burajirujin no henreki.* Tokyo: Ocha no Mizu Shobō, 1981.

———. *Imin no Nihon kaiki undō.* Tokyo: Nihon Hōsō Shuppan Kyōkai, 1982.

———. "Kaisetsu: imin bungaku kara mainoritei bungaku e." In *Koronia shōsetsu senshū,* vol. 1. São Paulo: Koronia Bungakukai, 1975.

Mamiya Kunio. *Saibara Seitō kenkyū.* Kōchi: Kōchi Shimin Toshokan, 1996.

———. "Taibei kehatsu undō to Imin Kyōkai no setsuritsu." In *Reimeiki Ajia Taiheiyō chiiki no kokusai kankei: Taiheiyō mondai chōsakai (I.P.R.) no kenkyū, Waseda Daigaku shakai kagaku kenkyūjo kenkyū shirīzu*, no. 33 (1994): 155–81.

Marshall, Oliver. *English, Irish and Irish American Pioneer Settlers in Nineteenth-Century Brazil*. Oxford: Center for Brazilian Studies, Oxford University, 2005.

Mason, Michele M., and Helen J. S. Lee, eds. *Reading Colonial Japan: Text, Context, and Critique*. Stanford: Stanford University Press, 2012.

Masterson, Daniel. *The Japanese in Latin America*. Urbana: University of Illinois Press, 2003.

Merrick, Thomas W., and Douglas H. Graham. *Population and Economic Development*. Baltimore: Johns Hopkins University Press, 1979.

Ministry of Foreign Affairs of Japan. "Japan-Brazil Relations." Accessed May 1, 2023. https://www.mofa.go.jp/region/latin/brazil/data.html.

Miyatake Kimio. "Hakurankai no kioku: 1904 nen Sentoruisu hakurankai to Ainu." *Hokkaido Daigaku Bungaku Kenkyūka kiyō* 118 (February 2006): 45–93.

Mizuno Ryū. "Imin jigyō to watashi." *Burajiru imin no 100 nen*. https://www.ndl.go.jp/brasil/text/t016.html.

Moog, Clodomir Vianna. *Bandeirantes and Pioneers*. New York: G. Braziller, 1964.

Morais, Fernando. *Dirty Hearts: The History of Shindō Renmei*. Translated with a Critical Introduction by Seth Jacobowitz. Basingstoke: Palgrave Macmillan, 2021.

Mori Sei'ichi, Yamamoto Kōsuke, and Suzuki Nao. "Burajiru Nihon imin no isseiki." *Jinmonken*, no. 7 (2009): 44–103.

Morris-Suzuki, Tessa. *Re-inventing Japan: Time, Space, Nation*. Armonk, NY: M. E. Sharpe, 1998.

Morse, Richard M. *The Bandierantes: The Historical Role of the Brazilian Pathfinders*. New York: Knopf, 1965.

Myers, Ramon, and Mark Peattie, eds. *The Japanese Colonial Empire, 1895–1945*. Princeton, NJ: Princeton University, 1987.

Nagano ken kaitaku jikōkai manshū kaitakushi kankōkai. *Naganoken manshū kaitakushi: sōhen*. Nagano-shi: Nagano Ken Kaitaku Jikōkai Manshū Kaitakushi Kankō Kai, 1984.

Nakamura Mihō. "Sengo Nihon no bunka kokka gainen no tokuchō: rekishiteki tenkai o fumaete." *Bunka seisaku kenkyū*, no. 7 (2013): 135–56.

Nakamura Shigeo. "Ōya sōichi no 'meigen' wo megutte." *Discover Nikkei*, March 29, 2007. http://www.discovernikkei.org/en/journal/2007/3/29/brazil-nippon-dayori/.

Nakano Kazunori. "Ezo kyōwakoku no tenmatsu." *Josetsu 2: Bungaku Hihyō*, August 2002.

Needell, Jeffrey D. "Identity, Race, Gender, and Modernity in the Origins of Gilberto Freyre's Oeuvre." *American Historical Review* 100, no. 1 (February 1995): 51–77.

Negawa Sachio. *Burajiru Nikkei imin no kyōikushi*. Tokyo: Misuzu Shobō, 2016.

———. "Senzen senchūki Burajiru ni okeru nikkei imin shitei kyōiku no shiteki kenkyū." PhD diss., Graduate University for Advanced Studies, Sokendai, 2013.

Nippon Rikkō Kai Sōritsu Hyaku Shūnen Kinen Jigyō Jikkō Iinkai Kinenshi Hensan Senmon Iinkai. *Nippon Rikkō Kai hyakunen no kōseki: reiniku kyūsai, kaigai hatten undō, kokusai kōken*. Tokyo: Nippon Rikkō Kai, 1997.

Nishita Toshihiro. "Shidehara Kijūrō no kokusai ninshiki: daiichiji sekai taisen go no tenkanki wo chūshin toshite." *Kokusai seiji*, no. 139 (November 2004): 91–106.

Oguma Eiji. *Nihonjin no kyōkai: Okinawa Ainu Taiwan Chōsen shokuminchi shihai kara fukki undō made*. Tokyo: Shinyōsha, 1999.

Okabayashi Nobuo. "Jinkō mondai to imin ron: Meiji Nihon no fuan to yokubō." *Doshisha hōgaku* 64, no. 8 (March 2013): 75–167.

Ōkōchi Kazuo. *Maboroshi no kokusaku-gaisha Tōyō Takushoku.* Tokyo: Nihon Keizai Shinbunsha, 1982.

Ōkuma Shigenobu. "Sekai no daikyoku to imin." *Nihon Imin Kyōkai hōkoku* 1. Tokyo: Fuji Shuppan, 2006. Originally published as "Sekai no daikyoku to imin," *Nihon Imin Kyōkai hōkoku,* no. 2 (August 1915): 6–9.

Peattie, Mark. *Nan'yō: The Rise and Fall of the Japanese in Micronesia, 1885–1945.* Honolulu: University of Hawai'i Press, 1988.

———. "The Nan'yō: Japan in the South Pacific, 1885–1945." In *The Japanese Colonial Empire, 1895–1945,* edited by Ramon Myers and Mark Peattie, 172–210. Princeton, NJ: Princeton University Press, 1987.

Pérez Meléndez, José Juan. "The Business of Peopling: Colonization and Politics in Imperial Brazil, 1822–1860." PhD diss., University of Chicago, 2016.

———. "Reconsiderando a política de colonização no Brasil imperial: Os anos da Regência e o mundo externo." *Revista Brasileira de História* 34, no. 68 (2014): 35–60.

Poets, Desiree. "Settler Colonialism and/in (Urban) Brazil: Black and Indigenous Resistances to the Logic of Elimination." *Settler Colonial Studies* 11, no. 3 (2021): 271–91.

Riall, Lucy. "Hidden Spaces of Empire: Italian Colonists in Nineteenth-Century Peru." *Past & Present* 254, no. 1 (February 2022): 193–233.

Rosenberg, Emily S. "Anglo-American Economic Rivalry in Brazil during World War I." *Diplomatic History* 2, no. 2 (Spring 1978): 131–52.

Ryang, Sonia. *Japan and National Anthropology: A Critique.* New York: Routledge, 2004.

Sakaguchi Mitsuhiko. "Kaisetsu." In *Nihon Imin Kyōkai hōkoku: kaisetsu, sōmokuji, shihisha sakuin,* 3–13. Reprint. Tokyo: Fuji Shuppan, 2006.

———. "Dare ga imin wo okuridashita no ka: kan Taihenyō ni okeru Nihonjin no kokusai idō gaikan." *Ritsumeikan gengo bunka kenkyū* 21, no. 4 (March 2010): 53–66.

Sakai Tetsuya. "Sengo shisō to kokusai seijiron no kōsaku: kōwa ronsōki wo chūshin ni." *Kokusai Seiji,* no. 117 (March 1998): 121–39.

Sand, Jordan. "Gentlemen's Agreement, 1908: Fragments for a Pacific History." *Representations* 107, no. 1 (Summer 2009): 91–127.

Satō Jin. *"Motazaru kuni" no shigen ron: jizoku kanō na kokudo o meguru mō hitotsu no chi.* Tokyo: Tokyo Daigaku Shuppankai, 2011.

Satō Yoshimaru. "Dainihon Bunmei Kyōkai shi shiron." *Waseda Daigaku shi kiyō* 21 (March 1989): 177–212.

Schuster, Sven. "The World's Fairs as Spaces of Global Knowledge: Latin American Archaeology and Anthropology in the Age of Exhibitions." *Journal of Global History* 13, no. 1 (March 2018): 69–93.

Shibusawa Ei'ichi Kinen Zaidan Kenkyūbu. *Jitsugyōka to Burajiru ijū.* Tokyo: Fuji Shuppan, 2008.

Shiga Shigetaka. *Nan'yō jiji.* Tokyo: Maruzen Shōsha Shoten, 1891.

Shimazu Naoko. *Japan, Race, and Equality: The Racial Equality Proposal of 1919.* London: Routledge, 1998

Shimizu Seisaburō. "Hokubei Tekisasushu iminchi torishirabe hōkoku." In *Gaimushō Tsūshōkyoku, Imin chōsa hōkoku.* Vol. 1, 1–28. 1908. Reprint. Tokyo: Yūshōdō Shuppan, 1986.

Shin Nichibei Shinbunsha. *Beikoku Nikkeijin hyakunenshi: hatten jinshiroku.* Los Angeles: Shin Nichibei Shinbunsha, 1961.

Shirane, Seiji. *Imperial Gateway: Colonial Taiwan and Japan's Expansion in South China and Southeast Asia, 1895–1945.* Ithaca, NY: Cornell University Press, 2022.

Siddle, Richard. *Race, Resistance, and the Ainu of Japan.* New York: Routledge, 1996.

Skidmore, Thomas E. *Black into White: Race and Nationality in Brazilian Thought.* Durham, NC: Duke University Press, 1992.

———. "Brazil's American Illusion: From Dom Pedro II to the Coup of 1964." *Luso-Brazilian Review* 23, no. 2 (Winter 1986): 71–84.

———. *Brazil: Five Centuries of Change.* New York: Oxford University Press, 1999.

Smith, Joseph. *Brazil and the United States: Convergence and Divergence.* Athens: University of Georgia Press, 2010.

Smith, Robert. "The Ethnic Japanese in Brazil." *Journal of Japanese Studies* 5, no. 1 (Winter 1979): 53–70.

Smith, Robert J., John B. Cornell, Hiroshi Saitō, and Maeyama Takashi. *The Japanese and Their Descendents in Brazil: An Annotated Bibliography.* São Paulo: Centro de Estudos Nipo-Brasileiros, 1967.

Staniford, Philip. *Pioneers in the Tropics: The Political Organisation of Japanese in an Immigrant Community in Brazil.* London: Athlone Press, 1973.

Sugimura Fukashi. "Hakkoku Imin Jyōkyō." *Burajiru imin no 100 nen.* https://www.ndl.go.jp/brasil/text/t014.html.

Summerhill, William R. *Order against Progress: Government, Foreign Investment, and Railroads in Brazil, 1854–1913.* Stanford: Stanford University Press, 2003.

Suzuki Masatake. *Suzuki Tei'ichi: Burajiru Nikkei shakai ni ikita kisai no shōgai.* São Paulo: San Pauro Jinbun Kagaku Kenkyūjo, 2007.

Szpilman, Christopher W. A., and Sven Saaler. "Pan-Asianism as an Ideal of Asian Identity and Solidarity, 1850–Present." *Asia-Pacific Journal* 9, issue 17, no. 1 (April 2011): 1–30.

Tachikawa Kenji. "Meiji zenhanki no tobeinetsu (1)." *Tomiyama Daigaku Kyōyōbu Kiyō* 23, no. 2 (1990): 1–30.

Tagawa Mariko. "'Imin' Shichō no Kiseki." PhD diss., Yūshōdō Shuppan, 2005.

Takushoku Daigaku. *Takushoku Daigaku hachijūnen shi: Meiji hen.* Tokyo: Takushoku Daigaku Sōritsu Hachijisshūnen Kinen Jigyō Jimukyoku, 1980.

Taylor, Lucy. "Four Foundations of Settler Colonial Theory: Four Insights from Argentina." *Settler Colonial Studies* 11, no. 3 (2021): 344–65.

Taylor, Lucy, and Geraldine Lublin, eds. "Settler Colonial Studies and Latin America." *Settler Colonial Studies* 11, no. 3 (2021).

Thornton, Michael. "A Capitol Orchard: Botanical Networks and the Creation of a Japanese 'Neo-Europe.'" *American Historical Review* 127, no. 2 (June 2022): 573–99.

Travaros, Paulo. "Modern Frontiers: Beyond Brasília, the Amazon." In *Latin American Modern Architectures: Ambiguous Territories*, edited by Patricio del Real and Helen Gyger, 191–211. New York: Routledge, 2013

Tsuchida, Nobuya. "The Japanese in Brazil, 1908–1941." PhD diss., University of California, Los Angeles, 1978.

Tsuda, Takeyuki. *Strangers in the Ethnic Homeland: Japanese Brazilian Return Migration in Transnational Perspective.* New York: Columbia University Press, 2003.

Tsunoyama Yukihiro. *Enomoto Takeaki to Mekishiko ijū*. Tokyo: Dōbunkan Shuppan, 1986.

Uchida, Jun. *Brokers of Empire: Japanese Settler Colonialism in Korea, 1876–1945*. Cambridge, MA: Harvard University Asia Center, 2016.

———. *Provincializing Empire: Ōmi Merchants in the Japanese Transpacific Diaspora*. Berkeley: University of California Press, 2023

Uetsuka Yoshio, and Nakano Yorio. *Uetsuka Tsukasa no Amazon kaitaku jigyō*. Chufu: Ten'en, 2013.

Usui Ryūichirō. *Enomoto Takeaki kara sekaishi ga mieru*. Tokyo: PHP Kenkyūjo, 2005.

Veracini, Lorenzo. "Is Settler Colonial Studies Even Useful?" *Postcolonial Studies* 24, no. 2 (2021): 270–77.

———. *Settler Colonialism: A Theoretical Overview*. Houndmills: Palgrave Macmillan, 2010.

Wago Shūngorō. *Baurū kannai no hōjin*. Bauru: Wago Shūngorō, 1939. Reprinted in *Nikkei imin shiryōshū dainiki, nanbeihen*. Vol. 25. Tokyo: Nihon Tosho Sentā, 1999.

Walker, Brett. *The Conquest of the Ainu Lands: Ecology and Culture in Japanese Expansion, 1590–1800*. Berkeley: University of California Press, 2006.

Webb, Walter Prescott. *The Great Frontier*. Boston: Houghton Mifflin, 1952.

Weinstein, Barbara. *The Color of Modernity: São Paulo and the Making of Race and Nation in Brazil*. Durham, NC: Duke University Press, 2015.

Wilson, Sandra. "'The New Paradise': Japanese Emigration to Manchuria in the 1930s and 40s." *International History Review* 17, no. 2 (May 1995): 249–86.

Wolfe, Patrick. "Recuperating Binarism: A Heretical Introduction." *Settler Colonial Studies* 3, no. 3–4 (2013): 257–79.

———. "Settler Colonialism and the Elimination of the Native." *Journal of Genocide Research* 8, no. 4 (December 2006): 387–409.

———. *Settler Colonialism and the Transformation of Anthropology: The Politics and Poetics of an Ethnographic Event*. London: Cassell, 1999.

Yamamoto Kiyoshi Hyōdan Henshū Iinkai. *Yamamoto Kiyoshi hyōdan*. São Paulo: San Pauro Jinbun Kagaku Kenkyūjo, 1981.

Yamamoto Shūsaku, et al. *Rejisutoro no rokujūnen*. Registro: Rejisutoro Rokujūnen Shi Kenkō Iinkai, 1978.

Yano Tooru. *Nihon no nanshin to Tōnan Ajia*. Tokyo: Nihon Keizai Shinbunsha, 1976.

Yoshitaka Hibi. "Chasing the Transnational Flow of Books and Magazines: Materials, Knowledge, and Network." In *The Japanese Empire and Latin America*, edited by Pedro Iacobelli Delpiano and Sidney Xu Lu, 191–207. Honolulu: University of Hawai'i Press, 2023.

Young, George F. W. *Germans in Chile: Immigration and Colonization, 1849–1914*. New York: Center for Migration Studies of New York, 1974.

Young, Louise. *Beyond Metropolis: Second Cities and Urban Life in Interwar Japan*. Berkeley: University of California Press, 2013.

———. *Japan's Total Empire: Manchuria and the Culture of Wartime Imperialism*. Berkeley: University of California Press, 1998.

Zaihaku Hokkaidō Kyōkai. *Zaihaku Hokkaidōjin shi: Hokkaidō hyakunen kinen*. São Paulo: Zaihaku Hokkaidō Kyōkai, 1968.

Zolberg, Aristide. *A Nation by Design: Immigration Policy in the Fashioning of America*. Cambridge, MA: Harvard University Press, 2006.

Founded in 1893,
UNIVERSITY OF CALIFORNIA PRESS
publishes bold, progressive books and journals
on topics in the arts, humanities, social sciences,
and natural sciences—with a focus on social
justice issues—that inspire thought and action
among readers worldwide.

The UC PRESS FOUNDATION
raises funds to uphold the press's vital role
as an independent, nonprofit publisher, and
receives philanthropic support from a wide
range of individuals and institutions—and from
committed readers like you. To learn more, visit
ucpress.edu/supportus.